# The M Room:

## Secret Listeners who Bugged the Nazis in WW2

### Helen Fry

MARRANOS PRESS

First Published 2012

Marranos Press: London

Website: helen-fry.com

Agent: Steph Ebdon, The Marsh Agency Ltd, London

*'No war can be conducted successfully without early and good intelligence,'*

1st Duke of Marlborough, 1715

Dedicated to

**the Secret Listeners**

who fled Hitler and worked for MI19

and

the memory of

**Thomas Joseph Kendrick**

Highly-respected MI6 officer

# CONTENT

# ONE

## DECADES OF SILENCE

BY THE SUMMER of 1939 Britain faced imminent war with Nazi Germany after the failure of Prime Minister Chamberlain's appeasement policy. With pragmatic foresight British Intelligence had already begun preparations for war the previous summer when Hugh Sinclair, head of the British Intelligence Service (soon to be known as MI6), purchased Bletchley Park in Bedfordshire from his own private funds. Here a dedicated team would break the German Enigma Code and shorten the war by at least two years. During 1938 Sinclair knew that war with Nazi Germany was inevitable – all intelligence pointed to it. It was not a matter of *if*, but *when*. As plans forged ahead to prepare British Intelligence for war, Bletchley was not the only unit in Sinclair's scheme. Another top-secret unit was being prepared to spring into action within twenty-four hours of the outbreak of war. It would prove to be one of the earliest deceptions of the enemy in the Second World War and one that would involve bugging the conversations of captured Nazi PoWs; some of them the German Generals.

Eavesdropping on the enemy was nothing new. British Intelligence had been doing it since the First World War. Now what Sinclair needed was a man whom he could trust to run the day-to-day operations of such a clandestine listening unit during the war with Nazi Germany. In his mind the job description was crystal clear. That man had to be fluent in German, have an intimate knowledge of German military capability, be acquainted with Germany's rearmament programme and yet understand human beings in all their complexities. He must know how to court high society – diplomatic, social, intellectual and cultural, and yet he could not be a diplomat. He had to be someone who could move with ease in any company and steer British Intelligence through the minefield of human egos and eccentric, stuffy demands of heads of departments with a devastating efficiency and subtle skill that would produce results. Sinclair had one man in his sight; a man who had already aided him in setting up Bletchley Park. That man was Thomas Joseph Kendrick – a military man and old master at organization and running a complex bureaucratic system.

Kendrick had been on the payroll of the British Secret Service since the 1920s. He was quick-witted, gregarious, and a gifted pianist whose sense of humour could entertain a room full of guests. He was discreet, trained in the mindset of Secret Intelligence Service (SIS) and yet able to think on his feet. Kendrick inhabited the world of John le Carre's *Tinker, Tailor, Soldier, Spy*. He was both soldier and spy, having served Britain at the end of the Boer War and during the First World War, often involving operations behind enemy lines. During the 1920s and 30s Kendrick became quite simply one of SIS's most important spymasters in Europe as the eyes and ears of the government in Vienna during the period when the city was the gateway of espionage into Russia and Germany. There Kendrick served as Passport Control Officer in the British Passport Office – a post to mask his clandestine SIS work. It was a dangerous, murky game of spies and double agents. With no diplomatic immunity if caught, Kendrick sailed close to the wind to gain Nazi secrets for the British during the 1930s. During Hitler's annexation of Austria from March 1938 he led a double life – saving Jews from the clutches of the Nazis on the one hand and running spy networks on the other. His luck did not last. In August 1938 he was betrayed to the Nazis and arrested. After four gruelling days of interrogations he was finally released and expelled from Austria.

Back in Britain, Sinclair deployed Kendrick in preparations for war at SIS headquarters in London. Alongside work on establishing Bletchley, Kendrick was tasked with setting up a unit to spy on Germany from within Britain's shores; a unit which by 1943 would employ nearly a thousand staff and 100 'secret listeners'.

* * *

London 2012: the capital is abuzz with preparations for the Olympics and Paralympics. Meanwhile at his home in North-West London a gentleman in his nineties is taken aback by the sudden explosion of interest in his wartime story. For decades Fritz Lustig never talked about his secret work in the 'M Room'. He had signed the Official Secrets Act and remained silent for over sixty years. Over the decades he often wondered whether the work had any impact on the course of the war and what sense it contributed to the Allied victory in Europe and defeat of Nazism. Now due to the declassification of thousands of reports and files at the National Archives it is possible to provide answers to these questions. But

Fritz is no ordinary veteran. He was born in Berlin in 1919 – a German, forced to flee Hitler's regime because the Nazis considered him a non-Aryan. In 1939 he arrived in Britain as a penniless refugee on the eve of war. He, like thousands of other German-Jewish refugees, quickly began to shed his German identity and settle into a new life. They fell in love with England and knew there was no returning to Germany once Hitler had been defeated. This was not a temporary exile and they aspired to being British subjects; something which many had to wait more than six years to obtain. These refugees quickly began to disassociate from their past and feel more British with a total loyalty to the country that had saved them from certain death in the concentration camps. Fritz, and thousands like him, felt a deep debt of gratitude to Britain and one which they were willing to repay once Britain was at war with the country of their birth. Concern for family members left behind and the terror unfolding across Nazi-occupied Europe was never far from their minds, although Fritz was one of the rare lucky ones whose immediate family all got out of Germany safely.

Fritz became one of 10,000 German refugees to enlist in the British forces in the early years of the war. These refugee soldiers found themselves 'digging for victory' in an unskilled labour unit, the Pioneer Corps. But there would soon be a vital role for veterans like Fritz and one in which their fluency in German was indispensable to the British Secret Service. In 1943 around a hundred veterans had the ultimate chance to do something special for their adopted country. In an ironic twist of fate they joined a clandestine unit and spied on the country of their birth. Little did they know then how important it would be for winning the war. They became the 'secret listeners' and worked at three sites deep in the heart of the English countryside. During their work for British Intelligence they never set eyes on a single German PoW, yet they came as close as possible behind the secret walls of the M Room from where they bugged enemy conversations – including 59 of Hitler's Generals held at Trent Park. The secret listeners spent three years eavesdropping on over 10,000 German PoWs: from U-boat crew, to Luftwaffe pilots and army officers to high-ranking Generals. The German prisoners were captured in many theatres of war, including North Africa, France, Greece and Italy as well as German pilots shot down over the English skies.

The hub of the work in the M Room proved to be 'one of the most valuable sources of intelligence on [German] rockets, flying bombs, jet propelled aircraft and submarines.' Secret recordings were made of intelligence which ranged from the first discovery of X-Gerät – the new ·Y beam technology fitted to Luftwaffe planes – to Knickebein, and the development of V2 rockets. Intelligence gleaned in the M Room related to all campaigns of the war, but most significantly included: German secret weapon development programme, new technology on Luftwaffe planes, Hitler's plans for a gas attack on Britain, German battle plans, U-boat bases and construction programmes and vital intelligence to win the Battle of the Atlantic, information on V2 rocket bases at Peenemünde, and the failed July 1944 attempt on Hitler's life. But the work of the émigrés who had once fled Hitler brought their trauma closer to home when it had an unexpected and deeply difficult side. The secret listeners picked up conversations on widespread atrocities against Jews and Russian PoWs as well as detailed plans of Hitler's 'Final Solution' for the Jews of Europe. They overheard in graphic detail the inner workings of the Nazi killing machine. What they picked up begins to challenge our known knowledge of the Holocaust at that time and most particularly the discovery of evidence of a mutiny amongst SS guards in a concentration camp as early as 1936/7.

The secret listeners were instructed by Kendrick to keep all 'cut' records of atrocities and heard extensive and explicit details of Hitler's annihilation programme long before the full reality was made known at the liberation of the camps. It was only in spring 1945 that the full extent of the horror became known when graphic newsreel was shown across the world alongside images in national newspapers. Today with the benefit of hindsight, it is easy to be complacent about what is now known. It is easy to forget that during the war itself some of the horrific evidence which was overheard was even doubted by British Intelligence officers. Comments to such effect appear occasionally in the transcripts of the secretly recorded PoW conversations. Today it is easy to overlook the significance of what the secret listeners discovered for British Intelligence in terms of atrocities and Hitler's wider programme for a pure Aryan race. However, it was one thing to gain intelligence, quite another to be able to use it. British Intelligence chiefs found themselves in a sticky situation at the end of the war. Much to the chagrin of the secret listeners, who themselves had experienced Nazi atrocities firsthand prior to 1939, their evidence gathered on war crimes and atrocities were withheld from the Nuremberg Trial and other War Crimes trials. A sharp exchange within British Intelligence circles at that time reveals that not everyone was happy with the decision to withhold the secret recordings from the prosecuting counsels. It meant that some war criminals never stood trial for their crimes against humanity.

Within the last two decades a wealth of material and books has been published on the extraordinary wartime activities at Bletchley Park. Their contribution has been admirably documented and acknowledged. However the clandestine work of the secret listeners like Fritz has never fully been told. The M Room operators often picked up information that had not been gathered by any other British wartime unit. On their first day in post they were told by their Kendrick that the work they were doing was 'more important than firing a gun in action.' They could never speak about their work, not even to fellow-workers in the camp. Having signed The Official Secrets Act they kept silent for over sixty years and many listeners have gone to their grave bearing the secrets of their work. It is now possible to tell their story and to see that their highly classified work protected Britain's shores from the greatest threat since the Spanish Armada in 1588. It became as significant for winning the war as cracking the Enigma at Bletchley Park.

# TWO

## WITHIN THESE WALLS

*'All the business of war and indeed all the business of life is to endeavour to find out what you don't know by what you do,'*

The Duke of Wellington

THE STORY OF the M Room is one of the earliest brainwaves of British Intelligence in the Second World War and began in the most unlikely of locations. Just two days before the outbreak of war, on 1 September 1939, Lt. Col. Thomas Joseph Kendrick arrived at the Tower of London to open his clandestine unit. Within these historic walls of the Nation's iconic fortress that had seen the deaths of royals, traitors and spies, he was tasked with coordinating a small team to bug the conversations of the first German prisoners after their capture. The idea of such a unit had originated from a joint meeting of intelligence chiefs from the Admiralty, War Office and Air Ministry who were only too aware that early intelligence was crucial. The stark reality was simple: *whoever won the intelligence game would win the war*.

Intelligence chiefs agreed on a coordinated strategy for providing information on enemy operations, military capability and weapons development, and it would be obtained by surreptitiously listening to the conversations of captured German prisoners. In a major new development it would be the first of its kind to work across the three services of Air Force, Army and Navy – services which usually acted autonomously and without inter-departmental cooperation on intelligence matters. The result was an inter-service intelligence unit called Combined Services Detailed

Interrogation Centre, or CSDIC for short. The unit originally came under the auspices of MI1(the forerunner of MI6), later became part of MI9 and then MI19. Kendrick's original team consisted of just five other officers from the Army, Air Ministry and Navy. Although their names are not listed in official reports it is known that alongside Kendrick himself, one was Flight Lieutenant S. Felkin who headed the Air Ministry Intelligence section known as AI1(K).

As head of the overall unit Kendrick liaised with the Post Office to supply special listening apparatus which was hidden in two rooms in the Tower. To maintain absolute secrecy the engineers who installed it were required to sign The Official Secrets Act. Operating from Married Quarters at the Tower and with its own 'miked room' known as the M Room, Kendrick's small team awaited its first prisoners-of-war. They didn't have to wait long.

On 20 November 1939 a Luftwaffe plane was shot down over the mouth of the river Thames and its pilot Lieutenant Wilhelm Meyer pulled out of the water and brought to the Tower for interrogation. A report dated 21 December submitted by Felkin provided Air Ministry with information on the crew's call-sign and the wavelengths used on their radio transmission (AIR40/3108). Meyer was interrogated about the meaning of codes transmitted between himself and his ground control. British Intelligence learnt that Meyer's crew had received no navigational aid on their flight to England but had flown by sight to just north of Borkum, and then on a plotted course between Deal and Dover where they crossed the coast. Assistance for their return flight (had they made it) would have been given over shortwaves. Felkin established that the type of wireless receiver used was a Fuge III A U which charged using a dynamo from the engine. A key priority at this stage of the war was to establish the kind of technology used on board Luftwaffe aircraft. A copy of Felkin's interrogation report was sent to the Air Ministry and also MI1(a), MI8 and MI6 which tells much about who within wider British Secret Service was receiving the classified information. Intelligence gained at this early stage of the war was pretty much piecemeal and a matter of gradually piecing together snippets from interrogations and secret recordings to gain an overall picture.

It became rapidly apparent that the Tower of London would prove insufficient to cope with the growing number of captured PoWs. With the Luftwaffe bombing raids on London and anticipated invasion of Britain, the War Office looked for new premises for its clandestine operations. Approximately ten miles north of the capital at Cockfosters lay a stately house in over 400 acres of woodland and park. A convenient distance from London, yet with easy access from the capital, the estate would be ideal to hide a clandestine unit. Here the work of British Intelligence could be carried out with no risk of public attention. The owner Sir Philip Sassoon had died that June of influenza and the War Office had seized on the opportunity to requisition the estate for 'special purposes'.

The Sassoons were Baghdadi Jews who had emigrated to India and traded in opium. Their success had turned them into millionaires. The Sassoon brothers ran part of the business from London and mixed with the wealthy European bankers, the Rothschilds. Sir Edward Sassoon married Evelyn de Rothschild and they had one son and a daughter. On the death of Sir Edward in 1912 his son and heir, Philip, inherited millions at the age of only 23. This included the beautiful Trent Park estate and the Sassoon business interests. After the First World War Sir Philip concentrated his efforts on reconstructing and redesigning the interior of the house to entertain politicians and rich guests. In an area at the front of the house he planted a million daffodil bulbs, still known as "The Daffodil Lawn". It was here at Trent Park in the 1930s that Sir Philip hosted parties for some of the most famous guests of his era; amongst them Winston Churchill who painted the Blue Room whilst staying there, Charlie Chaplin, Lady Cynthia Asquith, Stanley Baldwin and Mr and Mrs Neville Chamberlain. This also became one of the secret weekend retreats for Edward and Wallace Simpson in the days before their relationship became public knowledge. With so much history behind it, Trent Park was about to make history again when during the wartime it housed 59 of Hitler's German Generals with astonishing results for British Intelligence. The estate was never to be referred to as a prisoner-of-war camp but as 'Cockfosters Camp' or 'Camp 11'. Like Bletchley Park the fact that its existence remained unknown for decades, and is still largely unknown today, was a testament to its success.

## M ROOM APPARATUS

Before Trent Park could function for any intelligence purposes it had to be made ready. Preparations to install listening equipment in the house began before Kendrick relocated there. During October 1939 from his office in the Tower of London Kendrick liaised with other officers in MI1 to complete the plans. A handwritten report entitled *Listening and Recording Equipment at Country House* laid out the requirements. In discussion with Kendrick and a Capt. Buxton it was decided that five interrogation rooms and six bedrooms at Trent Park would be wired with concealed microphones. After consultation with BBC research recording engineers it was decided to approach the Radio Corporation of America (RCA) which had UK offices at Electra House on Victoria Embankment in London. The American company was known to British Intelligence, having previously carried out work for SIS. Correspondence between Kendrick and RCA Photophone Ltd reveals that the equipment for Trent Park was supplied by this company. A letter dated 26 October 1939 sent from MI1 to Kendrick at the Tower informed him that Mr Barton and Mr Clarke of the RCA would be ready for Kendrick to pick them up in a car at 10a.m on 27 October. It was proposed that Mr Barnes of the General Post Office Research Department at Dollis Hill (London) was to oversee the necessary wiring installation. Work got underway during the latter part of 1939 and most of the fitting of the bugging devices was carried out by Barnes' permanent staff at Dollis Hill. All installation staff were required to sign The Official Secrets Act and copies of their signed declarations, witnessed by Kendrick, have survived in government files. Thereafter the equipment was maintained and replaced by the Post Office Research Station to avoid any breach of security.

As the first Christmas of the war approached, Kendrick began the preliminary phase of the move to Trent Park even before the installation of equipment was completed. Two months later on 14 February 1940 Kendrick received a letter from the UK office of the RCA to inform him that, 'we have pleasure in handing over to you the complete installation at T.P [Trent Park] in full operating condition including both recording and reproducing or play-back sections... We have borne in mind the necessity for simplicity of operation together with the strictest economy both in original outlay and also in operating costs.'

Security and secrecy remained paramount as reflected towards the end of the letter which gives final hand-over to Kendrick. He was told in the letter: 'the only other copy of this letter and the attached report in existence is one in our own secret files which it is of course necessary for us to keep. We should point out that certain drawings are in the possession of the Post Office and the Office of Works and you will no doubt consider whether you want to collect them and destroy them.' These original drawings appear not to have survived in any official files and were destroyed as directed.

The Cockfosters Camp was kitted out with fifteen type 88A pressure microphones, nine portable disc recorders, five high quality headphones, one amplifier for loudspeaker monitoring, four switchboard assemblies, one main frame assembly and a transformer. The operators were supplied with five hundred and twenty-five 12" double-sided Acetate Recording Discs for recording conversations, and fifty-eight steel recording styli, ten sapphire recording styli and spare parts. The equipment was manufactured and supplied by RCA in New Jersey, America and shipped at the end of 1939 from the port of New York aboard *SS Lancastria*. On 6 December 1939 the then Director of Military Intelligence Sir R. Percival wrote to the Secretary of The Board of Trade in London asking him to issue an urgent import licence for the equipment which was granted.

The equipment allowed for complete versatility and flexibility for the intelligence work. Any or all operators could listen singly or together into any one of the bugged rooms, including the interrogation rooms and any of the eight machines could record conversations in any of the wired rooms. If necessary each operator was able to listen simultaneously into what was being recorded. Loudspeakers were also fitted to the equipment but had been disconnected for obvious reasons. A separate play-back room was equipped with four playback units with turntable and variable speed motor, amplifier, hypersensitive pick-up, power control switch and pilot lamps and twin output jacks. Eight headsets plus eighty silent styli were also part of the equipment supplied. This allowed for two translators to listen simultaneously to the recordings. Kendrick's own office also had a play-back machine similar to those in the M Room. At any time his office could be connected direct from the M Room to any of the bugged cells and interrogation rooms and listened in by headphones or loudspeaker. He also controlled by a switch, under lock and key the instruments in Interrogation Room 6. It also meant that if any of the machines in the M Room broke down, Kendrick's machine could be used as a replacement.

It was down to skilled carpenters and decorators to conceal the bugging devices in various places in the rooms at Trent Park, for example in light fittings or plants. None of the interrogation rooms were initially sound-proofed, neither were four of the secret recording rooms. The two long reception rooms of the house, S.1 and S.2, were fitted with false ceilings but in keeping with the rest of the architecture to avoid arousing suspicion by any PoWs held there. By May 1940 it was felt necessary to sound-proof various rooms and Kendrick petitioned Crockatt (MI9) to authorise funds to undertake work of partitioning and sound-proofing at the Cockfosters Camp.

The eavesdropping work at Trent Park was to prove indispensable for winning the intelligence game. Here the secret listeners eavesdropped on the conversations of German and Italian PoWs and picked up some of the most significant intelligence of the early part of the war during a period before the Enigma Code was broken at Bletchley Park.

## THE KING'S OWN ENEMY ALIENS

While Kendrick's attention was focused on setting up and running the nascent unit for MI9 (later MI19), twenty-year old Fritz Lustig was working in Cambridge. As a newly arrived refugee from Nazi oppression, with a visa for only 12 months which required Fritz to be trained in some trade before re-emigrating to Australia or New Zealand, he was not allowed to do any paid work. The local Refugee Committee found him an unpaid job with a jobbing builder. Having arrived just months before the outbreak of war there was no sense for him that he would ever go back to the country of his birth. 'I was pretty sure,' he says, 'that I would never return to Germany, for the Third Reich seemed so firmly established that nobody – at least in Germany – could imagine at that moment that a mere six years and a month later it would have disappeared. The proximity of war, and the possibility that it might entail a German defeat, was very far from my mind.' His parents had fortunately managed to escape and Fritz was able to write to them and receive letters frequently.

On 3 September 1939 the inevitable happened. Britain declared war on Germany after German troops had crossed the border into Poland two days earlier. Prime Minister Chamberlain's radio broadcast that day is etched on Fritz's mind forever. Perhaps, because of his German background, only Fritz could not miss the fact that it was the first time that Chamberlain publicly had not used the courtesy title "Herr" before Hitler's name. The outbreak of war changed everything and, along with around 75,000 other refugees from Nazi oppression, Fritz was classified as an 'enemy alien'. He suddenly found the country which had given him refuge at war with the country of his birth. Fritz, and thousands like him, had to bear the mistrust of a nation which sat uncomfortably with German speakers in its midst at such a time of crisis. 'We were not allowed to own cameras or maps,' recalls Fritz, 'and had to report to the local police station to obtain a permit if we wanted to stay away from our registered address or wanted to travel.' It would be nearly three years before his adopted country would trust him with some of its most highly valued secrets.

Fritz then took up work as a cleaner in Peterhouse College, Cambridge where the London School of Economics had evacuated from London. It meant an early start at 6a.m. to dust, sweep and clean the fireplaces in the Library. He says today, 'although it was galling to read and hear about the swift German successes in overrunning Poland, and seeing it carved up between Germany and its "ally" the Soviet Union, we still felt relatively isolated from the real war.' After two or three weeks his work changed to cleaning the students' rooms. At times Fritz became slightly envious of the privileged life of 'the young gentlemen', as the students were known. He looked longingly at the books on the library shelves and yearned to read some of them.

As a gifted cellist, Fritz came to England with very few possessions except his prized cello as one the few items he managed to get out of Germany. In his spare time he practised and channelled his emotions and anxieties into his music. When Professor Hutton at Cambridge learnt about Fritz's musical talent he recommended to the headmaster of Abbotsholme School in Derbyshire that Fritz join the establishment to offer private cello lessons to the boys.

On Saturday 4 May 1940, less than a week before the face of Europe dramatically changed, Fritz headed north from Cambridge to join Abbotsholme School. The enforced black-outs and food rationings were a daily reminder of war, otherwise he felt quite removed from the realities of war. Listening to radio news broadcasts became almost a compulsory occupation to keep up with the war. By now Hitler had overrun Norway and Denmark and set his sights on Denmark's neighbours.

On 10 May Hitler ordered his troops into the Low Countries and France. As German Panzer tanks rolled into much of Western Europe, back in London Winston Churchill took over the reins of government and became the new British Prime Minister. This belligerent politician who had once harangued the British government during the 1930s about Hitler's true intentions and rearmament programme now had his chance to lead Britain through its most vulnerable period. Hitler's face was firmly turned towards England and there was every expectation that a German invasion was imminent. The Invasion Scare brought panic in its wake. It was feared that Hitler would parachute German spies into England as he had in the Low Countries. These 'Fifth Columnists' could infiltrate the German refugees living in Britain and then it would be impossible to tell who was a spy or a genuine refugee. The British government reacted swiftly and in an emergency measure ordered the mass internment of German refugees living in Britain. Churchill coined the phrase 'collar the lot!' and around 27,000 German-Jewish refugees were arrested. They found themselves interned behind barbed wire in makeshift camps across Britain and on the Isle of Man. Other internees were transported to Australia aboard the infamous troopship *Dunera*.

On the morning of 4 July 1940 at the school where Fritz worked as a part-time gardener and part-time cello teacher, twenty-one year old Fritz received a visit from the local policeman. He was promptly arrested and interned as an enemy alien and potential risk to national security. Fritz was taken first to York Racecourse for a few weeks and held with other internees before being transferred to the Isle of Man. On arrival on the Isle of Man he and fellow internees felt the full brunt of the local civilian population's anger and mistrust, as he recalls:

'We marched from the harbour to the railway station and felt rather uncomfortable as the on-looking population was displaying a decidedly hostile attitude. They were obviously under the mistaken impression that we were "proper" Germans and therefore "the enemy". Another special train took us across the island to Peel, on the West Coast, where we entered a newly established camp, Peveril Camp.'

In an area behind barbed wire Fritz found himself in a boarding house with about twenty other internees, three of whom were not Jewish but had fled Germany as political opponents of the Nazi regime. He became less sympathetic with those internees who had had long established professions in Germany before emigration and who felt resentment towards the British for being 'locked up'. Fritz decided to make the best of a difficult situation and volunteered to help in the kitchen.

The internees were permitted little communication with the outside world. Letters sent from the camp had to be written on special paper and no more than 24 lines in total. All mail in and out of the camp was censored. Fritz was able to write to his sister in Cambridge who then passed on news to their parents who had fled to Portugal. It was a strange existence, largely isolated from the realities of the war. For weeks Fritz and fellow internees had no idea whether Hitler had successfully invaded Britain. But there was plenty of activities to occupy their time. Wherever mid-European continental refugees gathered they formed mini 'universities'. The camps on the Isle of Man were no exception. Amongst the internees were some of Europe's finest brains who offered master classes on their subjects.

Fritz's sister arranged for his cello to be sent from Derbyshire so he could join fellow musicians in putting on concerts in the camp. These proved extremely popular. The internees with whom Fritz shared a boarding house decided that his skills as a cellist were of greater benefit than his "culinary" ones and he stopped helping in the kitchen to spend most of his time rehearsing and playing in concert. In an extraordinary paradox the Continental internees who felt a profound sense of gratitude to Britain, even if mixed with resentment at being held behind barbed wire, played the National Anthem at their concerts, as was then the general custom:

'We played God save the King at the end of our performances and the audience of internees, so-called 'enemy aliens', all stood up. The irony of the situation must have been obvious to everybody there, including the camp officers who had been invited. Here we were, voluntarily honouring the head of the country whose government had put us behind barbed wire because we might be dangerous!'

On one level it seemed an idyllic life, far removed from the dangers of war. But many of the internees like Fritz felt a deep resentment at being unable to fight. This was their war and they did not want to sit back while others did the fighting. Fritz speaks about the sense of dissatisfaction at the time:

'The general mood was one of frustration at being interned in spite of having been declared "friendly" by a tribunal at the beginning of the war; and also resentment by the older internees at being separated from their wives and families who thereby had been deprived not only of the company of their husbands/fathers, but in many cases also of their breadwinners. Among us younger ones, it was mainly frustration at being unable to contribute in any way to the war effort since we considered ourselves to be motivated much more strongly to fight the Nazis than our British contemporaries.'

Little did Fritz know during the summer of 1940 that his chance to join the British forces was just around the corner. In October 1940 he seized one of the few opportunities to be released from internment early and enlisted in the British army. Along with thousands of other male internees who enlisted that autumn, he saw this as his chance to do something active for the war. Now he could fight alongside British soldiers and play his part in the defeat of Nazism. But it was to be a bitter-sweet revelation to discover that the only unit open to enemy aliens at that time was the Auxiliary Military Pioneer Corps which was essentially an unskilled labour corps. Still without British nationality Fritz donned the British Army uniform, swore allegiance to George VI and received the King's Shilling. He was one of around 6,500 German-speaking refugees to enlist in the Pioneer Corps between 1940 and the end of 1941. They became affectionately known as 'The King's Most Loyal Enemy Aliens', and as their individual war records show, they served Britain with total loyalty and were prepared to die for the country that had saved them from Nazi tyranny.

## DIGGING FOR VICTORY

For Fritz Lustig internment on the Isle of Man was over and he started a new life in the British army. During internment he had struck up a friendship with fellow refugee and internee Peter Ganz who was originally from Mainz. Twenty-year old Ganz was firmly agnostic; although his grandparents had converted from Judaism to the Lutheran Church. However this did not prevent him from being arrested by the Gestapo as a 'non-Aryan' and taken to Buchenwald concentration camp. He was released after six weeks and fled to England where he enrolled in 1939 as a student of German and Spanish at King's College London. His studies were interrupted in 1940 when he was arrested and interned on the Isle of Man. He, like Fritz, enlisted in the British forces from internment camp. On 8 October 1940 they arrived at Ilfracombe station on the North Devon coast, together with about twenty other internees, all ex-German refugees from Nazi oppression. An army lorry awaited their luggage. The men themselves marched nearly two miles down the steep hills of Ilfracombe towards their new barracks on the seafront. Not wishing to risk his cello on the lorry Fritz carried it on the long march down to barracks. These turned out to be in a number of requisitioned hotels on the seafront. As Fritz entered, a rotund Corporal with a strong Austrian accent noticed the cello and asked if he could really play. Given the affirmative, Fritz was ordered to report to Corporal Strietzel, a refugee musician and conductor in charge of the Pioneer Corps Orchestra. Before Fritz did so he had to collect his army kit:

> 'Our first job was to draw our uniforms and equipment from the Quartermaster Stores (this included not only the "battledress" but also underwear, a sewing kit and toiletries. Having donned these rather strange khaki garments, we were given some basic drill so that we could be let loose in the streets and knew how to walk smartly and - of primary importance - how to salute any officers we might pass!'

For these refugee soldiers any hope of fighting for the country that had saved them was soon dashed by the realization that they had enlisted into an unglamorous labour corps. Instead of firing a gun in action they found themselves in khaki battledress with a pick and shovel.

That autumn of 1940 the Victorian seaside town of Ilfracombe became a microcosm of German and Austrian intellectual life as many of the soldiers formed a mini-university in their spare time. In particular the older soldiers belonged to professions. They were doctors, engineers, surgeons, dentists, architects, mathematicians and scientists, and ironically the 'alien' Pioneer Corps became one of the most intellectualized units of the British army. During the initial three-week training Fritz and his friend Peter Ganz kept close together. In these uncertain times with many problems and worries they were able to provide moral support to each other and became 'kindred spirits':

'We found the basic training was tedious in the extreme - mainly square bashing, how to march, how to turn left and right, how to "turn about". It was pitiful to see that for a few poor souls nature had obviously not ordained them to be soldiers. They were unable to swing their left arm forward when moving their right leg, and would invariably try to move right leg and right arm together, attracting stern shouted rebukes from the British NCOs (non-commissioned officers) instructing us.'

At the end of the three-week training period Fritz and Peter were separated. Peter was attached to a 'working' Pioneer Company that left Ilfracombe. Once trained, a group of around 350 men formed a company and were sent all over the country on labour duties which varied from forestry work to mixing concrete, constructing Nissen huts, clearing the rubble in bombed cities or constructing coastal defences against a German invasion. The irony of the situation was not lost on Fritz – here they were – originally German and Austrian refugees, mainly Jewish, who had yet to be given British nationality, becoming part of the British Army. They had all sworn allegiance to George VI and began to see themselves as more British than German.

Because of his skills as a cellist Fritz was transferred to Headquarters Company in Ilfracombe as a member of the Pioneer Corps Orchestra which had been formed with other refugee musicians. They became part of the Entertainment Section and, under Corporal Strietzel and Russian-born Nicolai Poliakoff (aka Coco the Clown), they performed many concerts and musical stage-shows to provide morale for the local population and raise funds for the war effort. These shows always turned out a full house. Very quickly Fritz's role was not confined to playing the cello. He was considered the most promising member of the orchestra and was enlisted to help out in the stage productions. The first was a play *Murder on the Second Floor*, performed on three evenings in December 1940:

'I had a walk-on part as a police constable. The play was comprehensively written up in the *Ilfracombe Chronicle* under the sub-heading "Army Unit's Brilliant Play". At the end of February 1941 a play called *White Cargo* was produced, the action of which took place in Africa and depicted the problems faced by a white settler who fell in love with a half-cast woman. I was to take the part of a 'native', Jim Fish, appearing briefly in a few scenes. In one of these I had to sing what I imagined was a native song and allow myself to be beaten by the half-cast woman. As can be imagined, the part required that I was completely 'blacked-up' (apart from my middle-section, which was covered by a loincloth), and that was a lengthy procedure which I was unable to carry out on my own. Proper black make-up was not available, so I was literally painted with a paintbrush and black water-colour by an Austrian, Private Gurschner, who had also designed and painted the scenery.'

Although Fritz was providing a useful service in the orchestra and aiding the nation's morale he wondered where it would all lead. Would this be the sum total of his war? He wanted to fight properly and play his part in the defeat of Nazism. But Fritz would spend nearly three years in the Pioneer Corps before being drafted into British Intelligence where he, and other refugees like him, could make a real difference to the war.

# THREE

## THE M ROOM

WITH MUCH OF Western Europe under Nazi occupation in 1940 the need for intelligence had never been greater nor more urgent. Britain stood alone against the might of the Nazi war machine. Over the skies of Southern England the Battle of Britain pilots struggled in dog-fights with the Luftwaffe planes. Bombing attacks on the capital and other cities almost brought Britain to her knees. The fight at sea was equally intense. British shipping faced devastating attacks from U-boats which threatened to cut off food supplies.

From the outbreak of war until the end of 1940 Kendrick's M Room operators had already gathered an impressive amount of intelligence on Nazi Germany. But who were these secret listeners? At this stage of the war they were drawn from Commissioned Officers in the Army, Navy and Air Force who had either studied languages at Oxford or Cambridge University or were refugees who had arrived in Britain from 1933 onwards and already been granted British nationality. Only they knew about the existence of the M Room which was kept secret from other staff (like couriers, typists and bikers) working on site.

German PoWs from different services were held two to a room or cell in the hope they would talk to each other about what they had not told the British during their interrogations. The ruse proved correct. Limiting two prisoners to a cell also made it easy for the listeners to identify which prisoner was speaking at any one time. Transcriptions from the bugged conversations became known as Special Reports, or SRs. The Special Reports were exceptionally productive in providing the first information on new German technology, warfare, operations and military capability that could not at this stage of the war have been ascertained from interrogation alone. Until the first German General was captured in 1942, intelligence at this stage primarily came from lower rank German PoWs and a few Italians. The information was circulated to all sections of British Intelligence and crucially to commanders at Bletchley Park.

During 1940 Kendrick introduced the use of stool-pigeons (or SPs). Four stool-pigeons were selected from interviews with some eighty refugee soldiers who were serving in the 'alien' Pioneer Corps. Once selected they transferred to Trent Park where they took on their new identity, masking as a fellow German prisoner. They were placed in a cell with a genuine prisoner and primed to discuss and direct the conversation towards things which British Intelligence needed to know. The ruse worked. None of the German PoWs ever suspected the real truth. When people in high places at the Admiralty learned about the use of stool-pigeons they reacted quite badly to obtaining information 'from traitors'. MI19 ignored their concerns and continued on the steady path which it believed would achieve results for the war. And so the use of stool-pigeons was expanded over the course of the war, such that Kendrick would engage a total of 49 German PoWs to become stool-pigeons in return for preferential treatment, outings and rewards, all paid from the Special Fund [SIS fund]. The conversations between the stool-pigeon and PoW were always clandestinely listened to from the M Room. The greatest advantage of the combination of secret listener and stool-pigeon was summed up by Kendrick:

'Whilst direct interrogation may provide valuable information it cannot, as a general rule, reasonably be expected to provide the same insight into the prisoner's mind as is possible by the proper use of the listening method, which in addition to providing independent intelligence, often provides the Interrogators with a check on statements made to them. Careful mixing of prisoners in the cells must, however, be the keynote if success is to be achieved.'

From 1943, after the fall of Stalingrad, MI19 could have used any number of prisoners as stool-pigeons. Drafted into this ruse were German officers and a U-boat captain. What were they offered in return? One interrogator commented: 'we offered them blood, toil, sweat and tears for their efforts, and they served Germany and us magnificently.'

Kendrick himself drafted the six-monthly intelligence reports to Norman Crockatt (head of MI9) as well as weekly personal reports. As a highly efficient Commandant of the whole listening operation, he left nothing to chance. A weekly conference with operations staff was held to discuss their impressions of the material that was being gathered. In a memorandum to Crockatt, Kendrick wrote that the suggestions of his staff 'have been invaluable in enabling stool-pigeons to be properly instructed and any necessary modifications made in their modus operandi.'

Did the German prisoners ever suspect that the British were listening to their conversations? Interestingly they were warned back in Germany that if ever caught to be wary that their conversations might be bugged. But the prisoners soon became complacent and let down their guard. Kendrick was well aware of this. In a memorandum he reassured intelligence chiefs that security consciousness had been encountered amongst the prisoners, but 'this attitude was frequently broken down by careful grouping of PoWs and by devising ways and means of disarming suspicion.' The relaxed and relatively comfortable surroundings of the stately house of Trent Park did much to ensure the prisoners soon forgot their security worries. Later the listeners picked up a conversation between two security-conscious prisoners, one from an Able seaman from U-boat U-264 and the other from the battleship *Scharnhorst* (AIR40/3105):

> N.1552: What do they say in the security lectures?
>
> N.2243: So far it is correct. "You will come to a camp where you will be interrogated from all quarters, by English and American officers and when you are in your rooms you mustn't speak about your U-boat or about any service matters. There is even apparatus installed through which they hear everything, even the slightest sounds."

Only in one or two cases where a prisoner became particularly security conscious were they transferred off site to another camp to avoid 'rumours' spreading amongst the other prisoners.

By the end of the first year of the war Kendrick had submitted 1,533 reports, the majority from air intelligence. Reports were of two kinds: Intelligence Reports in the form of summarized intelligence under key headings, and Secret Recording Reports in dialogue form with German text and translation. It became a huge undertaking in clerical administration to keep, especially the SR reports coming out and circulated to intelligence departments shortly after the conversations were recorded. Kendrick's first Intelligence Report for the period 3 September 1939 to 31 December 1940 showed that his team of secret listeners had gathered extensive and detailed knowledge about Germany's military capabilities. An appendix to the survey gives a comprehensive list of the main topics on which reports were available from the bugged conversations. These included for example: aerodromes in German occupied countries, artillery, armour, Austria, Bulgaria, cavalry, enemy aircraft equipment, Gestapo, conditions in Germany, hand grenades, Hitler, Hitler Youth, Goebbels, Goering,

Himmler, identification of [German] units, Jews, losses (army, German air force and navy), Mussolini, navigation on aircraft, parachute troops, Poland, production of enemy aircraft, British PoWs, rockets, weapons, Western Front, Zeppelin, U-boats, tanks, "S" boats, small arms, SS, strength of enemy armed forces, aerial and magnetic torpedoes, and training of enemy forces.

In Kendrick's covering letter which was attached to the first Survey he outlined qualifying perspectives for intelligence chiefs and wrote, 'the report will enable those responsible for creating the Centre to get a fairly clear idea of its functions and production.' While not in a position this early in the war to estimate values of the intelligence gained, Kendrick assured chiefs that the whole idea of combining secret recordings with the use of stool-pigeons significantly improved the modus operandi of the Centre. F. H. Davidson, Head of the Directorate of Military Intelligence, was more than pleased with the results and circulated the following comments on Kendrick's report: 'I have inspected the whole show and thought it very efficiently run: and the general spirit of this Survey (and the weekly reports) shows the true spirit of attacking intelligence.' The most significant material came from captured Luftwaffe pilots. Gaining intelligence about technology used aboard Luftwaffe planes was going to prove essential. What the listeners overhead was used to corroborate information gathered from interrogations. To the end of December 1940, six hundred and eighty-five German airmen were captured and brought to Trent Park. What they provided was covered in over a thousand reports and often related to technology aboard aircraft. In this respect the secret reports from the listeners made 'their most important single contribution' in discovery of X-Gerät and Y-Gerät, Elektra and Knickebein. As the technology was in more general use by the German air force, so it was mentioned more frequently in the conversations between

PoWs. Impressive as it was then, the most significant discovery related to X-Gerät – the new technology fitted to Luftwaffe aircraft. It was this discovery that earned Kendrick an OBE.

## KNICKEBEIN, X-GERÄT AND Y- GERÄT

After interrogation the Luftwaffe PoWs were returned to their cell where they often bragged to their cellmate about what they had not told the interrogation officer. Revealing partial information during an interrogation was designed to plant a seed in the prisoner's mind such that he would talk in more detail about it to his cellmate afterwards. It was a ruse which rarely failed. Knowledge of the German system Knickebein was one such example. Knickebein made use of a radio navigation system developed for civil aircraft for use in bad visibility, broadcasting two adjoining radio beams in line with a runway. If the plane was to one side of the runway line the pilot would hear 'dot' pips in his headphones, if on the other he would hear 'dashes', and when they merged into a single unbroken tone he would know that he was approaching along the centre line of the runway. In the bombing aid system two such guide beams were sent from widely spaced transmitters, aimed to cross over the target. The bomber flew along one guide beam, and when the other beam signal could be heard (on another receiver) the pilot knew he was over the target. The British did everything possible to jam Knickebein and render it ineffective. In response the Germans developed a new technology. The ears of the secret listeners soon alerted to this new apparatus fitted on German aircraft. The prisoners began to talk about X-Gerät; Gerät meaning instrument. One of the earliest references to X-Gerät came in a conversation recorded between a Lance Corporal (A35) and a Wireless Operator (A38) in February 1940 in which they said [in translation, AIR40/3070]:

A38: He also enquired about the bombing apparatus

A35: Only you mustn't give it away that it is something for bombs. Otherwise they might still want to photograph it. They have just shot down a machine in which an X-Gerät is installed and they can try it out as much as they like, for it is so secret that only he knows about it, or the crew knows it and if the crew keeps its mouth shut they'll never find it out. They can try it out and examine it as much as they like. It is a sort of apparatus that they will never find out

A38: Is it an aiming apparatus?

A35: No, it is not an aiming apparatus. It is an apparatus in which the bombs are hung, that is the bombs hang in it and it is a contraption which hangs behind the W/T operator, and the W/T operator switches it on. And when the aviator has started, and on flying away – there are several transmitters in Germany – and you fly according to the landscape left and right, only in bad weather, it is in fact a bad weather apparatus. And a "Peilanlage" (?D/F installation) is made – and so a current is sent down from the machine, downwards, then you know whether you are over a village or a town, or towards the objective which you are trying to reach. And when you are over this, the order comes from over there, over this "guiding ray" (*Leitstrahl*) to the "Gerät", and so the bombs drop: quite automatic.

A38: I never heard anything about this.

X-Gerät was developed when the British became too good at interfering with Knickebein. It was an early radar system which enabled German pilots to conduct more precise bombing raids across England. Using a main guide beam for the bomber to fly along, intersecting beams were placed at a set distance from each other and from the target. On getting the signal from the first intersecting beam a timer was started, on crossing the second a second impulse would be fed into the timer. As the distance between the intersecting beams was known, this showed the ground speed of the aircraft irrespective of headwind or tailwind, so at the moment the bomber reached the target (again at known distance from the second intersecting beam) the timer automatically released the bombs. Armed with information about X-Gerät from the secret recordings, the Air Ministry was able to develop counter-technology and build a profile of German war capability. In one bugged conversation after an interrogation the following was picked up between a bomber pilot, codenamed A.807, captured on 10 April 1941, and another pilot A.777, captured on 13 March 1941 (WO208/3457):

A.807: Did he ask you about X-Gerät?

A.777: No, only about the night fighters

A.807: 'we used to fly by Knickebein at about 11 or 12 o'clock but we don't do that any more.

A807 then proceeded to tell his cellmate that the interrogation officer seemed to know that two beams were sent out from a base in Cherbourg but nothing more detailed than that. Pilot A.777 replied, 'They know that all the construction work is carried out by the French. He has a rough idea of it, but he doesn't know exactly, especially about the new Y-Gerät.'

Y-Gerät was devised to overcome English interference, since it was harder to jam than a system of cross beams. Y-Gerät allowed ground controllers to determine the position of the bomber by measuring time delay of responding (reflecting) signals from the aircraft, giving distance from the ground station (the ground station's directional receiver aerial showed the plane's direction) and instructing the pilot by radio. For bombing purposes Y-Gerät was claimed to be accurate to within an area of 200 square yards. The prisoners did not appear to know the precise location of the beam transmitters, but they did know that there were two positions: Zentrale A and Zentrale B. 'A' was west of Cherbourg and 'B' in the neighbourhood of Kassel. Once British Intelligence knew the location of these transmitters they passed the information to the RAF who authorised air sorties to attack the transmitters. One Luftwaffe pilot spoke in his cell about the Lotsenpeiler. This mystified British Intelligence until it was explained in a secret recording by another air force PoW. The Lotsenpeiler worked on the VHF wave-band and was the method by which aircraft were guided from the aerodrome to the Y beam, and again on its return flight, from the point where the aircraft left the beam back to the aerodrome. It was never used when aircraft were flying on the beam. The use of the Lotsenpeiler necessitated keeping to an exact height but this also prejudiced the crews against its use. By 1941 all aircraft of the Gruppe had been equipped for the Y-system. Although a map of the system had been captured by the British it was barely legible. It was only from the bugged conversations that British Intelligence was able to reconstruct most of the lines of the Y-system. The Y-system operated from Kassel to Hull, Sheffield, Liverpool, Birmingham and London, and from a point just west of Cherbourg to London and Sheffield. At least four tracks were drawn from Poix and at least seven from Fécamp. This system was effective for the Luftwaffe until the British learned to transmit false 'reflecting' signals from Alexandra Palace in North London. The German pilots did not know their location. Some landed on RAF airfields, thinking they were in France.

The discovery of X-Gerät was one of the most important pieces of intelligence in the early part of the war. Kendrick received a glowing letter from Norman Crockatt, dated 10 April 1940, conveying his thanks: 'to congratulate those officers under you who contributed so largely to one of the most successful pieces of intelligence investigation I have ever come across.'

Information gathered was not solely about German technology. It was important to understand the mindset of the enemy. In this respect the unguarded conversations of the prisoners revealed some unexpected attitudes. The listeners began to pick up a growing respect amongst Luftwaffe pilots for the British Spitfire which was holding its own in the skies over England during the Battle of Britain. The following extract comes from a conversation secretly recorded between a wireless operator (A26) and a pilot (A29). British Intelligence has given them a reference rather than use of their real names (AIR40/3070):

> A26: the Spitfire overtakes us
>
> A29: a first class machine! What a pity we haven't one like her
>
> A26: She has better manoeuvrability and ...
>
> A29: (interrupting) goes faster?
>
> A26: Yes...
>
> A29: if the Spitfire goes up to 10,000 metres, or even 9,000 metres, the fighters will not catch up so easily; even the 109 will find it difficult enough

It became clear that Luftwaffe pilots now pinned their hopes on Germany's new Focke-Wulf fighter which was expected to go into action shortly. In the same conversation from above, pilot A29 admitted to his cellmate that he had flown the new Focke-Wulf fighter. Cellmate A26 then commented that there was another new machine. To which pilot A29 replied, 'The HE177 dive bomber; it is to go to the formation that I was to join. But they [the British] mustn't find out anything about it and we mustn't talk about it in camp. It is still being kept dark, even in Germany.' On 20 August the following was overheard about the Spitfire but also about Luftwaffe formations for attack on coastal cities and docks (AIR40/3070):

A344: The Spitfire is better at banking than the "110". Our W/T operator only has four weapons in the moveable turret. He can't shoot straight in front. The Air Force has equipped the "109" with bombs. It is a marvellous idea and works quite splendidly. During the attack we flew in *Staffel* formations. One *Staffel* always flies 2000 metres lower than the other. We set fire to all the oil stores in Portland, Weymouth and Plymouth. They shot down six of us.

Luftwaffe crew appeared keen to share their experiences of the moment when they were shot down by Spitfires. The following conversation took place between an Observer (A44) and Pilot (A46):

A46: I came down near Aberdeen – on the sea. I was attacked at 9500m by 3 Spitfires.

A44: We were attacked by 10 Spitfires. My Mechaniker [mechanic] was killed. We had a spare W/T operator with us. Our engines were done in. My swimming-jacket was bust.

A46: I am the only survivor. My observer, Lt. Frose, could not cling on to the boat and was drowned. We were unable to inflate the boat properly, because the compressed-air container was only half full. Our boat was half full of water. We had landed in a minefield.

These snippets of information are amongst tens of thousands that were gathered by the M Room operators. Isolated references on their own may seem insignificant, however it enabled British Intelligence to keep track on German losses and air strategy, but also the enemy's attitude towards British forces. Updated news of the continued rearmament programme was also gleaned as demonstrated in a comment from a Luftwaffe pilot to his cellmate on 28 March 1940 in which he said: 'The whole of North Germany is one big aerodrome. The further north one goes, the worse it becomes.'

## NAVAL INTELLIGENCE

As valuable as air intelligence was, it could not be gathered in isolation. MI19 also relied on naval intelligence to combat the increasing U-boat menace at sea. During the period of Kendrick's first survey to the end of 1940, 447 German Naval officers and 31 Italian Naval officers passed through Trent Park, the majority from U-boats. Italian naval PoWs provided very little by way of intelligence except to give an indication of low morale amongst crews. From the M Room the listeners were able to establish details of the strength and movement of German U-boats as well as their losses sustained in the Norwegian campaign, for example. From information gathered from the PoWs throughout the year it was also possible to monitor the progress of Germany's new battleship construction programme. On technical matters the most important naval information of this period was the discovery of the magnetic torpedo about which some PoWs spoke in detail.

## ARMY INTELLIGENCE

Relatively few army prisoners were captured during the first phase of the war. Their influx did not gather momentum until after the successful British campaigns in North Africa in 1942. Kendrick's first survey draws on information provided from only 113 German officers and other ranks. What was picked up in the M Room related mainly to detailed descriptions of tank battles in France prior to the evacuation of the British Expeditionary Force at Dunkirk in June 1940. Other conversations dealt with the type of tanks used, railway guns and the 'liquid air' weapon. Some army PoWs spoke about the landing of German troops by air during the invasion of Holland and the heavy losses of men and aircraft. All types and sizes of bombs were mentioned. The size of bombs used during 1940 by the German Air Force were gradually increasing in weight to 3,600 kg per bomb. In addition to high explosive bombs, references were made to other special types of bombs such as liquid air, oxygen, cable and flame bombs. The PoWs expressed doubt that Germany could win the war by bombing techniques alone. This provided an important indicator to Kendrick on the reality of the German military capability.

The most frequent discussions concerned a possible invasion of Britain, the use of gas in warfare and matters concerning morale in the German forces. As expectations of an invasion heightened, so too the subject became more frequent in discussions between the prisoners, especially in July, early August 1940 and from mid-September to November 1940. Listeners soon picked up preliminary references to the possible cancellation of the autumn invasion plans and carefully monitored any signs of its truth. It provided British military command with the first signs that Britain's shore may yet be safe. Even so there was no room for complacency and the intelligence gathering continued as a top-priority.

Concerning morale in the German armed forces, British Intelligence picked up the impression that it depended largely on their faith in Hitler. In the majority of cases the prisoners expressed what amounted to 'a blind worship' of Hitler. A downward trend in morale could only be expected by a decisive defeat or if anything should happen to the Führer. 'Fighting morale' was still defined by the belief in an early victory against Britain and that the prisoners would be home by Christmas. As this became more unlikely a mood of pessimism began to prevail until renewed hopes of an invasion of England's shores surfaced in their conversations. In his report Kendrick concluded that 'any future developments in morale are likely to depend on the military situation.'

The largest number of references in Special Reports on any one subject apart from invasion and morale concerned enemy losses. British Intelligence was keen to verify and learn about the losses sustained by the Germans after a campaign. During the autumn of 1940 the listeners at Trent Park gained a more general picture of the extent of German losses incurred in the heavy daylight raids, but also continued references to losses on night flights, mainly during take off and landing. In one report a PoW quoted Kesselring [German Field Marshal] as saying that during 1940 Germany was losing 280 aircraft a month from accidents alone. The clandestine recordings appeared to be particularly valuable in giving information about killed or missing airmen. At this stage of the war it was difficult for British military commanders to gain this kind of information by any other method.

The listeners also picked up that around May 1940 the Germans had tried out a type of 'nerve gas' with temporary soporific effect at Maastricht. Although the majority of references to the use of gas were of a general kind, British Intelligence discovered from these conversations that Germany would not employ gas in an attack against Britain unless used by Britain first. Other PoWs spoke about the alleged use of an 'anaesthetising gas' in Belgium. In the period up to July 1940 the morale of the German Armed Forces appears to have been at a consistently high level. The M Room operators picked up tensions between the army and SS. In a special report dated 23 July 1940 a conversation was recorded between two lower ranks, Obergefreiter (Lance Corporal), codenamed M99, and Oberfeldwebel (codenamed M98) that became quite heated:

M98: It was the same in Poland. Many of the SS were stood against the wall for disobedience by the Army Commanders.

And the Germania regiment was a complete failure. The Germania made the most terrible mess of things.

M99: Well, an Army Officer told me that the SS were the best infantry regiments in Germany. And it was an officer who said it.

After a further brief exchange prisoner M99 referred to the young Wehrmacht (army) subalterns as contemptible rats. To which M98 replied, 'Balderdash!' The conversation continued:

M98: The scraps between the SS and the Wehrmacht will never end!

M99: What happened in Poland? One mustn't talk about the casualties. But I can at least tell you that our SS formations had heavy losses! And the army left us in the lurch! It was lamentable! At any rate the SS will never again be subordinate to the army, that is clear! To give some decrepit old general the right of doing whatever he likes with an SS regiment! They gave us the dirtiest work…

At this point he was interrupted:

M98: I suppose you are not trying to insinuate that the other Infantry regiments had no losses? They lost just as heavily as the SS – you can take it from me! Well, anyway on the Western Front the SS did nothing decisive.

M99: (shouting) You don't know anything!

M98: (also shouting) Oh but I do! Every child knows that!

M99: You don't know it. The SS fought just as bravely… (interrupted)

M98: But it did nothing decisive.

M99: (Quite excited) Of course, of course, only the Army … but you seem to forget who commands in Germany today – the Army or the Party.

M98: (Annoyed) Well, you seem to think that the Party and the SS rule Germany and the Army has to play second fiddle! That is where you are entirely wrong!

And so the argument went on. What MI19 were gaining from conversations like these was an insight into the inner workings and politics of the military and SS that could not be ascertained by any other means. British Intelligence could begin to piece together the views and realize that there was a less than unified front in Germany, especially by those who ran the Nazi regime. Tensions such as these could be manipulated for propaganda purposes, but provided an important key to understanding the mind-set of the enemy.

## ATROCITIES

During 1940 the secret listeners picked up the first references to atrocities committed by the SS in Poland. The subject was raised again in Kendrick's six-monthly survey at the end of 1941 where he wrote: 'a few PoWs have had some experience of, or heard about, the situation in Poland. Several spoke of atrocities committed against the Poles. One PoW who had passed through Poland on returning from the Russian front said that the whole of South Poland was 'lying fallow owing to the refusal of the peasants to cultivate the land; bread was unattainable and both children and adults could be seen looking for scraps among the refuse of Germany Army messes' (WO208/4970).

At this point there appeared to be no specific mention of concentration camps. Kendrick knew from his period of office as British

Passport Control Officer in Vienna during the Nazi occupation in 1938 that thousands of Jews disappeared, were rounded up by the Gestapo and sent to concentration camps. He had mixed in Viennese social circles and had a number of Jewish friends in the city. Kendrick knew the risks for Jews. He and his staff had spent every spare hour trying to issue as many visas as possible to get Jews out of Austria. Now at Trent Park he primed the listeners to record any conversations about atrocities. Such references would intensify after 1942 when Hitler formalized his "Final Solution" for the Jews of Europe.

## GERMAN TROOPS IN OCCUPIED TERRITORIES

Secret recordings during 1940 monitored the behaviour of German troops in Nazi occupied countries. In Holland and Belgium troops requisitioned whatever they wanted. France was the only country which provided economic cooperation with the occupying regime when the Schneider-Creusot company agreed to construct 140 locomotives for Germany. These locomotives had been built in Vienna but that factory was now engaged on constructing parts for submarines. It was noted that the first German officers to arrive in Paris in July behaved so badly that they spoilt it for their successors. In September a German soldier raped a fifteen year old girl and was shot for it. By February 1941 one PoW at Trent Park revealed that the behaviour of German troops cost them two murdered men a day. The Trent Park listeners recorded conversations about acts of sabotage in France. Telephone wires were cut and aircraft damaged at night. In the neighbourhood of Hitler's headquarters lights were down and it was reported that 350 persons were shot as a result. Interestingly British Intelligence picked up two further important pieces of information known to the German PoWs: French inhabitants were hiding English airmen, and 'telephone wires tapped and information transmitted to England by an espionage organisation, 20 members of which have been arrested in Brest.' In Holland Dutch soldiers were being compelled to salute German officers. In Amsterdam there were reports of brawling between German soldiers and Dutch civilians. In January 1941 an SS battalion was on its way to the country to preserve order and prevent anti-Nazi outbreaks after serious shootings in the capital. One PoW commented that in Amsterdam 'practically all our rear-gunners have gonorrhoea... efficiency was noticeably reduced.' Two months later industrial unrest led to the shooting of strikers.

Thirty-six Italian PoWs passed through Trent Park during the period of Kendrick's first survey. They yielded virtually nothing in the way of intelligence, except comments which revealed that they had a poor opinion of Italy's war capabilities. Most recognised that Mussolini had made a great mistake in entering the war, and all were anxious about internal developments in Italy. The news of the British successes in North Africa, which they received while at this Centre, added to their depression.

## EXPANSION OF THE M ROOM

British Intelligence never once entertained the notion of defeat against Nazi Germany. During the late spring of 1940 it instigated plans to expand the secret listening programme, anticipating successes in the war that would bring more German PoWs under British military control. It was obvious that Trent Park would prove inadequate for an influx of prisoners. Neither would the relatively small team of listeners be able to deal with the volume of intelligence-gathering. It was proposed to use two other sites. Making them ready for proper use would take time but with foresight the plan would pay off at the right time.

Two estates were chosen deep in the heart of the Buckinghamshire countryside – Latimer House at Chalfont & Latimer near Amersham, and Wilton Park near Beaconsfield. Both sites had a stately house and were close to a railway station which afforded a ready rail link to the capital. The sites were chosen because they were well hidden and would preserve the secrecy surrounding the whole operation. Kendrick was tasked with their set-up and governance of the intelligence staff. The stately houses of Latimer House and the White House at Wilton Park were requisitioned for special purposes. These were chosen 'in consultation with the Admiralty, the Air Ministry and A.A. Command (Anti-aircraft) as being the most suitable.'

Over the course of the next two years the sites were made ready for use in what became a massive undertaking and one which was overseen by Kendrick. Work included the construction of cells, Nissen huts in the grounds, the construction and wiring of an M Room for the listeners, and bugging the complex. As with Trent Park, both new sites had to be wired and bugging devices fitted. In addition to the permanent camps four semi-mobile units, mounted in converted 32-seater coaches, were provided for use by Kendrick's team. The units were designed to fulfil a twofold purpose: that should the centres be bombed, the mobile units could move to any premises and provide emergency facilities within twenty-four hours.

Just how important was the clandestine listening programme is highlighted in a series of memoranda by the Joint Intelligence Sub-Committee in Cabinet Papers (CAB121/236). The memoranda were marked 'strictly limited circulation', and unlike the secret reports from the listeners, had to be 'KEPT UNDER LOCK AND KEY'. In a memorandum dated 7 October 1940 the huge priority given to the unit is indicated by the authorization of unlimited funds for the expansion to two new sites. Only earlier in the year the intelligence chief of the committee agreed that the unit 'is of the utmost operational importance, vital to the needs of the three fighting services.' If anything was required by Kendrick it had been further agreed that he did not need to go through the usual channels for authorization. That memorandum stated:

> 'Its requirements should be given the highest degree of priority, that the normal formalities regarding Service plans and tenders should be waived and that any work required should be put in hand at once forthwith irrespective of cost and completed by the earliest possible date.'

Construction of the two sites and making them operational was estimated at over £400,000 – a huge sum of money at that time which further underlines the importance of the whole operation. But the special requirements did not stop there. Two aerodromes which were in the process of being constructed near Latimer House and Wilton Park came under scrutiny. Intelligence chiefs were so concerned that once the houses were operational the noise of the aircraft would interfere with the listening work that they even contemplated moving the aerodromes. The Joint Intelligence Committee met on 5 November 1941 and discussed the problem of the airfields. It had already been suggested that the aerodrome near Wilton Park should be abandoned. However over £300,000 had already been spent on the construction of the aerodrome at Bovingdon which was 60% complete. To minimize interference with the work at Latimer House it was decided to use the airfield as a ground training station. However it was expressed that in the Committee's opinion, 'financial considerations should be subordinated to the requirements of these Interrogation Centres.' Rear-Admiral Godfrey of Naval Intelligence emphasised the great importance of the work at the centres and the effect of interruption by flying operations in the vicinity.

Sir Charles Portal of the Air Ministry informed the committee that the Ministry had agreed to give up the aerodrome near Wilton Park. It was proposed to keep the Bovingdon aerodrome operational because it was four miles away from Latimer House but that a Bomber OTU (Officer Training Unit) would be located there instead with flying restrictions. Sir Dudley Pound reiterated the view that financial considerations and the large sum of money already spent on the aerodrome at Bovingdon should not be a deciding factor in whether to save it or not. The first priority had to be the interrogation centres where the listeners were to work. The issue was settled with a decision not to construct an aerodrome near Wilton Park; and restrictions would operate at Bovingdon to completely minimise any effect on the work at Latimer House. Until Latimer House and Wilton Park became fully functional, Trent Park continued to be the only clandestine centre with M Room operations.

# FOUR

## SPILLING THE BEANS

DURING 1940 BRITISH merchant shipping, warships and submarines battled hard for supremacy at sea. Losses in attacks by German Navy and U-boats inflicted serious damage on the British Navy and supply lines into Britain. It was a difficult battle that would last most of the war. Although life at Trent Park carried on with the slow, painstaking gathering of intelligence, the results were to prove crucial during 1941, especially for the Battle of the Atlantic. Hours of patient listening from the M Room would pay off and give British Intelligence the information it needed to gain the upper hand. PoWs during this period were mainly prisoners from U-boats brought into ports by the Royal Navy or Luftwaffe personnel shot down over Britain. All intelligence was shared with commanders at Bletchley Park. Much of the interrogation during this period, even of U-boat crews, was undertaken by staff directly under Wing Commander Felkin of Air Intelligence at Trent Park. Felkin sent regular transcripts of interrogations to Kendrick to collate with other intelligence.

In the period of Kendrick's first six-monthly report for 1941 the number of prisoners captured from the German Navy amounted to 288, and only five from the Italian Navy. Intelligence was gleaned from 238 captured German Air Force personnel. Kendrick's report summarized intelligence from the secret recordings of conversations and interrogations as well as information collected from captured documents. Three German army PoWs passed through Trent Park, all other ranks, who were captured in British raids on the Lofoten Islands (off Norway). Invasion of Britain was no longer a major theme of conversation amongst the PoWs and if mentioned, they expressed doubt that it would take place at all. The focus of conversation in the cells in the first two months of 1941 gave British Intelligence the first indication that the enemy was planning to intensify his U-boat attacks from March and carry out a blockade of Britain. Hitler intended to starve Britain into submission. However during May a very different pictured emerged from the bugged conversations. PoWs spoke about the heavy U-boat losses that had been inflicted on the German Navy and the increased difficulty of attacking British shipping from the air because of improved defence by the RAF.

Throughout 1941 Luftwaffe pilots were continuing to devastate cities in their bombing raids across Britain. The city and dockyards of Plymouth came under intense attack. Much of the city centre would be left completely flattened during the blitz. Fritz Lustig was still based in Ilfracombe with the Entertainment Section of the Pioneer Corps, but now their duties included travelling to other towns and cities to perform in concert. In March one of the tours took them to Plymouth to perform in two shows in the Royal Marine Barracks. It was here that Fritz experienced firsthand the blitz on the city, and ironically details of which the M Room operators would later pick up from captured Luftwaffe pilots. During the second performance Fritz noticed a small red lamp in the centre of the footlights suddenly lighting up while Coco the Clown was in the middle of his act:

'Immediately large numbers of the audience got up and left. Coco brought his act to a swift end and we were told to pack up and proceed to an air-raid shelter. The red lamp indicated that an air-raid warning had sounded, which could not be heard in the theatre itself. The warning was justified: the Luftwaffe had selected Plymouth as their target that night. In the shelter we heard the bangs of the exploding bombs, some of which were close enough to cause the underground shelter to shake and clouds of dust to be raised. The shelter had no toilet and I was obliged to go up to ground level. It proved to be close by, but these two or three minutes out of the shelter were pretty frightening: the bombs were still dropping, and now I could hear the terrible, threatening "whine", going down in pitch the nearer they came to the ground. None struck the immediate surroundings while I was out of the shelter, but I was very glad when I had reached the relative safety of being underground again!'

The following months proceeded without further incident. But the fate of Europe's Jews was never far from the surface. Towards the end of the year Fritz heard news from a friend that she and her sister had news via America that their parents whom they had left behind in Berlin had committed suicide prior to being deported by the Nazis to a horrifying fate. Fritz comments, 'From my remarks when I related this to my own parents in a letter I can see that as early as the end of 1941 the fate of the Jews who had remained in Germany was known – certainly to those of us from Germany.' It would not be long before full graphic details of the annihilation programme for Europe's Jews would be picked up by British Intelligence via the M Room operators.

## GERMAN WARSHIPS AND U-BOATS

For now all focus remained on the vital Naval intelligence that was necessary to fight the U-boat menace and win the Battle of the Atlantic. The intense battle at sea continued. In the first six months of 1941 two prize crews from the *Admiral Spee* passed through Trent Park. Members captured from the warship *Gneisenau* discussed the movements, tactics and exploits of the vessel and also the German battleship *Scharnhorst*. Listeners picked up important information about how the battleships refuelled at sea. Other PoWs provided vital descriptions of the damage inflicted on German vessels at Brest. In secretly recorded conversations the listeners overheard the survivors of the battleship *Bismarck* describe her last voyage in considerable detail, including the damage inflicted on her during her fight with British warships *Hood* and *Prince of Wales*. British Intelligence gathered that the Bismarck had managed to scuttle. What was needed now was information on her condition and ability to fight again. That kind of news did not take long to emerge from other PoWs just brought to Trent Park, and it soon became apparent that the *Bismarck* was undergoing repairs ready for operations again. German naval personnel helpfully leaked technical details aboard specific battleships, i.e. their armour, armament, construction and engines for the *Bismarck*, *Tirpitz*, *Scharnhorst*, *Gneisenau* and *Admiral Spee*.

Due to U-boat losses an interesting shift in attitude was emerging amongst the prisoners who began to doubt the use of the U-boat as a decisive weapon in deciding the outcome of the war. Captured crews provided precise details of losses and numbers of U-boats still operational at sea. In May 1941 one prisoner, described in an MI19 report as an anti-Nazi, discussed with his cellmate precise numbers of U-boats, saying that its full strength was 50, of which 20 were at sea, 20 in port and 10 in dock. It also emerged that there was a shortage of trained U-boat crews. Other PoWs confirmed that more than 70 U-boats had been in operation but 35 had been sunk. References to the loss of a specific U-boat often reached the ears of British Intelligence through the M Room weeks before any official announcement had been made in the German press. It underlines the importance of the whole listening operation.

## GERMAN AIR FORCE

Naval PoWs from two Kondors discussed the new German *109* fighter and the long distance bomber *HE177*. Further discussions on navigation and communication on aircraft provided really useful information to MI19. PoWs continued to mention Knickebein, Elecktra and X-Gerät, and Britain's interference with navigational beams. However one of the most significant pieces of intelligence received during this period related to the new heavy bomb termed 'Max' (2,500kg) and mine-laying techniques. Kendrick reported that secret recordings uncovered 'the introduction of 1lb incendiaries with a small explosive charge.'

The most outstanding contribution of the listeners during this period was in the field of mines and torpedoes. It was discovered that the Germans had introduced a new type of mine with delayed action, acoustic and water-pressure as well as an improved version of the magnetic mine. Listeners picked up the target areas for mine-laying in British waters. Accompanying this information was considerable detail about the various heights from which German aircraft dropped the mines. Due to the improvement of British defences the enemy had largely abandoned dropping mines from a low altitude. To maintain accuracy from a higher altitude it was discovered that the Germans were developing a "mine-bomb", fitted with fins and without parachute. Just how significant this intelligence was is outlined in a letter from B. F Trench at Naval Intelligence Division of the Admiralty in Whitehall to Kendrick on 6 February 1941. Trench informed Kendrick that the Director of Torpedoes and Mines was especially pleased with intelligence in the Special Reports and wrote: 'the type of mine mentioned as being "stirred up by propellers" seems to be a new type and any information regarding this is of utmost importance. Especially important is any indication regarding its external appearance and whether it is similar to other aircraft mines' (WO208/3460).

Further praise was received when John Godfrey, Commander-in-Chief of the Naval Intelligence Division at the Admiralty, wrote to the Directorate of Military Intelligence on 11 February 1941: 'Without them [the Secret Reports] it would have been impossible to piece together the histories of ships, their activities and the tactics employed by U-boats in attacking convoys.' He admitted that the hardest naval information to obtain with any degree of reliability concerned technical matters and finished by congratulating the workers: 'convey to the staff at the CSDIC my warm appreciation of their work.'

By May the value of the Naval intelligence was clearly spelt out by the Admiralty in a letter to Major-General F.H.N. Davidson. Information picked up in secret recordings and interrogations revealed that the enemy was about to make alterations in his mining attack. The Admiralty liaised with Felkin and Kendrick to advise them of the technicalities of the mines and what exactly to try to get out of the PoWs. As a result it enabled the Director of Torpedoes and Mining to form an accurate picture of the situation and 'recognise the new object directly it arrived and have an officer on spot without any delay and to issue a warning and guidance at home and abroad.'

It was not only the Admiralty that was benefiting from the work in the M Room. Most of the information was of direct relevance to the Air Ministry and 'enabled Air staff to keep abreast of enemy technical developments and in some instances to take effective counter measures.' The increase in staff at Trent Park at the beginning of 1941 was justified by the results from the M Room. Getting the various Intelligence Departments of the Army, Navy and Air Force to liaise was never going to be an easy job but Kendrick had succeeded. Boyle of the Air Ministry in Whitehall told Davidson at the War Office: 'I am very grateful for the most helpful attitude of Colonel Kendrick and his staff in dealing with the problems of the Air side. I feel sure that equally valuable results will be forthcoming in the future.'

Two days later Stewart Menzies, Head of MI6, wrote to Norman Crockatt of MI9 and reinforced the importance of the work at Trent Park. Menzies wrote: 'From my point of view, the reports are of distinct value, and I trust the work will be maintained and every possible assistance given to the Centre [CSDIC]. It is essential that the Service Departments should collaborate closely by providing Kendrick with the latest questionnaires, without which he must be working largely in the dark.'

## STRATEGY AND MORALE

Gauging the effect of RAF bombing raids on German cities was not easy once a pilot had completed his sortie and returned to base. It was here that British Intelligence relied on the M Room operators to pick up such details. The bugged conversations revealed that substantial damage had been inflicted on places such as Kiel, Wilhelmshaven, Hamburg, Mannheim and Berlin. Morale amongst the German Air Force was in decline due to heavy losses sustained during their attack on British shipping and raids over Britain. PoWs began to criticise Germany's bombing strategy. Kendrick noted, 'Outspoken pessimism about the outcome of the war is rarely met with, but occasional discussion of the possibility of losing the war is in strong contrast to the prevailing mood during 1940, when such talk was virtually unheard of.'

A conversation between a British army officer and U-boat

Commander, previously serving on the battleship *Scharnhorst*, revealed a idolisation of Adolf Hitler. Prisoner N511, as he was known in the secret transcripts, had been present at the launching of battleship *Prince Eugen* and the Führer stepped on board and met the crew (WO208/3455):

> 'I shall never in all my life forget the moment when I saw the Führer. An electric shock went through and through me and it is just the same when he speaks... As he stood there on the platform and looked around it was really quite unforgettable. The Führer casts a spell over anyone he looks at... and when you have once heard the Führer speak, there radiates from him a compelling influence which cannot be described. You can't hear him on the wireless, you must see him. He takes possession of you.'

The weakening of belief in an early victory often promised by Hitler led some POWs at Trent Park to express a considerable measure of political criticism. Party Leaders were frequently attacked and references made to strained relations between the German armed forces, SS and SA. Kendrick noted that, 'Hitler remains for the majority of PoWs above controversy, but towards the end of the period under review there were several unusually irreverent references to Hitler by Naval personnel.'

In terms of German military strategy, Naval PoWs spoke freely in their cells to each other about the movement of aircraft to Romania and U-Boat personnel to Bulgaria. Relations between Germany and Russia were said to be strained and heavy fortifications were being constructed on Germany's eastern front. There was talk of the deployment of a new long range bomber *HE177* against cities like Moscow and increased references to the movement of troops to the East. This was accompanied by some withdrawal of aircraft away from the West. British Intelligence could monitor the build-up towards Hitler's invasion of Russia, a major change in military strategy that could ultimately change the course of the war and direct troops away from an invasion of England. British Intelligence was already prepared when news broke of the German invasion of Russia on Sunday 22 June.

## HITLER INVADES RUSSIA

Just days before the news of Hitler's invasion of Russia, Fritz Lustig was back in Ilfracombe at the headquarters of the Pioneer Corps. Prima ballerina and ex-refugee Hanne Musch, also married to a refugee soldier in the Corps, organised a dance recital in Ilfracombe's Garrison Theatre in which she and others in the Entertainment Section took part. Twenty-two items were performed; from musical items to dance. Again Fritz found himself on stage alongside actor Carl Jaffe and baritone Karg-Bebenburg in a performance of *Bolero Phantastique* (music by Ravel). Hanne Musch played the part of a Senorita in a bar who was being courted by the above three gentlemen. In a letter to his parents Fritz described his costume: 'long black trousers, white shirt with open collar, coloured sash, red head scarf, big black Spanish hat made of cardboard, big gilt ear-rings, long painted-on black side-boards'. He comments in his unpublished memoirs: 'I suppose we looked suitably Spanish. The steps we had to perform were not very complicated or difficult, but as I had to take part in the musical numbers as well, it required a quick change before and after my stage appearance.'

Although immersed in entertainment activities, politics and the events unfolding across Europe were never far from Fritz's mind. News of Hitler's invasion of Russia caused great apprehension and he discussed his concerns with a fellow Pioneer soldier Roy Henderson, a young Englishman and conscientious objector whose pacifist position had landed him in the Pioneer Corps. Roy was prepared to don the army uniform on condition it did not mean taking part in the fighting. As an actor, Roy was also drafted into the Entertainment Section. Fritz recalls:

'We knew that Churchill was well-known for his strong anti-Communist views. After the invasion of Russia, we wondered whether Churchill would now side with the Germans to fight the hated Bolsheviks. A radio speech by the Prime Minister had been announced for the evening, and all soldiers in Ilfracombe were invited to assemble in the Garrison Theatre to listen to it. Roy and I did so and were greatly relieved to hear that Britain was now considering herself an ally of the Soviet Union in the fight against Nazi Germany.'

Back in the M Room at Trent Park the listeners continued to track German military campaigns in Russia and the fierce U-boat battles at sea. British Intelligence firmly held on to the belief that only the intelligence game could, in the end, win the war against Hitler.

## M ROOM INTELLIGENCE: JULY – DECEMBER 1941

In the six month period from 1 July 1941 to 31 December 1941 the listeners transcribed 1,324 individual Special Reports from the M Room. Most of it came from the bugged conversations of U-boat crew, German naval personnel and Air Force PoWs. Although no German army PoWs were captured during this period, matters relating to army intelligence were often provided by U-boat crew or Luftwaffe pilots. For example, in Holland and Norway which were under German occupation, they provided evidence of civilian resistance and Germans fears of sabotage, and in North-West France there were suggestions of attacks on U-boats in their pens. Conditions in Germany itself seemed favourable with little evidence of any hardship being suffered from the war. In Southern Germany and Austria food conditions were less favourable and there were suggestions that religious persecution of Jews was unpopular.

Kendrick's six-monthly survey shows that his unit dealt with 341 personnel from the German Navy and U-boats. Other ranks amounted to 301 who were captured from various vessels: the *Bismarck, Alstertor, Gonzenheim, Egerland, Lothringen* and prize ship *Ketty Brövig*. Also from Raider 35 (Pinguin) and Raider 16, as well as the following U-boats: U-651, U-138, U-556, U-570, U-501, U-111, U-95, U-433 and U-574. Amongst the details overheard by the listeners was information from survivors about the sinking of the German battleship *Bismarck* on 29 May. Attempts had been made to send sea and air assistance to the ship but without success. Its final moments are unclear and still subject to debate amongst historians. The transcripts may shed light on this and provide historians with eye-witness accounts, albeit from the German perspective. The *Bismarck* and her sister ship *Tirpitz* were two of the largest battleships ever built by Germany. British commanders had their eye on tracking their every movements, often off the Scandinavian coast.

*Bismarck* was tasked with raiding British shipping from North America to Britain and became one of the main surface threats in the North Atlantic too. She engaged and destroyed the prized British battleship *HMS Hood* at the Battle of Denmark Strait. Two days later *Bismarck* was pursued relentlessly by the Royal Navy and attacked by torpedo bombers from *HMS Ark Royal*. It was reported that the following morning British battleship *Dorsetshire* destroyed the *Bismarck*. German accounts provide an alternative explanation and say that she was scuttled. However survivors were spotted in the waters and the British destroyer *Maori* moved in to pick them up. In total the ship rescued 110 survivors from an original crew of 2,200 before leaving the scene because of threats from a U-boat. Bismarck's surviving crew were brought to Trent Park for interrogation and clandestine monitoring by M Room operators.

The Admiralty was particularly concerned for information on any of the German battleships. Special Reports revealed that a new fearsome warship *Tirpitz* had completed her trials and was ready for Atlantic operations. Damage from RAF bombing of the battleships *Gneisenau* and *Scharnhorst* were also mentioned, as was the refit of the *Hipper* which was set for a tropical cruise. Criticism was expressed from both U-boat and other Naval PoWs that the German High Command had shortened the period of training for new recruits and was drawing heavily from the Hitler Youth. During the period under review Kendrick's Centre dealt with survivors from nine U-boats. The volume of intelligence was not only impressive but vast. Vital information was gleaned on the movements and exploits of the U-boat fleets. Estimates of the number of U-boats in operation varied between 25 to 50. References were made to various U-boats having been sunk by Britain. In some cases the Admiralty had had no accurate confirmation of these losses until one particular PoW, a former W/T operator, said that sixty U-boats had been lost. MI19 considered the transcripts from his conversations to be reliable because he had been engaged in passing messages from Kondors to U-boats and was therefore judged to be well-informed. Another PoW, captured from a U-boat on 27 August, revealed that the Germans had around forty U-boats in operation with another twenty undergoing repair. He placed the total number of U-boats at 200, with the vast majority being used for training purposes.

In a new development the M Room operators discovered that Italian submarines stationed at their base at Bordeaux in the south of France were to be replaced by German U-boats. It was also said that new U-boat pens were being built at Lorient and St Nazaire. Confirmation of such bases could only have come from listening into the conversations of PoWs. RAF reconnaissance of these bases which were so well hidden could not detect details from aerial photography. By the end of 1941 there was concern that Germany had U-boat bases in Italy and a U-boat flotilla based in Greece. Of concern too was the knowledge that German U-boat construction was speeding ahead with a construction company in Hamburg turning out one new U-boat a week. References to small U-boats, like E-boats, were also made. The construction programme did not end there. Large and medium tonnage mine-laying U-boats were also in production and in terms of new technology the Admiralty learnt that U-boats were being fitted with wireless-controlled torpedoes. Any details about U-boats were seized on by British Intelligence which was particularly eager to learn how they were refuelling without returning to base. Surprisingly, these kind of details were soon forthcoming in PoW conversations. It turned out that other German ships were engaged in supplying under-water and surface raiders with food, munitions and fuel.

Towards the end of 1941 it was learned that a German merchant ship was moored at Vigo, to which U-boats could fasten at night and take on fuel and other supplies. Knowledge of replenishing of supplies and fuel to U-boats was a vital piece of information in how the German Navy kept its vessels functioning. A PoW who had once served on Raider 16 provided details of German tactics and armament of their raiders which, it was discovered, operated from a base on the island of Kerguelen in the Southern Ocean. One surviving crew member of the *Pinguin* [a wireless operator] talked at great length with his cellmate about German Naval Wireless Transmissions (W/T) and codes, and the extent of knowledge within the German Navy about British Naval codes. A captain of a German supply vessel spoke about raiders located in the vicinity of Panama in the South Atlantic. From this information the Admiralty was able to sink a raider off the coast of South America in the summer of 1941. Snippets of information in themselves seemed insignificant but gradually they completed the jigsaw puzzle for intelligence chiefs.

German Air Force PoWs captured during this period were considered relatively small at a total of ninety-seven, however some were from specialised units – from Kondor, night fighter and torpedo and mine-laying units. One PoW gave away details about the operational flight areas over Britain and how it was divided for German night fighter patrols. He spoke to fellow PoWs about the code used for W/T communication between the night fighter aircraft and the home station as well as interception of British W/T messages. Establishing exactly what the enemy knew about British operations and technology was as vital as knowing about the enemy.

Another report offered new information from the Naval crew of a Kondor about the re-training of Luftwaffe pilots for attacks by aircraft with torpedoes. The PoW provided an important insight into the difficulties Germany was having in attacking Atlantic convoys because of the protection by British aircraft, including the use of the balloon barrage and improved Anti-aircraft barrages. Germany had suffered substantial Air Force losses on the Russian Front, usually from those engaged on low-level attacks. As the year ended it was learnt that, due to heavy aircraft losses, the enemy had withdrawn its planes from action on the Russian front. The question uppermost for British Intelligence and commanders was to establish where those aircraft would be re-deployed and whether that would be over the skies of England. Details of the strength of the German Air Force also emerged. A PoW captured in July stated that Germany only had 40-50 bombers available to attack Britain.

During the period of Kendrick's survey there had been a number of technological advances on German aircraft. PoWs who had flown in operations on the Russian front spoke of a small anti-personnel bomb used in low level attacks. Another bomb was fitted with a photo-electric cell to correct deviations from the desired target during the fall of the bomb. Copies of reports of the technological information gathered from the listeners was sent to Professor Jones, one of the foremost scientists to work with British Intelligence during the war.

Although there had been some decline in morale in the German forces since 1940 and discontent about conditions at sea, the majority of PoWs still maintained an absolute loyalty to Hitler. It did not prevent many expressing concern to each other about the war with Russia and its outcome. Doubts were also now expressed that Germany could not win the war by an Atlantic blockade alone. Such shift in opinion was welcome news to British Intelligence and showed that Germany may yet not gain naval supremacy.

Losses sustained by the German Air Force had begun to affect morale amongst pilots. They realised the difficulties in attacking Allied shipping and complained that air attacks on Britain were now 'tantamount to a death sentence.' It gave the most significant indication yet to British Intelligence that Germany was losing grip on any chance of air and naval supremacy.

## CONCENTRATION CAMPS

Thus far little had been picked up in the M Room about concentration camps which at that time were located within Germany's borders. That would soon change after the Wannsee-Conference of 1942. However in December 1941 the listeners recorded a conversation between two PoWs captured in the British raids on Maaloy concerning the existence of Bergen

Belsen camp which at this point had not become a full death camp. One was an infantry soldier, the other an artillery soldier. The infantry soldier appears to know nothing of the camp's existence:

> M119: There's a PoW camp near Hameln. I saw how the Poles were living at Bergen – first-rate housing. I should say that, without exaggeration, there were at least fifty thousand PoW there – what a camp!
>
> M130: At Bergen?
>
> M119: Yes, Bergen in Germany, near Fallingbostel
>
> M130. Oh I see. I thought you meant up near Oslo
>
> M119: You wouldn't believe what the camp was like! There was a high barbed wire fence, then the ground sloped down, and then there was another fence which was 2 metres high; there was one 1.25 metres high, and then another 1.5 metres high. They were all 1.5 to 3 metres and the spaces between them were filled with coils of barbed wire so nobody could get through. At each corner there was quite a high tower with machine guns and huge searchlights on all sides… the ones in Bergen can move about freely. There were a few sentries marching around the camp – it was a poor sort of camp.

## JUSTIFYING THE M ROOM

The whole M Room operation and use of stool-pigeons was expensive in terms of both finance and manpower. Norman Crockatt, the ultimate head, felt it necessary to remind all heads of British Intelligence of the need for its continued existence. In a detailed memorandum which he circulated he told them (WO208/3455):

'The regular and continuous supply of SR and SP reports over such a period provides accurate and completely untendentious information on the general topics outlined. Providing a regular supply is maintained, these methods produce better results than would intensive direct interrogation of PoWs who have already been subjected to this by Navy and/or Air Force. Value on the technological side – the secret recordings produced some of the earliest information (March 1940) of the German experiments in Air Navigational aids, and has played an important part in the successful development of the British counter-measures.'

The technological information gleaned enabled the Admiralty to take preventive action to meet the new German "mine-bomb" even before the Germans made operational use of it. The third and final major justification given by Crockatt may be surprising. It related to the use of material which had no Service value 'but which deals with Party scandals, local colour, erotic stories and low-class jokes. Such material, we are assured, is of great propaganda value.' This provided one of the first indications that British Intelligence intended to use the results of the M Room for propaganda. In that respect it would prove to be highly significant during the course of the war. Feedback was essential to the ongoing success of the whole operation. Kendrick requested whether F. Davidson at the Directorate of Military Intelligence could ask intelligence departments direct for a frank assessment of the material coming out of the Centre. He felt that if he contacted them himself they might only give polite answers. A set of questions were circulated by the Directorate to ascertain reactions to the listening programme:

1.      Is the information contained in these Reports of vital importance? Of importance or merely of interest from your point of view?

2.      Do you obtain technical knowledge from these Reports?

3.      Do you feel that you are getting your requirements from this source or are there any points of interest to you that are being overlooked?

4.      Would you prefer the information contained in SR Reports to be paraphrased, summarized and passed to you in the form of Intelligence Reports, or is the present dialogue form in the Secret Reports of greater value?

5.      If the latter, do you find the German text of great value, of value, or of no value?


Every department within Military Intelligence received copies of the questionnaire and that included for example MI4, MI5, MI6, MI8 and MI14. Some sample responses are looked at here below. MI5 replied to the above that the reports were important; technical knowledge was gained but 'only as referring to espionage' and the German text is of great value. MI6 confirmed that both Interrogation Reports and Special Reports 'are of considerable importance and their method of presentation is excellent.' The Special Reports from the M Room were described as 'of vital importance' and technical knowledge definitely gained from them. MI6's reply further stated: 'The present dialogue form of SR reports is excellent and could scarcely be improved upon. The German text is frequently of great value. From time to time it would be of value if further questions could be put to the PoWs amplifying some of the statements made.'

The response by MI10 to the questionnaire was lengthier. The majority of reports were deemed: 'of interest only. About 10% are important and we have had a few of vital importance... rarely, with the exception of A.A [anti-aircraft] on which our operational methods have been influenced by these reports.' Dialogue form of the reports was most useful because it gave 'the background and stability of the prisoner. Important points are apt to be overlooked by non-technical compilers.' Having a copy of the German text was considered essential to the intelligence work of MI10. The following final comments were made:

'We should like to be assured of being informed promptly if any prisoner has knowledge of the subjects in which we are interested, viz weapons, vehicles, works. I think it should not be left to us to deduce from SR or I.R [Interrogation Reports] since there is then delay and the prisoner may be moved on before he can be got at.'

Comments received from MI14 were also insightful for Kendrick because of the level of detail in the response. MI14 found the reports generated by Kendrick's unit 'of vital importance in connection with enemy preparations for combined operations. It is of importance in adding to our records of personalities, Field Post Numbers, locations, etc... concerning enemy morale, the German scene, relations between party and the army, political opinions, etc. In this connection these reports are frequently of considerable interest in so far as they provide possible material for the broadcasts to the German army.' This intelligence department found Interrogation Reports immediately useful but Special Reports 'of greater value in dealing with intricate matters.' The German text was of special value 'in certain cases where the English text unavoidably leaves a doubt in the reader's mind as to the exact shade of meaning.' Guidance about the kind of information needed from the M Room was fed back to Kendrick. This included knowledge of tactics of German Air Force bomber and reconnaissance pilots by night and day, heights at which they attack targets, routes most frequently used and methods of identifying targets, use made of beams, and Flak.

Copies of reports were also sent to the Political Intelligence Department of the Foreign Office. The department's reply to Kendrick's questionnaire highlights the importance of M Room intelligence for propaganda purposes, especially for information which they could not obtain any other way: 'These reports are our *only first-hand* information concerning the state of mind of the clients for our propaganda.'

A further response from the Foreign Office went on to say that 'the present dialogue form of SR reports is of greater value, but in order to conceal the method by which these reports are obtained we are glad to have the summarized Intelligence Reports as it enables us safely to give them a slightly wider, though still restricted circulation.' The War Office confirmed, 'not only do we obtain technical knowledge from the reports but we get also a line on the standard technical training given to German Air Force personnel… The German text is of great value, not because there exists grounds for criticism of your translations, but because the text in the original language occasionally conveys something which is lost in translation.'

Much of the success of this period was down to the inter-personal skills of Kendrick himself. At Trent Park Kendrick entertained the top brass of British Intelligence as well as intelligence chiefs from the Admiralty, Anti-aircraft Command, War Office, Foreign Office, Air Force and Army. By hosting lunches he could build up the necessary rapport for total cooperation between himself and other departments. A tour of parts of the site, within limits, enabled them to see firsthand the nature of the work and how it had a bearing on their own intelligence gathering. Lt. Gen. Sir Frederick Pile of Headquarters of Anti-aircraft Command, Stanmore wrote to Kendrick after one such luncheon and told him: 'In future, when I read the reports I get, their value will be enhanced at least fifty per cent by knowing how these reports are arrived at. I told you when I saw you how useful I found your reports, and I would like once more to emphasise that I get more value out of them than out of any of the Intelligence summaries which reach me.' Lt. Gen. Pile reiterated his unqualified support of Kendrick's work and assured him of complete cooperation in all matters. Whatever Kendrick needed would be provided. He had only to ask.

Since the beginning of the war Kendrick had skilfully built up a network of cooperation and trust with the heads of intelligence departments whilst running a highly efficient operation. The sheer volume of intelligence now coming out of Trent Park, especially the clerical work that it generated, necessitated the engagement of ATS officers to maintain continuity and to cope with the workload. In the end the intelligence being gathered saved the lives of British servicemen and civilians in Britain's town and cities.

# FIVE

## PRIZED PRISONERS, IDLE CHATTER

*'The difficulty of finding suitable M Room personnel cannot be over stressed.'* Kendrick

THE BOMBING OF Pearl Harbour by the Japanese on 7 December 1941 finally brought America into the war. Within a matter of weeks American personnel began to arrive at Kendrick's unit to conduct their own interrogations and share in the intelligence results of the unit. Over the course of the next three years Kendrick and his officers oversaw the training of a number of American Intelligence personnel at Latimer House which became operational in July 1942. Kendrick also aided personnel from the FBI, Washington. That September a grateful Edgar Hoover wrote a personal letter of thanks to Kendrick, addressing him as 'my dear Colonel': 'I am writing to express to you my deep appreciation for the assistance which you rendered to Mr H. M. Kimball of this Bureau during his recent visit to London. It was very good of you to be so helpful, and you may be sure that your kindness is sincerely appreciated by me.' It was the continuation of what became a long wartime collaboration with the Americans. During the first six months of 1942 the unit at Trent Park dealt with a total of 122 PoWs from six U-boats and two E-boats, including PoWs taken during the Smallscale Raiding Forces' raids into parts of Norway. These highly risky operations into key costal areas brought vital information from interrogations and bugging of their cells. Although the numbers may not seem large, the intelligence which was gained form these particular PoWs was significant, especially on the German Order of Battle and new Naval construction work. Some prisoners were taken during the

Vaagsø Raid and this included from merchant vessels; also other PoWs in the Lofoten Raid. In this same period the number of German Air Force personnel totalled twenty-seven, some of which had been captured after the Bruneval Raid. In terms of army, twenty-six military PoWs were taken during the Vaagsø Raid, two from the Bruneval Raid and two from the Middle East. With the exception of two officers they were all ordinary ranks. Although the number of PoWs could be deemed relatively small, this period generated 936 reports from the listeners and stool-pigeons. An idea of the kind of piecemeal intelligence that was being gathered by the listeners during 1942 is given here below, and by the end of the year there would be some surprising turn of events in the war.

## NAVAL INTELLIGENCE

During this period the listeners picked up that the new German battleship *Tirpitz* was ready for action. Damage had been successfully inflicted on warships *Gneisenau*, *Scharnhorst* and *Prinz Eugen*. A large number of references to other German ships under construction were made in PoW conversations, especially a new kind of E-boat which could travel half-submerged. Amongst those mentioned were the *Lützow*, *Hipper*, *Scheer*, *Seydlitz* and *Graf Zeppelin*, and talk of repairing a captured Russian battleship for use in the German fleet and of destroyers under construction.

The most detailed reports of German naval organisation came from the crew of E-boats which provided information on the operations of E-boats in the Channel and Baltic as well as the transfer of E-boat by canal to the Mediterranean. E-boat tactics in torpedo attacks and mine-laying was also described. Significantly, British Intelligence learned that new shelters were being built for E-boats at St Nazaire and other French ports and the Low Countries. This was the kind of information that had not been to ascertained from RAF reconnaissance missions and underlines the importance of these snippets of intelligence that the listeners were carefully gathering. Other PoWs spoke about the difficulties the Germans were having in recruiting new officers to serve on U-boats, which was largely due to conditions in the German Navy.

Significantly too, MI19 learned that a major construction of U-boats was underway at a number of locations in Germany. Some sites were already known, others were new. It was suggested that U-boats were being constructed at Blohm & Voss and in Hamburg at a rate of three a fortnight. Other places of construction included the key ports of Danzig, Kiel, Wilhelmshaven, Rostock, Lübeck and Flensburg. The concern for Allied commanders was that Germany was managing to keep up with its U-boat losses. References were picked up about U-boats and their operations in the Arctic, Mediterranean, Vigo and Azores. PoWs captured en route from France to the Mediterranean spoke about operational groups of U-boats in the Mediterranean, including bases in Greece and Sicily. Other reports mentioned that U-boats were being restocked with supplies from a German supply ship at Vigo. Mention was also made of U-boats making contact with the indigenous population of the Azores. This vital information provided the Admiralty with an overall picture of U-boat areas of operation as well as tactics, and how it was gaining new supplies for the crews.

At the Admiralty British commanders had no clear idea how many losses had been sustained by Germany's Kriegsmarine in British attacks. The secret reports generated during the first six months of 1942 show that through the M Room, British Intelligence gained knowledge of the extent of U-boat losses which the Admiralty had hitherto not known. Losses were placed at as many as 47 by one PoW and 65 by another. However the most significant data came from details of a major change in U-boat tactics. It was revealed that the protection of British convoys had been so highly successful that U-boat crews were undergoing a period of re-training for mass attacks on British shipping and submarines. The British navy would have been unprepared for the new strategy in which between twenty to thirty U-boats would attack en masse.

## GERMAN AIR FORCE

Although the number of Luftwaffe PoWs captured in early 1942 was small, they provided enough tactical information, especially on the "Baedeker" air raids, as to be significant for Felkin to report back to the Air Ministry. Germany began to bomb sites in Britain listed in the famous tourist guide books, Baedeker. These became known as the Baedeker raids. The listeners gained details of the number of aircraft and units employed on these raids. Interestingly, the PoWs began to complain about the strain which was being placed by the Baedeker raids on the already depleted German Air Force. It was an important indication for the Air Ministry of the state of the German Air Force and its continued decline.

Information was also given by PoWs on the flying routes employed by the Luftwaffe and the heights used by enemy aircraft when approaching England. Also discussed amongst the PoWs were the tactics employed in German attacks on British shipping and the nature of aerial reconnaissance missions to check out the shipping routes ready for an attack. During this period the PoWs talked about the RAF raids and devastation wreaked on the major German cities of Hamburg, Cologne, Lübeck, Essen and Münster. Some admiration was expressed for the strategy of the thousand-bomber raid on Cologne, however in general terms most PoWs spoke in dispassionate terms about the raids. On the Russian Front it was learned that the Germans had dropped hundreds of Russian-speaking parachutists behind the Russian lines. They had brought back valuable information on the disposition of Russian troops. The strength of the German Air Force in Russia, Finland and Italy was also established through SR reports and the attention being paid to training 5,000 German Air Force officers to be attached to an aerodrome in France.

It was through the listeners that the Allies picked up information on new German aircraft and bombers as well as technology being developed for use on aircraft. Germany was trying to develop a navigational beam that was not subject to British interference. Naval and air PoWs discussed known types of bombs and new explosives. There were several references to gas warfare that would be instigated on Hitler's order. Men were sent to Celle to attend a gas course.

## ARMY INTELLIGENCE

In terms of the German army those PoWs captured in the raids on Norway and France spoke about the operations in great detail. The defenders of the Vaagsø district agreed that they had been taken by complete surprise by the British attack. Artillerymen on the island of Maaloy had been fooled into thinking they were being subjected to an air attack and had hidden in the caves. References to the situation in Africa was made. Several PoWs complained about the hardships which the German troops were suffering from continuous bombing, shortage of water and plagues of flies. However, as the report said, 'there was no wavering of confidence in Rommel and the belief expressed that he would in a short time be in Cairo.' Details were also forthcoming on the deployment of German troops on the Bulgarian-Turkish border which would break through to Palestine and the Suez Canal to link up with Rommel's forces. Such outlines of projected battle campaigns provided important information to British commanders.

A recurrent theme in the discussions related to the "Second Front" and speculation of when and where the Allies would mount an invasion of Europe. They expressed the view that German forces in the West were inadequate to prevent defeat and should be reinforced from troops serving on the Russian Front. PoWs were divided on whether the threat of a "Second Front" was merely bluff on the part of the Allies. Conversely, talk of a German invasion of Britain declined during 1942. Some PoWs admitted that the time for an invasion had passed. The only talk of an invasion came from an Oberleutenant who was captured at the end of 1941 who spoke about a German invasion plan along the flat coast around Brighton with the use of barges protected by two old battleships, the Schlesien and Schleswig-Holstein. This six-monthly report brought details of tank reinforcements being sent by special aircraft to Rommel in Africa.

The reports generated by Trent Park did not only cover military matters but enabled commanders to gain a wider picture of the war. The secret listeners overheard conversations about resistance amongst the civilian population in France, including acts of sabotage. On one occasion inhabitants of Northern France displayed lights to help British night-fighters. Members of two E-boat crews who had been stationed in Holland were able to leak information about conditions there. PoWs taken during the Lofoten and Vaagsø raids were depressed by the hostility of the Norwegian people who had carried out acts of sabotage and attacks on German troops. The report states: 'In Trondheim it was said that soldiers were found with their throats cut and a hidden arms dump discovered. In Bergen German troops fired on Norwegians who made the V sign. In Oslo the leaders of a disturbance in a factory were shot' (WO308/3455).

One of the primary areas where intelligence was needed was on conditions within Germany itself. A number of references were made in PoWs' conversations to the use of PoWs and foreign workers for labour.

Food was getting short in some of the larger towns. Hitler and the SS had tightened their grip on power with Gestapo guards being stationed at key factories. Criticism of the Hitler Youth Organization was also mounting. At this stage of the war there was no serious breakdown of civilian morale. It was learnt that areas in Germany that had been subjected to heavy Allied bombing were issued with a liberal amount of supplies which were normally restricted under rationing, as a way of keeping up civilian morale.

Sporadic outbursts from Communist sympathizers were known to have occurred. Although there was resistance in Germany to the Nazi regime there was no strong leader who could organize and effect opposition. The eyes and ears of the Gestapo and SS ensured that no such opposition could take a foothold.

The SR reports during this period reveal a shift in attitude amongst the German PoWs, in particular they were beginning to question the infallibility of Hitler. This was a marked difference from the previous six months and they began to express concern over the Russian campaign and there was increased pessimism over the outcome of the war, with a growing fear of defeat. Japan and the war in the East played little part in their conversations. It was noted by Kendrick that the morale of PoWs from Norway and France had worsened. German airmen were becoming the most outspoken against the regime.

Information obtained by the secret listeners was passed to the Foreign Office and used in propaganda. Intelligence chiefs had no idea how effective their propaganda campaign was until the secret recordings from Trent Park confirmed that BBC programmes were being widely listened to by German forces. In particular German airmen tuned in to the BBC to receive news about comrades missing in action. British Intelligence had the confirmation it needed – via radio broadcasts it had an extremely powerful tool at its disposal. Now they knew for certain that the news broadcasts were being heard in Germany itself. It meant that a phoney radio station could be set up via the BBC and mask as a German radio station broadcasting within Germany, although it was based at Milton Bryan not far from Bletchley Park under the directorship of MI6 officer and former journalist Sefton Delmer. Regular and reliable information, which could only really be gained from prisoners' conversations via the M Room, would be vital to this propaganda machine.

## SOUTHERN COMMAND

Rumours circulated amongst the Entertainment Section that No.3 Training Centre of the alien Pioneer Corps at Ilfracombe faced imminent closure. The future of the Entertainment Section was thrown into doubt. A series of farewell concerts were given and, on 23 January 1942, Fritz was amongst those Pioneer soldiers who moved to Bulford, not far from Salisbury, to join Southern Command. They travelled by train which had two extra carriages, one for instruments, the other for the soldiers. Fritz was still no nearer to doing something with a direct impact on the war. Instead the Entertainment Section found itself in new quarters, consisting of a wooden building just large enough to accommodate about 30 beds, fairly close together, and each with a small locker. Fritz recalls the primitive surroundings: 'There were two small iron stoves, one at each end of the hut, which provided sufficient heating only if you were quite near to them.' He and fellow refugee soldiers now became part of Southern Command Orchestra.

On 21 June the orchestra gave a concert in the town of Swindon. Between rehearsals and the concert Fritz and the other musicians heard news on the wireless that Tobruk in North Africa had fallen to Rommel's Afrika Korps. It was a disastrous blow for the British. Rommel went on to capture El Alamein and came within 65 miles of Alexandria. Hitler rewarded him with the rank of Field Marshal. One question was uppermost in Fritz's mind – were the Allies now in danger of losing Egypt? That would open the way for the Germans to sweep eastwards and to the Middle-Eastern oilfields. On 1 July Fritz wrote to his parents:

*Unfortunately the war situation does not look too rosy. It seems to me that the end is less foreseeable than ever. But unfortunately it does no good at all to worry about that. But my temperament does not allow me to adopt a carpe diem [take each day as it comes] attitude which would be desirable at such times and in such situations.*

Fritz became increasingly frustrated by the monotony of life in the orchestra. These were extraordinary times of life and death in the struggle against the evil which he had had to flee and he felt he had no useful part in the fight. He tried to console himself – if only the conductor could play chamber music it might distract them and relieve the boredom. Then Fritz suddenly heard from the company office that a new Army Council Instruction had come out asking for volunteers to train as glider pilots. Furthermore he heard that the British government had lifted the ban on enemy aliens serving in the fighting forces. This was his chance to fight properly.

An interview in Oxford was set for 8 September. Fritz sailed through the written tests and medical examination. Then received the disappointing news from the Medical Officer that his eye-sight was not good enough to go further. Rather despondent, Fritz returned to Southern Command and muddled his way through an uneventful autumn of boredom and frustration. In mid-December the orchestra went on a fortnight's concert tour of Oxfordshire. Poorly housed and feeling very uncomfortable during the tour, morale became extremely low. Fritz developed a severe cold and did not get out of bed. A medical orderly was sent to his bedside to ask routine health questions, one of which was whether he had opened his bowels that morning! 'It was a pretty depressing time,' comments Fritz.

However spirits were soon lifted. On New Year's Day 1943 the orchestra played in the presence of Queen Mary, widow of the late George V, at her residence at Badminton House in Gloucestershire. It was to prove a good omen because the year dawned on a period that would see significant change in Fritz's life. Fritz wrote to his parents after the concert:

> *The Queen came in, tall and upright, and very well preserved for her 75 years or so, and said with a clear voice: "I wish you all a very happy New Year, and a victorious one". We played for her and an audience of about 100 male and female soldiers for about an hour, and afterwards our conductor, Hans Geiger (the leader), the pianist Stiasny (who had played a solo) and the tenor Rudolph Jess were presented to her. She spoke briefly to each of them, even a few words in German. Before the concert and afterwards we got an excellent meal in a posh hotel. We got back to our garrison at 3 a.m!*

Frustration at a wasted life in the army orchestra did not abate. Fritz wrote a philosophical letter to his parents that his experiences during the past 2½ years had cured him of any desire to become a professional musician. He comments, 'I no longer considered it the most desirable path to follow.'

## LATIMER HOUSE

In July 1942 the headquarters of MI19 moved to Latimer House, hidden deep in the Buckinghamshire countryside. Close to Amersham railway station with a fast link to London, it was ideal. Kendrick was joined there by Ft Lt Felkin who ran the Air Intelligence Division AI1(K) and a small number of American Military Intelligence personnel. Kendrick was still in overall charge, now of both Trent Park and No.1 Distribution Centre, as Latimer was named. He was supported by two assistant Commandants: Lt. Col. CM Corner M.V.O as Assistant Commandant (Intelligence) and Lt. Col. F. Huband, M.B.E., M.C., D.C.M as Assistant Commandant (Administration).

Since the unit's foundation Kendrick's team of secret listeners had gradually risen to forty. However, Kendrick now faced a problem. Not only were there insufficient numbers of M Room staff to run operations at Trent Park and Latimer House, but also for Wilton Park which was due to be fully operational by the end of 1942. Latimer House and Wilton Park each had 30 miked rooms, plus the bugged rooms at Trent Park. Furthermore it was proving impossible to recruit a sufficient number of British officers with a requisite knowledge of colloquial German. Even those with a degree in languages struggled with the German dialects of the PoWs. Operations were at a critical phase and MI19's work was only set to become more important as the war progressed. Kendrick wrote in a report to bosses:

'The difficulty of finding suitable M Room personnel cannot be over stressed. Very frequently it was found that Englishmen with a perfect academic knowledge of German were quite unsuited for M Room work. Apart from the obvious prerequisites (i.e. a 100% knowledge of the colloquial idiom and perfect hearing) an operator must be mentally very alert and adaptable. In addition he must acquire an extensive knowledge of service slang, conditions and technical gadgets. This of course takes time, and experience has shown that at least three months are required to train an operator.'

Kendrick didn't have time on his side. What he needed was native German-speakers. He required no reminder that Britain was in the middle of a war with Germany. Where could he find such people? The answer came in the form of German-speaking refugees serving in the alien Pioneer Corps. With the same diplomacy and discretion which had marked his secret service career thus far Kendrick petitioned 'those in the know' for native German personnel. A major shift now occurred. MI19 authorised that the listeners could be Non-Commissioned Officers, not limited to Officer rank, and this enabled German-speaking refugees to be drafted into the unit. There was no time to train them through Officer Training Units and commission them.

On the payroll of MI6 and heading one of Military Intelligence's most important operations Kendrick was privy to the wider military situation. The Allies were in the process of planning the invasion of Sicily and Italy for the following year and could expect a large influx of PoWs. Kendrick knew that it was only a matter of time before the PoWs would not be limited to petty officers and others ranks. The turn of the tide in North Africa would finally yield some of the most important and top-ranking PoWs for MI19. The drama that would shortly unfold in Trent Park provided a scenario that kept MI19 busy for the duration of the war and afforded them a unique insight into the mind of the enemy. 'The stage' was now set to receive the first German Generals and some of British Intelligence's most prized prisoners.

# SIX

# BATTLE OF THE GENERALS

*'General Crüwell says, "we have the best philosophers, but no statesmen."*
*I say, we have the best Generals and are losing the war.'* Bassenge to
Neuffer, Trent Park

IN MAY 1942 the first German General from the African campaign was brought as a prisoner to Trent Park. General der Panzertruppen Ludwig Crüwell was captured after his plane was shot down whilst being escorted by his pilot over North Africa. For British Intelligence this was just the beginning of what would become the saga of the German Generals. Crüwell's personal file at Trent Park noted that he 'tried to impress everyone with his own importance and knowledge, a trouble-maker and a bore'.

In November Crüwell was joined by fifty-one year old General Ritter von Thoma, commander of a Panzer tank division, who had been taken by the British at Tel-el-Mapsra west of El Alamein. In the opinion of MI19 von Thoma was 'very intelligent and exceedingly well read.' He was a cultured man whose hobbies included the study of art, history and politics. It was noted that 'he has a striking personality and is violently anti-Nazi, a man who does not suffer fools gladly. He could have been a great leader if he had possessed the ability to coordinate his ideas with action.' If he thought a principle to be correct he said so calmly, even in the face of the most bigoted critic. If an opponent still did not see reason he let the matter drop but continued in his own way. He preferred to spend time alone in his room reading books on art, politics and history. MI19 noted:

'his reminiscences are as interesting as his political views and he has had many and varied contacts with all sorts of eminent people from New York actresses to Balkan monarchs – not to speak of the Führer!' Von Thoma could read English well but spoke little English in conversation.

Within twelve months eleven more captured Generals joined Crüwell and von Thoma, often accompanied by their batmen. For them, the war was over and they quickly became depressed with their captivity that they knew would last until the end of hostilities. That turned out to be three long years. By the summer of 1943 the Generals held alongside Crüwell and von Thoma were Hans-Jürgen von Arnim, Hans Cramer, Theodor Graf von Sponeck, Gotthart Frantz, Gerhard Bassenge, Fritz Krause, Georg Neuffer, Kurt Freiherr von Liebenstein, Friedrich Freiherr von Broich, Schnarrenberger, Heinrich-Hermann von Hülsen; and other lower ranks Dr Carius, von Glasow, Bülowius and Bock. Crüwell, von Thoma and Cramer, the three senior Generals, were given a single bedroom and a sitting room. Cramer was allocated a particularly large bedroom. The other Generals were allocated single rooms, except the lower ranks who were accommodated two to a room.

Bringing the German Generals directly to Trent Park began one of British Intelligence's most cunning deception plans of the war. They expected to be interrogated and held in a rudimentary prisoner-of-war camp. But British Intelligence knew that the Generals would yield very little information in interrogations at this stage of the war. Instead the Generals found themselves escorted by car down the mile-long drive through a sumptuous parkland from where they got their first glimpse of an impressive red brick stately house. How could they not fail but be impressed with the scale of it with its long elegant windows and grand entrance, with statues in the gardens and front court? It played right into the Generals' sense of self-importance and inflated egos. Duped into believing they were being held here as befitted their military status, the German Generals quickly became off guard. Their every need was catered for and they began to relax into their surroundings. They devoted time to learning languages and other subjects. A room was set aside for creative activities – for painting and drawing, also for playing cards, table-tennis and billiards. Little did they suspect that even the billiard table had a bugging device hidden in it. They had complete freedom to roam the house and grounds; received newspapers and were able to listen to BBC radio broadcasts. One officer even wrote home to his wife that he would love his family to stay there with him, but without the barbed wire! However the Senior German officers did not know about the labyrinth of passages and cellars in the basement of the house which had been carefully sealed off with a false wall to prevent them straying into the area where the secret listeners were ensconced.

The Generals had been warned back in Germany that if they were ever captured, the British would be listening into their conversations. The caution went unheeded. Very quickly they didn't limit their discussions to the English weather. During the first week there was a feeling of constraint amongst them. The Generals reflected on whether they were in any way responsible for the defeat in Tunisia and North Africa. Some blamed the Italians for not using their fleet; others felt the responsibility lay with German High Command. Von Arnim, appointed Camp Leader by the other PoWs, expressed the opinion that reports of the true military situation had been withheld from Hitler. Von Arnim's real allegiance was somewhat of a mystery to MI19. He continued to profess a belief in a German victory, was fervently anti-Jewish and anti-Bolshevik, but there was no overt evidence for his Nazi views while at Trent Park. Bülowius and Krause were depressed by the turn of events and their capture, but soon became resigned to their situation.

The Generals were offered the opportunity of having their portraits painted by an official war artist. They discussed the matter amongst themselves and von Arnim decidedly told British Army officers that permission would not be given for such an activity. However von Thoma took another approach. He was interested in art and suggested that the artist may be glad of a model and that he, von Thoma, had all the time in the world and would welcome the entertainment. As the most highly decorated General in the camp he was entitled to wear the most medals but he declined. When the question arose of what he would wear for the portrait, he said he preferred to be painted in his bush shirt without badges of rank or decorations, just as he was when he was captured in the desert. Von Arnim disapproved of von Thoma sitting for the artist.

The most important dimension of this whole bugging operation was that it provided unguarded conversations between the top ranks of Hitler's military. British Intelligence was overhearing raw, unadulterated opinions of the German Generals on a range of political and strategic information. It also gave an important insight into the mind-set of the enemy, enabling British Intelligence to understand that mind-set and fool the Generals into a false sense of complacency and spilling more secrets.

Just how much MI19 understood the characters and mind-set of their prisoners is demonstrated in notes at the bottom of each individual personal report on the Generals. From the confines of the M Room installed in the basement and cellars of Trent Park the listeners recorded their conversations. They quickly came to recognize the individual voices and could distinguish which General was speaking.

It would not be long before the M Room yielded some priceless results.

# LORD ABERFELDY

What British Intelligence gained from bugging the Generals was much more than military secrets. These were the top echelons of the military high command and British Intelligence was not going to miss a single opportunity to get all it could from them. Nothing was left to chance. Everything was carefully choreographed down to the very last detail. It represented a multi-layered deception plan. Nothing was what it seemed on the surface. The deception went as far as creating the fictional character of Lord Aberfeldy. Lord Aberfeldy was no real 'Lord' but an intelligence officer who masked as a welfare officer. He befriended the Generals and pampered to their every need; making trips into the city once a week to buy items which the Generals had requested: shaving cream, chocolates, sweets and cigarettes. The Generals were permitted to run their own small 'tuck-shop' or canteen for extra items they wished to purchase from an allowance given to them by MI19.

Documents held at the National Archives give no clues as to the real identity of Aberfeldy. Was it an intelligence officer who had never served for the British Secret Service? Or was it someone in the inner circle? Could it have been Kendrick's own brother-in-law Rex Pearson who served with SIS during the First World War, having been recruited with Kendrick from South Africa in 1915? Pearson was a strong, likeable, dependable character who didn't have the obvious panache of a daring agent. He had operated behind enemy lines during WW1 because his knowledge of pigeons gave valuable service to the nascent British Secret Service. He had coordinated the dropping of pigeons and messages behind the lines from France from 1916 onwards. As part of a group known as the 'Suicide Club' he had worked alongside handsome adventurer and balloonist Beau Maschwitz who ballooned at night over enemy lines in

1918 on behalf of British Intelligence. In the early 1930s he was posted to Vienna for a time with another SIS agent Charles Dick Ellis, and then from 1936 drafted into Claude Dansey's Z Organization, and involved from Switzerland in industrial espionage on behalf of SIS. Pearson had some involvement again with pigeons during the Second World War but this may have been much later. He was also known to stay at Kendrick's house in the country.

Or was it another mysterious figure and intelligence officer 'Barnes' who has never been properly identified? Barnes was the third man assigned as one of the minders to Rudolf Hess, alongside Kendrick and Frank Foley, at Hess's incarceration at Mytchett Place in 1941. Did Barnes leave in 1942 to become the Generals' friend and 'Lord'?

Could it have been Charles 'Dick' Ellis? An SIS operative who prior to the end of the war and afterwards lived in the house next door to Kendrick in Oxshott, Surrey? Ellis had spent time in Vienna with Kendrick's brother-in-law in the early 1930s working for British Intelligence and keeping an eye on the Russians, probably as part of Kendrick's network of spies. During the early part of the war he was serving at the SIS post in New York but his movements after 1942 are somewhat unclear and he may have returned to London. Ellis' life is surrounded by no small amount of mystery. Thought once to have betrayed Kendrick to the Gestapo in the late 1930s, he was later thought to have finally confessed to his MI6 superiors of betraying secrets, not to the Germans, but to the Russians.

Lord Aberfeldy may well have been none of the above characters. But nearly seventy years later he is still a puzzling figure and one who probably continued to work for the British Secret Service after the war.

# BATTLE LINES: PRO-NAZI V. ANTI-NAZI

As the German Generals settled into their life of captivity they began to form into two distinct groups: pro-Nazi and anti-Nazi. Crüwell headed the vehemently pro-Nazi group which consisted of Gotthard Frantz, von Hülsen and, by June 1943, also Naval Captain Meixner. Von Thoma led the anti-Nazis who clustered around him. They were Sponeck, Cramer, Bassenge, Neuffer, von Liebenstein and von Broich. Their personal files provide an insight into their characters. Every idiosyncratic detail was picked up by British Intelligence to build a physical and psychological profile of the prisoners.

Heading the Nazi group, Crüwell continued his allegiance to Hitler whom he had only met twice. British Intelligence described Crüwell as an 'ignorant, stupid, sentimental, narrow-minded, conceited, vain and self-satisfied type of Prussian senior officer.' Crüwell was supported by the tall, slim Major-General von Hülsen who was always urging him to cause as much trouble as possible for the British. Crüwell had a ready ear and listened to von Hülsen who busied himself trying to persuade the others to cause trouble. Hülsen was 'a hanger-on of the worst type and always trying to be with Arnim.' Hülsen perpetually moaned about something, legitimate or not, and every letter or card written home to his wife contained some sly dig at conditions in the camp. His complaints, usually pure fabrication, were always delivered in a polite yet petty and annoying way.

The idiosyncratic characters which unfolded in the camp could not have been created better in fiction. No more was this true than with Lieutenant-General Gotthard Frantz, an ally of the Nazi clique. Somewhat neurotic he was described as a stage caricature of a Prussian General and never without his monocle which had deformed his eye. Only once had he been seen without his monocle, and that was when he took it out to wipe it after an emotional moment. British officers noticed that he even wore it under sunglasses and seemed to sleep in it because it was always in place when he was counted in bed in the morning. At fifty-five, Frantz was of medium height, slim, with a beak nose, wrinkled face and thin lips. Having heard the news that he had been awarded the *Ritterkreuz* [Knight's Cross] while in British custody, he could not wait to receive a real one from Germany. His puffed-up ego was impatient, and so in the meantime he borrowed a *Ritterkreuz* from one of the other Generals and always wore it around his neck. While at Trent Park Frantz wore so many decorations from the Great War that he had to 'button up his tunic and then fasten them on over his buttons.' He duplicated some of the ribbons with medals which hung in profusion all over him. Bizarrely he even went to bed with them on. In a clipped voice he moaned constantly to British officers and fellow prisoners. At first he tried to lay down the law to the former but gradually learned that he could not do that. Bluntness was the only way to deal with him. It took three weeks for him to learn that it was not the duty of a British officer to search the London shops for red-brown boot-polish even for a German General. Frantz made himself the most unpopular prisoner and was disliked by the batmen.

Also amongst Crüwell's ardent supporters was Paul Hermann Meixner who had been captured on 11 May 1943. He was brought first to Latimer House in Buckinghamshire, where MI19 had re-located its headquarters, and then to Trent Park on 16 June. Fifty-two year old Meixner had served in the Austrian Navy during the First World War and offered his services to the German Navy in the Second. First impressions of him were of a benevolent rosy-faced man whose white hair seemed to heighten this perception. But he was found to be too polite and gushing which masked him as 'an Austrian Nazi and a dangerous man.' He tried to please his fellow officers but when in the company of the anti-Nazi camp at Trent Park he was much less the ranting politician. MI19 were surprised to find that his colleagues thought him a man of fine character. Meixner was paired up to share a room with Major-General von Hülsen. In spite of his pro-Nazi beliefs Meixner was sneakily spotted one evening by a British officer who entered his room, reading a copy of Lord Vansittart's *Lessons of my Life* which he had borrowed from von Thoma. Meixner's English was considered to be very good, such that on two evenings he translated material for the other Generals. Most evenings he spent playing bridge with a group formed by von Arnim.

After the arrival of Meixner, Crüwell began to canvass for support from the anti-Nazis to get them to change allegiance. Schnarrenberger and Krause seemed to take no part in the political battles in the communal rooms of the house. It seems hard to imagine the Generals partaking of any cultural activities, but Krause, described by MI19 as pleasant but rather unintelligent, preferred to engage his time in playing chess, table tennis and bridge. He was an ardent member of the Camp 11 String Quartet.

The anti-Nazis around the pillar of General von Thoma quickly outnumbered the Nazi clique and gained the upper hand. Their diverse characters soon became obvious. General Hans Cramer's file shows him to be 'anti-Nazi and a monarchist who detested the Nazi Party and wanted the Hohenzollern dynasty restored to the Throne'. Forty-seven year old Cramer had been decorated with the Iron Cross during the First World War having served in an infantry regiment. Under Hitler he served as Commander of the German Afrika Corps and was captured by the British in Tunisia on 12 May 1943. Four days later he was brought directly to Trent Park with Georg Neuffer and Gerhard Bassenge. He preferred to isolate himself from the others by often remaining quietly in his room.

Cramer's outward appearance was somewhat deceptive. Of middle height, his sparse hair was drawn tightly back and he always wore a monocle. A neat and straightforward figure, he gave the impression of being a typical Prussian officer. He turned out to exceed expectations and MI19 found him to be a pleasant and interesting conversationalist who talked too fast such that no one could get a word in. He seemed amused by the petty complaints raised by his comrades. He was tired of the war and yearned for peace between Britain and Germany.

Bavarian-born Neuffer made no secret of his anti-Nazi views. He was found to be good-natured, well read, intelligent and exuded a certain charm. He was the only senior officer who had a good word to say for the Russians and understood what democracy stood for. A veteran of the Great War, Major-General Gerhard Bassenge offered to collaborate with the British in getting rid of Nazism and stopping the war. He tried to convince British officers that no selfish motives lay behind his offer and was overheard by the listeners, saying to Neuffer: 'General Crüwell says, "we have the best philosophers, but no statesmen." I say, we have the best Generals and are losing the war.'

Another German veteran of the Great War was Lieutenant-General Sponeck who had been recognised by Germany's Field Marshal Rommel as a leader-type. Sponeck had led his Division in difficult defensive actions and retreats in North Africa with 'prudence, skill and determination.' At Trent Park he was prone to be neurotic, moody on the one hand, and exceedingly talkative on the other. A talented painter he spent most of his time in captivity on his art. A defeatist, monarchist and anti-Nazi he sometimes 'snoops around the place like a dog with his tail between his legs.' On 1st June 1943 they were joined by Fritz von Broich and Kurt Freiherr von Liebenstein. The son of a General, von Broich was a 'jolly ex-cavalry man with a twinkle in his eye'. Having transferred from the

German cavalry to command the 10$^{th}$ Panzer Division, von Broich too surrendered with the German army in Tunisia. He was not particularly intelligent but always amusing and charming. Widely travelled in Europe he displayed a pride in his aristocratic blood. From Trent Park he wrote strong anti-Nazi letters home to his wife which caused her no small amount of aggravation from the Gestapo. MI19 noted that he had a weak will and 'a horror of Communism only equalled by his horror of Nazism.' In captivity von Broich envied the English political system and sought to understand democracy and its significance. In that respect he was not dissimilar to von Liebenstein who admired English democracy and French culture.

The most un-German-looking of the Generals, forty-four year old Liebenstein was a talented artist who painted credible watercolours during his time at Trent Park. In June 1943 von Arnim appointed him as deputy camp leader. Although he read little, he began to support the cause by taking up the reading of anti-Nazi literature supplied on request by the British officers. A great lover of horses Liebenstein expressed gratitude when hunting scenes were provided for the walls of his room. Politically he declared himself a monarchist who admired the British and their traditions, detesting dictatorship in all its forms.

The anti-Nazis were described by MI19 as the most intelligent, widely-travelled and most cultured officers who looked eagerly to a restoration of the Monarchy in Germany. Von Thoma petitioned to be allowed to read books which had been banned in Germany. The Commandant granted the request. Being divided along political lines von Thoma tried to entice the Nazi group to read the literature. It was also possible to see a split in attitude towards their incarceration. They never complained about their treatment and often told their captors how grateful they were for the excellent treatment. The Nazi faction had no interest in literature, and frequently complained and moaned about their conditions. They likened Trent Park to a sanatorium for tired Generals rather than a PoW camp. Carius and Bock left on 11 June, both considered 'unpleasant specimens'.

Most of the Generals now believed that Germany had little chance of victory. They seemed uninterested in military advances made by the Russians. For them the war was as good as lost and they spent their time discussing how the complete collapse of Germany could be avoided. Politics seemed a far more engaging topic. Crüwell and Arnim were horrified by the defeatist attitude and suggested that the disloyal Generals would be shot when they were repatriated. The other Generals isolated Crüwell and Arnim as 'windbags' who refused to engage in reasonable debate. British officers monitoring the transcripts of the bugged conversations felt that below the defeatist exterior the Generals really harboured the idea of world domination and planned for the next war. In spite of defeat von Thoma believed that Germany would recover. Of all the Generals he was the one who engaged readily on politics with British officers at Trent Park. British Intelligence saw straight through von Thoma's two-pronged propaganda: that as soon as possible Britain should make a statement of intention for Germany, and second that they should reach Berlin before the Russians so that 'Germany may be saved from Bolshevism.' Fear of Russia became one of the most persistent themes of their political discussions. One of the Oberstleutnants commented, 'as long as our Army is intact the English, with us, would be in a position to march against the Russians.'

The German Generals discussed the belief that the next world struggle would be between Communist Russia and the Western Capitalist powers. History would, of course, prove them right. It was only a matter of a few years before Europe and America were thrown into the Cold War.

Bassenge and von Thoma expressed the view that in the next struggle Germany would side with Russia against the West.

## A LIFE OF GENTLEMEN

On 16 June 1943 the number of high-ranking German officers at Trent Park increased with the arrival of Colonel Schmidt (German Air Force), Colonel Buhse, Colonel Reimann, Lieutenant-Colonel Köhnke (German Air Force) and Lieutenant-Colonel Wolters. With the exception of Buhse whose views remained unknown, they joined the anti-Nazi group; although Reimann seemed not to have the moral courage to stand up for his views against the opposition. MI19 commented that Reimann insists that as a Silesian, he must not be mistaken for a Prussian. He was found to be an excellent manager of the PoW canteen. At the beginning of July the Generals were joined by Colonel Drange and Colonel Heym of the German Air Force. Von Thoma surprisingly found the German Air Force men inclined towards anti-Nazi views, having erroneously believed they were a stronghold of the Nazi Party. By now the Generals had structured themselves along lines which recognised von Arnim as their Camp Leader. At noon on 25 June the Commandant summoned von Arnim and von Liebenstein to his office to announce two major changes at Trent Park.

Firstly, those below the rank of Lieutenant-General were required to share a room with another PoW. Secondly, the War Office had issued instructions that rations were to be reduced. Von Arnim and Liebenstein had already drawn up a list of complaints for the Commandant but the news completely took the wind out of their sails. They were visibly shocked by the announcement and asked for time to think about it. They left after requesting to see an interpreter later that afternoon. In the interim, during the course of the afternoon, Arnim and some of the senior Generals tried to bully the warders into giving them empty rooms in another part of the house, but their request was refused.

The interpreter later entered the common room to find Arnim seated with some of the other Generals. They had worked themselves up into quite a frenzy. An enraged Arnim laid down their demands and concluded uncompromisingly, 'we will sleep in the corridor rather than share rooms!'

'Do you really mean it?' said the interpreter.

'Yes!' Arnim replied indignantly.

The interpreter made an excuse to leave the room briefly. On his return he made the situation perfectly clear.

'You must remember,' he told them, as they hung onto his every word, 'as prisoners-of-war in Germany our own Generals are not treated in the same excellent way that you are treated here. Some of ours are still in shackles. We are in a democracy here where Parliament still has a say. Questions are being asked already in Parliament about the comfortable lifestyle which you enjoy here. So gentlemen, if you prefer to sleep in the corridor, you may do so. But, you will not be permitted to remove any furniture from the rooms.' The interpreter turned and looked directly at Arnim. 'Remember that as a prisoner-of-war you must submit to British military discipline.' With a cursory nod, the interpreter left the room.

The Generals engaged in an intense discussion. At the end they decided that they had better give in. Later during the evening, possibly in an unofficial discussion with Lord Aberfeldy, they were given friendly advice that it would be wise to accept the situation. Most of the German Generals agreed that they were receiving excellent treatment. However the pro-Nazi group grumbled in letters home to their families and also made sarcastic remarks to their British minders about the reduction in food rations. They saw it as an admission that things were in a bad way in

England generally during the war. Quietly amongst themselves when they didn't realise they were being eavesdropped on, they admitted the food was still good and ample. Krause even conceded that the food was better than anything they had had in Germany since 1914. He added: 'there is good coffee and tea at all meals.' The battle of the Generals left a sour and strained atmosphere for a few days but it was all soon forgotten. In reality they had little to complain about. They were taken on trips to central London and on occasion dined at Simpson's on the Strand where they were served a plate of meat and heaps of vegetables, followed by a pudding. This was all part of the multi-layered deception by British Intelligence to make them feel completely relaxed and loosen their tongues in private. The Generals were taken on a three-hour excursion which ended in tea at Kendrick's house in the secluded village of Oxshott in Surrey. Their stiffness soon began to melt as the day progressed and they finally relaxed in the company of their escorting officers. During their open conversations they complained that they had suffered an honourable defeat but had been outnumbered by Allied men and tanks. They offered critical comments on the Allied offensive and dissected the battle plan that had led to their defeat. General Krause complained that the barrage before the final breakthrough was overwhelming and worse than at El Alamein. He criticised British strategy of taking up positions on forward slopes which he felt went against all modern German teaching which preferred reverse slopes. All the Generals agreed that the amount of equipment and ammunition behind Allied lines was impressive. General Bassenge was found to be a valuable talker, full of self-confidence. It was felt by British handlers that General Krause was the most reliable and could probably be persuaded to unburden himself in due course. When asked questions by the accompanying officers, the Generals politely waived them aside and continued to talk about matters which they decided upon.

Other rank officers were also periodically taken on trips to London. On one occasion they were treated to a day in Whitby on the coast. The day did not quite work out as planned because some of the prisoners consumed too much beer. A crisis threatened to ensue when a U-boat captain and his First Lieutenant started shouting firing orders for torpedoes as ships went past in the bay.

By all accounts the trips were deemed a success. When Churchill found out about them he was furious. The belligerent, indignant Prime Minister banned the 'pampering' of the Generals. MI19 ignored his orders in the belief that they knew exactly what they were doing. It wasn't long before the plan paid off and MI19 gained its most important coup which led them to discover Hitler's secret weapon programme.

## BATMEN'S REVOLT

Life at Trent Park continued along the drawn battle lines of pro-Nazi and anti-Nazi. After dinner on 9 July von Arnim as Camp Leader gave a rather long-winded 'pep' talk directed against the anti-Nazis who were seen as defeatists. Von Arnim's true political position continued to baffle British Intelligence. His speech was noted for its absence of any reference to Hitler. Afterwards von Thoma added his opinion that 'old men blind themselves before the blatant facts.' Shortly before von Arnim's speech General Cramer had been discussing politics with a British Army officer about possible leaders for a revolution in Germany. After von Arnim's speech Cramer shouted loudly from the corridor outside the dining room: 'I look forward to continuing this discussion!' Arnim and Cramer had become much closer during that last week. Von Arnim had invited some of the defeatists to his room to play bridge and Cramer was always noted to be present. Was von Arnim moving into the anti-Nazi camp?

The effect of the speech was interesting. Rather than deterring the anti-Nazis it had the effect of drawing them out. Anti-Nazi literature was no longer read secretly behind closed doors of their bedrooms. For example Colonel Borcherdt openly read Braun's *Von Weimar zu Hitler* in the courtyard in front of the other Generals. The following day Liebenstein read the book in his room and quoted chunks of it to a British officer in front of his batman – a great crime according to von Arnim's speech the previous evening. The Colonels all appeared to have joined the anti-Nazi camp.

Trouble with the batmen had been simmering for a while. During the week of von Arnim's after-dinner speech they began to grumble that they should receive the same comforts as the Generals because they were all equal as PoWs. It came to a head over the distribution of cigars from the German-run canteen or 'tuck-shop'. The Generals discussed the behaviour of the batmen and made a written request to their British minders. They asked for the removal of three batmen: Schmidt, Dittmar and Wodtke. Of all the batmen Erich Schmidt was the most disliked. His personal MI19 profile is not very flattering. A Nazi and rather an odd character, he frequently found something to complain about which he put down to British incompetence. He had innumerable physical complaints (WO208/3433):

> 'The first being caused by being hit in the stomach by a medicine
> ball. This caused him to lie on the ground groaning. He was taken
> to hospital where after an X-ray examination it was ascertained
> that he had merely been winded and the groans immediately
> ceased. Next he decided that rheumatism was killing him. The
> English climate was to blame. He retired semi-permanently to bed.
> When talk of repatriation arose he became permanently

incapacitated. He only got up to draw nudes.'

The British officers did not place too much stress on the inability of the Generals to keep the batmen in order because they had caused no small amount of trouble for the British. The batmen had another go at persuading Crüwell to makes things unpleasant for the minders. Although Crüwell had already agreed to get rid of the three batmen he petitioned von Arnim to make out that the British were riding roughshod over the Generals and forcibly trying to remove their batmen. He suggested to von Arnim that he should put his foot down. Von Arnim was wise enough to keep quiet about the whole affair. He began to tire of Crüwell's nagging. Von Arnim had long talks with Cramer and Crüwell about the war situation. In spite of their disagreements they agreed not to give in to defeatism but to support the regime to the bitter end. Von Arnim continued to sign his letters, which were censored by British Intelligence, 'always your old optimist.'

During the summer months of 1943 Meixner began to show leanings towards the anti-Nazi defeatists. The batmen continued to contribute to the scene. Von Broich had an interesting defeatist talk with his batman who happened to be head batman in the camp. Von Hülsen revealed his hand as a monarchist and against Hermann Goering, although publicly he still professed to be in the anti-Thoma group. Discussions amongst the Generals included speculation about their role after the war. The anti-Nazis believed they would still hold on to their military positions. The pro-Nazis suggested that they might be forced to retire in disgust and take up bee-keeping, poultry-farming or work as estate agents. Political literature continued to be circulated and provided for them by their British minders. This included: Heiden's *Europas Schicksal* (Europe's Fate), Rauschning *Vernichtung des Nihilismus* (Revolution of Destruction), Lochsner *What about Germany?* and Langhoff *Moorsoldaten* (the story of a concentration camp). Crüwell borrowed Spengler's *Preussentum und Socialismus* (Prussianism & Socialism). A few German newspapers were circulated by the British – perhaps a rather surprising move but designed to enable the Generals to relax further into their camp life, be totally off-guard in their conversations and think that the British were stupid. The alter-ego of the Generals could not entertain the idea that British Intelligence was pulling the strings of their stage-set in a situation where the melodrama turned into an almost comical charade.

# SEVEN

## MAD HATTER'S TEA PARTY

AN ALMOST FARCICAL scene faced British minders on a daily basis. The German Generals provided no small amount of entertainment as they continued to battle their political leanings and fan the feathers of their egos like peacocks strutting around the grounds of a stately home. On the afternoon of 15 July von Hülsen was taken by truck to the dentist. His escorts expected him to react to what he saw on his journey but they did not expect his comments to degenerate into the pure ridiculous. Von Hülsen made absurd comments about how badly people were dressed and how decrepit the houses looked – all due, in his opinion, to the war. To add to his smug confidence, that day was early closing and the shops had already pulled down their blinds. He added that this was because the war was going badly and they had nothing to sell. The myth was soon shattered when they passed some open shops further down the road. When he saw a trolley-bus he declared it had been electrified because the country had a serious shortage of petrol.

Frustrations ran high. Crüwell displayed an outburst to a British officer over his treatment in the camp. He knew from letters from Germany that life for some German PoWs was much better in camps in Canada. The British officer offered to arrange a transfer. Crüwell quickly rescinded and complained that the lack of food was making him thin. To this he received the response that he looked less flabby and much healthier.

During July 1943 new military blood arrived in the camp in the form of German Colonels Egersdorff and Borcherdt. They came with fresh ideas about how the running of the camp could be improved. It was suggested that for the greater happiness of everyone the PoWs should be given parole for pheasant-shooting and have a plentiful supply of whisky, amongst other things. The British minders ignored the request. This was the middle of wartime. Did the Generals really think they could get whatever they demanded? It didn't stop them trying. Always the British kept the upper hand.

Von Arnim requested a meeting with the new camp Commandant in charge at Trent Park while Kendrick was based at Latimer House. He produced further requests on behalf of the Generals – a German cook, a German tailor and a German dentist. He considered British methods of dentistry old-fashioned. Complaints were made about the quantity of rations. It was pointed out to him that the other PoWs had already expressed contentment with the rations. That was the swift end of that. It did not prevent von Arnim asking for more cigarettes, cigars and tobacco until he was promptly told that such rations for PoWs were far less in Germany. The camp Commandant played the Generals at their own game.

The following day von Arnim was escorted to the hospital for a problem with his feet. Whilst there he was permitted to visit another PoW and inmate Lieutenant-General Frantz who was in hospital for an unknown complaint. Von Arnim expressed disgust at the methods of treatment which he considered old-fashioned. When the specialist asked him who had treated him in Germany von Arnim squeaked 'some little man.' When he was then attended by a female doctor he almost collapsed into an apoplectic fit of shock and objected to her tending to him. These reactions appeared in British Intelligence files.

On the afternoon of 23 July the Generals received a visit from Mr. Barwick of the British YWCA and Tracy Strong of the American YMCA. No secret was made of the presence of the PoW camp – it had eventually come out in the British press when the Generals had been taken on trips into London. But what was kept completely hush-hush was the whole bugging of the conversations and Secret Service aspect. Access to the site was strictly controlled. The YWCA visitors promised to ameliorate life for the prisoners by offering to provide a grand piano, gramophone, golf clubs and a range of literature from Liverpool University.

News of Mussolini's resignation on the night of 25 July rendered the Generals speechless. The announcement soon travelled through the camp to the other officers. The consequence was shattering for them and completely unexpected. Even the defeatists were seriously affected. In response Hülsen declared that Germany's position was precarious; to which von Arnim and Crüwell agreed. During the first few hours after the news Crüwell despaired and declared, 'I am no Nazi!' This quick change of heart was typical of him. British Intelligence recorded in its report of the following morning:

'It would have been difficult to have found a gloomier collection of people than our guests here. The only smiling face was von Thoma's and he went about with an "I told you so" air, much to the annoyance of the anti-defeatists. Thoma told a British officer he had discussed the news with Crüwell and said to him "which of us has made a fool of himself, you or I?" Which of course must have poured salt into Crüwell's already smarting wounds.'

That same day the G.O.C (General Officer Commanding), London District, was due to inspect the camp. As camp leader von Arnim had been informed the previous evening and advised by the Commandant that he and the other Generals might like to remain in their rooms because the G.O.C may want to see their rooms and would also be inspecting the guard in the courtyard. Von Arnim reacted badly to the news as a restriction on their freedom of movement. He was politely reminded that the last time the guard was inspected he had requested advance notice so the Generals could chose to stay in their rooms out of the way. The reaction of the other Generals to the impending visit by the G.O.C, whom they would respect as military men, is not without its humour. Hülsen and Meixner, who shared a room, decided to hide their cigarettes in the hope that the G.O.C would think they were badly treated and had none. The G.O.C did visit the upstairs rooms but, much to von Arnim's disgust, did not stay to talk with him. That evening von Arnim complained to every British officer he saw that the G.O.C had not given him the time of day – all this on the same day as one of the batmen gave a Nazi salute to a British officer in the corridor, then swiftly apologized.

Von Arnim and Cramer requested a walk that evening in the grounds with a British officer. It was a gloomy affair. Von Arnim appeared to have drastically aged and all he wanted to do was sit and dig holes in the grass with his stick. They were in no mood to discuss Mussolini in spite of much prompting by the British officer. Cramer merely commented, 'yesterday was indeed a red-letter day for you!' Meanwhile, the other Generals sat alone in their rooms to contemplate the day's events.

## APPEALING TO THE SWISS

A few days later on the morning of 29 August the Commandant gave the Generals a few hours advance notice of a visit to the camp by Dr Preiswerk, the Swiss representative. Switzerland was officially a neutral country. The news sent the Generals into a frenzy of preparatory activities. Nothing focused their attention better than being motivated by their own cause. They began to work on a plan of campaign to bring various complaints before the Swiss representative. Every part of their 'privately-planned' strategy was ironically recorded by the secret listeners. The

Generals constantly tried to run rings around their captors but there was nothing happening in the camp that British Intelligence did not know about. The Generals agreed amongst themselves to complain about the Major-Generals being assigned two to a room. Also on their growing agenda: the question of parole and taking walks outside the wire fence; the unequal treatment of batmen – they get no beer and are only allowed to write two letters and four cards a month, whereas the Generals may write three letters and four cards. They requested provision of a German doctor and dentist to be provided from amongst German PoWs being held in Britain, and asked for specialist officers from other PoW camps to come to Trent Park to give lectures on various subjects. They asked why only one lower-rank officer was permitted to go for a walk at a time, whereas two Generals could go?

The Generals agreed not to offer the Swiss representative any cigarettes so he would think that the British were not giving them any. Crüwell went so far as to suggest that they should not be too nasty to Dr Preiswerk because he was their last hope but that they should only ask him to tea in one of their rooms if he was already proving helpful. Crüwell suggested to von Arnim that he should wear full uniform and decorations so the special visitor would be impressed. Also it was urged on von Arnim that Dr Preiswerk should be steered clear of those Generals and officers who did not approve of the grumbling campaign. Of course British Intelligence was monitoring their plan through the listeners and decided to intervene behind the scenes by ensuring that Dr Preiswerk visited von Thoma who would be much more appreciative.

Eventually when Dr Preiswerk visited von Arnim he threw him off guard by asking to see him alone. Isolated from the others, von Arnim kept to the plan and brought up the list of complaints. Dr Preiswerk proved unhelpful and pointed out that the German government was largely to blame. He advised von Arnim not to press matters too much because it might provoke an investigation which could turn out unfavourably against the Generals. Clever and robust counter-strategy on the part of Dr Preiswerk. Von Arnim told several downright untruths. On one occasion, he told the visitor, an officer PoW had signed a parole form but was still accompanied to the dentist by a British escort.

'Why should we be accompanied by a British officer at all if we have signed a parole form and the whole park is surrounded by barbed wire?' von Arnim asked.

'You are mistaken,' replied Dr Preiswerk. 'It is a normal peacetime fence and under the Geneva Convention the power holding the prisoner has to protect them from hostile demonstrations. It is in your interests to be accompanied by a British officer.'

Von Arnim had nothing to say in response. Dr Preiswerk asked to see the other Generals but von Arnim swiftly assured him that they had nothing to discuss with him. Dr Preiswerk was not deterred and managed to see von Thoma.

At the end of the month Lieutenant-General Frantz was fetched from hospital and brought back to Trent Park. The nurses told the British officer that they had tried to discharge Frantz earlier. They had never come across such an unpleasant, domineering and 'thick-skinned patient'. Some of the nurses refused to go into his room. On his return Frantz seemed happy with the medical treatment but complained bitterly that he had been insulted with a sentry posted outside his room at all times. He also took the opportunity to complain about the food and went so far as to suggest to the other Generals that it was a sign of how badly the war was going for the British.

# SNAKE IN THE GRASS ACTIVITIES

During August 1943 the Generals seemed as disunited as when they first arrived. After Sunday lunch on 15 August von Arnim gave another of his 'pep talks' and warned the others against defeatist talk. He announced that he suspected a British Army officer of listening into their talk from his window – why else had a British Army officer moved to a room on the first floor? He also declared suspicions that their conversations might be overheard by the establishment. The speech created uproar amongst the other Generals. Even the pro-Nazis objected to the tone and language of von Arnim's rhetoric.

The following day von Arnim added more fuel to the fire when he said that all he was trying to do was save the defeatists from court-martial when they finally returned to 'the glorious Fatherland'. The other PoWs objected strongly to what they termed 'the Gestapo-style' methods contained in von Arnim's speech. The result had the opposite effect and turned the PoWs' views of von Arnim to suspecting him of suffering from psychosis, and Crüwell was deemed to be unbalanced. The British Army officer who was the subject of von Arnim's comments received sympathy from the other prisoners who later discussed amongst themselves how he could not possibly be a British Intelligence officer because he was not subtle enough. That must have brought a smile to MI19 when they read it.

Crüwell began to work against Liebenstein to get him deposed as Deputy camp leader, perhaps hoping that he himself would be selected. It didn't happen and he was bitterly disappointed. He continued to vent anger and a hatred of von Thoma and did his best to win over supporters. His efforts were wasted. The other PoWs showed no interest at all. Meixner thought it ridiculous for Crüwell to suspect von Thoma of being a bad influence on the young. Hülsen added that there were no young men in the

Camp, only men of experience who were perfectly capable of thinking for themselves and forming their own opinions.

The Generals continued to be supplied with literature. Crüwell complained that the anti-Nazi books had been supplied by the British authorities and should in no way be distributed in wartime without being censored by the German authorities. The other Generals quickly responded - who did he mean by the 'German authorities'? British Intelligence commented in a report 'he [Crüwell] probably meant himself!'

On 20 August Frantz, Schnarrenberger, Heym and Drange were informed that they were being transferred to an American camp the following day. The announcement naturally took the attention of the other Generals who could not resist commenting on the reasons for the unexpected transfer. Frantz bizarrely decided he was being exchanged for some American machinery and that he had been chosen because he was the senior Luftwaffe General in the camp and the Americans wanted him for reasons of prestige. Heym decided he was being exchanged for forty old destroyers. Drange suggested that he and Heym were on the American 'Black List' and shouldn't be transferred to the Americans whom they despised. Then the M Room listeners overheard an extraordinary comment which gives an insight into the brain-washing of the Nazi regime. The four prisoners feared that they were victims who might fall into the hands of the Jews in America and be paraded through the streets of New York.

## WINTER FESTIVITIES

As Christmas approached British Army officers turned to plans for festivities in the Camp. On 9 November the 'guests', as they were politely referred to in general intelligence reports, had group photographs taken to send to their next-of-kin as a Christmas present. In a move which surprised

Intelligence staff, the Generals organised themselves along political lines for their official photograph. Clustered in one group was von Arnim, Crüwell, Hülsen, Meixner, Schmidt, Buhse, Egersdorff, Borcherdt, Boes, Glasow and Hubbuch. The other group was composed of Sponeck, Broich, Liebenstein, Bassenge, Neuffer, Krause, Reimann, Wolters and Koehnke. Von Thoma refused to have his photograph taken at all because he did not want a reminder of his time in a PoW camp or to be seen with 'old Blimps' as he termed his colleagues.

A short time later a British Army officer stumbled across an advertisement for Trent Park written by one of the Generals. Its priceless tongue-in-cheek humour must have brought a smile to British minders and reads in translation (WO208/4363):

PARK SANATORIUM

First class accommodation, running hot and cold water at all hours of the day, also baths on the premises. Four generous meals daily, first class English cuisine.

Regular walks under expert guidance

Large library of carefully chosen literature of all countries.

Table-tennis tournaments, billiards, chess and bridge circles.

Instruction in art and handicrafts.

Alcoholism cured without extra charge.

Moderate terms, varying according to social position.

Best society assured at all times!

Internal rivalry continued unabated. Crüwell endeavoured to have the deputy camp leader von Liebenstein removed from post, proposing to have him replaced by Bassenge in the hope of bridging the rift between the diehards and defeatists. His strategy was aimed at isolating von Thoma and

and giving the Nazis more influence over the defeatists. Bassenge discussed Crüwell's offer with Neuffer who urged him to accept. Bassenge in accepting the position declared that he would frame a clear-cut policy and put it into operation in the camp.

Towards the end of November Generals von Broich, Sponeck and von Liebenstein were informed by a British Army officer that the Führer was sending a gift of money to all prisoners. Their response to Hitler's 'generosity' was somewhat 'uncomplimentary and unprintable'.

Christmas celebrations began following afternoon tea on Christmas Eve. That evening the Generals and Senior German officers sat down to Christmas dinner. Afterwards the various groups retired to their rooms to celebrate quietly. Only von Thoma spent the remainder of the evening alone. Major Boes, one of the most violently-Nazi officers in the Camp, received news from his wife by letter that he had been promoted to Lieutenant-Colonel. British Army officers noted that his 'Anglo-phobia gets more marked each day'. The festivities were marred only by von Arnim who, even on Christmas Eve, felt it his duty to annoy the British officers by raising complaints again about their treatment. Bassenge took a firm stand and told the British that the others were only too grateful for what had been done for them in the Camp.

On Christmas Day the Generals listened to the King's Speech. Cramer commented how impressed he was and how the King provided a figure which a nation could rally around in times of crisis. He blamed the removal of the Kaiser for all Germany's subsequent ills. The others said little. At this time it was brought to the attention of von Arnim by the British minders that the prisoners had shown a tendency recently to waste electric light and water. Arnim discussed the matter with Cramer, both of them agreeing that they would not want the British to retaliate by cutting rations.

New Year's Eve saw no particular celebrations apart from the Generals gathering in the common room to listen to the German wireless at midnight. Goebbels' speech and Hitler's proclamation did nothing to lift their sombre mood, except an agreement even amongst the defeatists, that they would support their motherland to the bitter end. They needed no crystal ball to tell them that the events of 1944 would decide the fate of the war and they faced the beginning of the end.

Two weeks into the New Year, Dr Haccius of the International Red Cross visited Trent Park to report on conditions in the Camp and was received on behalf of the German Generals by Bassenge. Ever mindful to know what the Generals thought of the Camp and what was being said to the Red Cross, the conversation was bugged by the listeners. Haccius was overheard expressing mild criticism of American methods and lack of understanding at an American camp which he had visited at Oxford. Bassenge gave a description of the Christmas festivities at Trent Park and told Haccius: 'the British made a great effort to ensure our celebrations were a success.' Haccius suggested that there ought to be a vegetable garden in the camp. Bassenge seemed unenthusiastic and stated that food was ample. They discussed long delays in prisoners' mail and censorship. Haccius asked about interpreters in the Camp. He was reassured that the two interpreters were excellent and had arranged English and Mathematics lessons for the prisoners. Haccius promised to send more cigarettes for the batmen.

A separate conversation took place between Haccius, von Arnim and Bassenge. MI19 noted that Haccius told them his life story. They proceeded to discuss the chances of exchange of German internees and prisoners. Von Arnim continued his complaint about English dentistry and insisted on a German dentist and doctor. Coffee was served. Over coffee von Arnim thanked Haccius for the Red Cross parcels and then asked if it was possible to buy wrist-watches from Switzerland. A discussion about the difficulties of this ensued. The meeting ended with mutual expressions of goodwill.

Two days after Haccius' visit, MI19 headquarters received a transcript of the conversations during his visit and also impressions gleaned from the M Room listeners. A covering letter stated: 'The general impression made on the M Room operators was that Dr Haccius did not observe a strictly neutral attitude. His remarks on other camps, censorship and exchange of PoW gave the impression of being more pro-German than neutral.' After Haccius' visit the batmen were given the opportunity to work in a vegetable garden on the estate, for which they would receive payment. Five pro-Nazi batmen refused, saying it helped the British war effort. New deputy camp leader Bassenge pointed out the ridiculous nature of the argument and said that everyone benefited from the work. He went on to suggest that, if they rejected work in the vegetable gardens, logically they should refuse English cigarettes which helped the British war effort through taxation. Neuffer and Bassenge dismissed the batmen's attitude as pure stupidity and ludicrous.

News of the sinking of the German battleship *Scharnhorst* at the end of the previous year brought some surprise and speculation amongst the Generals that Hitler had intentionally sent her to her doom because all was not well with the Navy. Discontent continued amongst the batmen who had also formed into two distinct groups of pro-Nazi and anti-Nazi. British Intelligence officers had difficulty with General von Hülsen who, according to the camp-diary, 'seems to think that camp orders do not refer to him.' Instead of arranging an afternoon walk with his minders he just turned up at the allotted time and expected to be accommodated. Neuffer was already irritated by Hülsen and 'gave him a piece of his mind', leading to a very public row in front of the batmen. Hülsen went so far as to call

Neuffer an 'imprudent fellow'. British Intelligence General-Report for January 1944 commented, 'the fat was in the fire and the whole camp buzzed with excitement.' The Commandant warned Hülsen that if he carried on as before, he would be subject to 'special treatment'. The Generals proceeded to speculate on the meaning of 'special treatment' and concluded that it may mean transportation to Russia.

Suspicions ran high with the arrival on 22 January of Lieutenant-Colonel Müller-Rienzburg, a German Air Force officer. Not understanding the politics in the camp, Müller-Rienzburg made the mistake of airing his defeatist and pro-British views to some member of the pro-Nazi group. Now the pro-Nazi group suspected Müller-Rienzburg of being a British Secret Service agent – which of course was not the case and they had, ironically, failed to suspect that most of the British officers in the camp were from British Intelligence.

By now Crüwell began to realise that he had become the most unpopular man in the camp. The others avoided sitting with him at mealtimes. A dejected Crüwell only came downstairs for dinner, taking other meals in his room and becoming more and more isolated from the others. British officers found him mainly in his room, staring into the distance or playing a game of patience. It was noted that he and von Arnim were 'heading for mental disaster if they don't change their attitudes'.

Lieutenant Hubbuch and ardent Nazi Lieutenant-Colonel Boes left for a PoW camp in Canada. This caused a stir amongst the Generals who feared they might be sent to Canada too; something which they saw as a backward step. In spite of their grumblings, life in Trent Park was comfortable. In a surprising U-turn, the Generals petitioned British officers against leaving Trent Park. When alone together it did not stop them speculating who might be next to be transported across the ocean.

The end of January marked the 11th anniversary of Hitler coming to power in Germany. The Generals gathered around a wireless set and listened to the Führer's radio speech. None of them appeared impressed by it. Reimann summed it up as like 'a worn-out gramophone record'.

## HITLER'S BIRTHDAY CELEBRATIONS

By early April 1944 Crüwell began to make preparations to mark the Führer's birthday on 20th; all this permitted by MI19 who were listening in to their plans. Crüwell sounded out the other German officers and suggested that he himself could make a short speech at dinner. They would have to drink the Führer's health with beer. 'Pity it has to be English beer,' he added, 'but that can't be helped.' An anxious Crüwell fretted that von Thoma might refuse to stand up and participate in the toast. He feared too that Bassenge might not make proper camp arrangements. Crüwell had a ready solution to these problems. If Bassenge messed up preparations for the Führer's birthday and von Thoma refused to toast, the Generals would expel them from the Officer' Corps and prohibit them from eating in the Officers Mess. He believed the other Generals could take matters into their own hands and apply rules which may be contrary to Camp Regulations.

On the morning of 20 April it was clear to anyone observing that this was no ordinary day. The German batmen were dressed in their 'Sunday best' but the officers were not. At 12.30pm von Arnim and Captain Meixner visited the batmen's dining room – the first indication in British Intelligence reports that the batmen dined separately from the Generals. A toast was offered up to Hitler and a short speech given by von Arnim. Meixner and von Arnim then entered the other dining room (aka Officers Mess) and repeated the speech with a toast to Hitler. For the British minders it had become a camp within a camp. The Generals liked to believe they had autonomy. In return, the British were happy for them to believe it because the whole operation gave MI19 far more intelligence than they could ever have imagined. While the Generals wrangled over political divisions and etiquette, the secret listeners spent hours recording their unguarded conversations – conversations which yielded some of Hitler's most closely protected military secrets; the most precious of which related to the deadly rocket programme and the development of the atomic bomb.

# EIGHT

## SECRET LISTENERS

On 13 December 1942 the third of Kendrick's operational centres became fully functional at Wilton Park. Its day-to-day running on site was left to Major L. St. Clare Grondona who was ultimately answerable to Kendrick. The Wilton Park camp was built around a large manor house known as the White House, in which captured Italian Generals were accommodated.

Events were taking a dramatic turn on the Russian Front. At the end of January 1943 German Field Marshal von Paulus, in charge of the German 6th Army trying to take Stalingrad, had surrendered to the Soviets. The tide began to turn for the Allies. The RAF and US Air Force hammered the enemy's industrial centres in successful air raids across Germany. In early March 1943 Fritz Lustig was staying on leave in London. His mother's cousin had introduced him to two of his friends in the capital, Norman and Christel Marsh. Christel was of German origin; her husband a barrister by profession and now a Captain in the Intelligence Corps. Fritz visited them several times during his army leaves and often expressed frustration at not being able to do something worthwhile for the war effort. Norman listened patiently and gave nothing away. Then on one particular visit he asked Fritz if he would be willing to transfer to the Intelligence Corps because a special unit was looking for fluent German-speakers. Fritz was enthusiastic at the prospect. He left that day with a promise from Norman that he would put his name forward.

With leave over, on 17 March Fritz travelled to Waterloo Station for his return to Southern Command in Bulford. Amongst the busy throng of soldiers on the platform Fritz suddenly heard his name. He turned to see a friend rushing up to him. She explained that a telegram had arrived for him that morning ordering him to attend an interview in Northumberland Avenue the next day. Fritz left the station and returned to central London.

The following morning he arrived outside the Metropole Building in Northumberland Avenue for the interview. Inside he found about a dozen other candidates waiting for interview, all ex-refugees from Germany or Austria. Some had already transferred to other units and were no longer in the alien Pioneer Corps. Fritz was ushered into an interview room where a board of six officers (one a woman) sat around a horseshoe-shaped table. He made a sufficiently good impression to be asked to come back for a second interview after lunch:

> 'The second interview was with two civilians who I am convinced were from MI5. There was little they did not know about me – they knew for instance that I had corresponded with my parents while they were still in Germany, and that they were now in Portugal. As far as I can recall, I was not interrogated about my political views at all.'

Fritz left with no idea whether he had been accepted. He returned to Bulford and life carried on in the orchestra as before. In the coming weeks Rudolph Jess, a tenor and fellow refugee-soldier in the Entertainment Section, told Fritz that as security officer of the section (something Fritz was unaware of) he had been asked about Fritz's political views by the intelligence authorities. Jess had assured them that all was in order. Fritz heard nothing further. In mid-May the orchestra was on tour in Somerset, covering concerts in Burnham-on-Sea, Wellington, Taunton and Bristol. On 17 May the officer-in-charge, Lieut. White, received a telegram instructing Fritz to report again to the Metropole Building in London. Fritz instinctively knew this was acceptance into the Intelligence Corps, but had no idea what that would entail. That evening he and the orchestra were giving a concert at a Convalescent Depot in Sherford, near Poole in Dorset:

> 'I was very conscious of the fact that this was the last time I would be playing with the orchestra, and with the people who had been my comrades for the past 2½ years. The last item on the programme was the overture to *Orpheus in the Underworld* by Offenbach, which has a cello-solo of about 16 bars. I tried to play it better than ever before as my "farewell" to the orchestra.

Judging from the comments afterwards Fritz had succeeded in making a memorable last performance. The following day he travelled to the Metropole Building in London where intelligence staff told him he was to take the Metropolitan Line to Chalfont & Latimer where he would be met at the station. Given the necessary train ticket, Fritz left the building none the wiser about his new unit. That same day he penned a letter to his parents, uplifted by new military successes in North Africa after Montgomery's 8<sup>th</sup> Army had taken Tunis:

> *'We have been reading the reports of English journalists about Germans streaming into captivity, who this time - for the first time - have not been fighting to the bitter end, as if they were fairy tales - too good to be true. Let's hope that German morale will soon start to break in other places as well.'*

The next day was 19 May – his father's 70<sup>th</sup> birthday – and the day that Fritz took the Metropolitan Line to Chalfont & Latimer. At the railway station he was met by a driver in military uniform and driven to a nearby 'camp'. As they drove along the country lane through the rolling lush green countryside Fritz got his first glimpse of a red-brick stately home,

Latimer House. Little did he imagine that this was to be his new base. On arrival he discovered that the unit was not just military personnel but also comprised of men and women from the Air Force and Navy, and that it was in fact a special prisoner-of-war camp. Nothing else was revealed then. Fritz was immediately issued with three stripes – the sleeve insignia of a Sergeant. 'I was stunned,' he says, 'by the fact that I had been promoted from Private to Sergeant – three ranks in one go!'

The contrast from life in the Pioneer Corps could not have been more stark. Sergeants and Sergeant-Majors had their own Mess which had easy chairs for relaxation and a wireless to listen to radio broadcasts. Sergeants of the intelligence staff had their own Mess and were kept apart from ordinary camp Sergeants. Again for security purposes nothing had been left to chance. Non-intelligence staff did not mix with Intelligence staff. No one was allowed to speak of their particular classified work to anyone else in the camp. Fritz found sleeping quarters much better, now sharing with six or seven others, rather than twenty soldiers as in the huts of the Pioneer Corps.

The following morning Fritz came face-to-face with his new Commanding Officer in an interview. Lt. Col. Kendrick explained the nature of his work and impressed on him the importance of not telling anyone about his work, not even family or close friends. Kendrick passed him a form and asked him to sign. Fritz read the terms of The Official Secrets Act carefully, then signed. Now he was bound by oath to keep whatever classified information came his way. This unit's existence had to be kept secret at all cost. Before dismissing him, Kendrick said something to Fritz which he has never forgotten: 'your work here is more important than firing a gun in action or joining a fighting unit.'

Fritz had been selected to become one of Kendrick's secret listeners. The irony was not lost on him. Back in November 1938 when the

Nazis had unleashed Kristallnacht, the Night of Broken Glass, he and his family had feared for their lives. Like many Jews, they had gone into hiding. That terrifying night they were expecting a telephone call from Fritz's brother who had escaped to America. The Gestapo [Secret Police under Himmler] were known to tap the telephones of Jews and political opponents of the regime. Fritz recalls:

> 'Many people even suspected that secret microphones had been attached to their telephones which would enable the Gestapo to listen-in to conversations while the receiver was on the hook, and therefore piled several cushions on top of their telephones in order to muffle the sound reaching the supposed microphone.'

At the height of the terror being inflicted on the Jews of Germany that fateful night in 1938, Fritz's family managed to get a telegram to his brother warning him not to telephone them for fear of the consequences. Nearly five years later Fritz found himself working for British Intelligence against the Nazis. His loyalty to the country which had saved him was never in doubt, but now his adopted country finally trusted him with their most closely guarded secrets. In an ironic twist of fate the man who once feared being bugged by the Gestapo was himself about to bug the conversations of Nazis.

## ÉMIGRÉ LISTENERS

Since 1938 Kendrick's life had been inextricably caught up with the lives of Europe's émigrés. Back then in Vienna he and his staff at the British Passport Office had worked tirelessly for over twelve hours a day to save Austria's Jews from the Nazis. Now during the war itself he looked to the

German-speaking refugees living in Britain to provide British Intelligence with the tools for keeping ahead in the intelligence game. From the end of 1942 and during 1943 over eighty refugee-soldiers transferred from the alien Pioneer Corps to become M Room operators in Kendrick's unit. They formed a tight-knit team, all united in being able to do something exceptional towards the downfall of the regime they had once fled.

After almost three years Fritz was reunited at Latimer House with his friend Peter Ganz whose name he had suggested as a possible listener for MI19. After a short time at Latimer House, Ganz transferred to the M Room at Trent Park and there, with other Jewish émigrés bugged the conversations of the German Generals and Senior officers. One of those émigrés was Eric Mark. Born in Magdeburg, Germany as Erich (Meyer) Mark he fled the Nazi regime in January 1935. During the war he enlisted in the alien Pioneer Corps and served with 93 Company until his transfer to the Intelligence Corps on 1 March 1944. He was sent first to Wilton Park and then Trent Park. He recalls life at Trent Park and eavesdropping on conversations about the V-2 rocket bases at Peenemünde and also the reaction of the Generals to the failed assassination attempt on Hitler's life. Nine months later he was promoted to Sergeant-Major.

Back at Latimer House Fritz struck up a friendship with another new arrival at the unit. George Pulay was younger than Fritz and had arrived in the Intelligence Corps via a different route. Born in Vienna on 5 March 1923, George was the son of Ida Pulay and eminent skin specialist Dr Erwin Pulay. After Hitler's annexation of Austria in March 1938 George's father was immediately at risk because of the Gestapo round-up of Jewish intellectuals and professionals. Dr Pulay came to England during 1938 ahead of his wife and children, aided by Kendrick's staff at the British Passport Office in Vienna. The family always felt that he had abandoned them and never really forgave him – they harboured a sense of betrayal at leaving them to the horrors that were unfolding for Jews in Austria. By 1939 Ida managed to come to England with son George and daughter Uli, again aided by the British Passport Office. Ida and Dr Erwin Pulay separated. Life was hard for newly-arrived refugees, not least for George's mother in a strange land, with no knowledge of the language and raising two teenagers. At the outbreak of war George was not old enough to enlist in the British forces and therefore did not come to MI19 via the usual route. He was also probably too young to be interned in the summer of 1940. In 1943, possibly as a result of voluntarily enlisting in the British forces, George was drafted into the Intelligence Corps and sent to Latimer House. There he joined one of the M Room teams working alongside Fritz Lustig.

Another listener was Rudi Oppenheimer, a lawyer, who had fled Nuremberg with his wife in 1934. His son Peter was born in London in 1938. After a brief spell in internment, Rudi joined the Pioneer Corps and trained in Ilfracombe. He served from 10 September 1940 until May 1942 when he joined the Royal Army Service Corps (RASC). Then from 18 March 1944 he transferred to the Intelligence Corps and was based in the M Room at Wilton Park. He remained with MI19 until 28 December 1945.

Teddy Schächter, who eventually anglicised his name to Teddy Chester, never spoke about the nature of his work to his family. All he ever told them was that he worked for MI5 and could not speak about it. They accepted that. During the writing of this book his family finally discovered that Teddy had been one of the secret listeners.

## M ROOM OPERATIONS

In the specially constructed M Room, which consisted of three rooms and six listening stations in each, the listeners worked in eight-hour shifts. Through bugging devices in the lamp fittings of the cells they listened into the conversations of the PoWs. It was a clever ruse and one which the prisoners appeared never to have suspected. Part of MI19's deception involved placing two prisoners from different services in a single cell together in the hope that they confided to each other about what they failed to tell British officers during interrogation. It worked. The thousands of transcripts which survive in the National Archives are testament to that. The prisoners relaxed and chatted freely with no sense of security. Fritz comments, 'Only two prisoners to a cell – otherwise it would have been almost impossible for us to distinguish properly between the voices.' On occasion more than two German Generals chatted in a communal room and transcripts show that it was sometimes difficult to distinguish between them. However on the whole, the listeners at Trent Park became familiar with a particular General's voice and that made the work straightforward.

In overall charge of the M Room was Major Cassels. Other officers in charge of the squads of listeners were Capt. Brodie, Capt. Hartje, Capt. Davis, Capt. Serin, Lt. Blyth, Lt. Rowe, Lt. Read-Jahn, Lt. Reynolds, Lt. Gross, Lt. Bauers and Lt. Weber. Technical side of recording and listening-in was taken care of by Capt. Copping of the Royal Corps of Signals. Psychologist Lieut. Col. Dicks advised on interrogation of particular prisoners.

Prisoners were not permitted to leave their cells for any length of time to avoid discussing critical information out of range of the hidden microphones. Apart from half an hour in the exercise yard and occasional visits to the toilet, they remained in their rooms. The environment was always geared towards encouraging the prisoners to talk and therefore they were only permitted one newspaper a day to stimulate conversation between each other. Literature was kept to a minimum so the prisoners spent time talking rather than reading. An exception to this was at Trent Park where the German Generals were given complete freedom and access to the house and grounds. Not a single period of the prisoners' waking hour was left unmonitored as Fritz recalls:

'We were organised into squads of up to twelve operators; each squad divided into two shifts of 6 operators and an officer in charge. We worked in two shifts: early and late. The early shift started after breakfast at 8 am and ended at 4 pm. The late shift began at 4 pm and finished whenever the prisoners stopped talking and had gone to sleep. This could be as late as 11pm or midnight. Overnight a night duty officer always slept in the M Room in case of an emergency.'

Weekends were counted as normal working days but operators were given one day off a week which had to be booked in advance so that there was always sufficient cover in the M Room. Access to the M Room remained highly restricted – the key to it only given to staff working there. Other intelligence staff did not know of its existence.

'We sat at tables fitted with record-cutting equipment – this was before electronic tapes were invented. We had a kind of old-fashioned telephone switchboard facing us, where we put plugs into numbered sockets in order to listen to the PoWs through our headphones. Each operator usually had to monitor two or three cells, switching from one to the other to see whether something interesting was being discussed. As soon as we heard something which we thought might be valuable, we pushed a switch to start a turntable revolving, and pulled a small leaver to lower the recording-head onto the record. We had to identify which prisoner was which by their voices and accents and keep a log, noting what our "charges" were doing or talking about. In that log we noted down the time of day and the subjects that we had recorded, so that the next shift could see at a glance what had been happening. As soon as a record had been cut, somebody else had to take over the monitoring, and the operator went to a different room to transcribe what he had just recorded. At the end of duty the log-sheet was handed to the next shift so the other listeners could tell what had happened on the previous shift. Whenever a record was 'cut', a note was made in a column on the log sheet. It enabled the day's activities to be seen at a glance for any of the cells.'

The listeners did not take shorthand notes because MI19 needed to record every detail, not personal judgments. Each record held up to seven minutes of conversation. A carefully transcribed text could take up to an hour and a half to transcribe and then translate from German into English. If it was not possible to identify certain words, then a gap with dots indicated on the transcript the inability to recognise a certain word or phrase. The listeners were not permitted to guess what the word might be. After transcribing the conversation, a senior operator checked the draft for any errors, omissions or superfluous material, and then it was passed to the draft room for typing. Finally it went to Kendrick, often via Felkin, for distribution to various select intelligence centres. These included, for example, Air and Naval Intelligence, the War Office, Political Intelligence Department, MI5, MI6, MI8, MI9, MI14, commanders at Bletchley and the Joint Intelligence Committee. The 'cut' record was kept for two months before being returned to the Post Office Research Station for re-conditioning and re-issue. Records with evidence of wartime atrocities were kept permanently.

## LAYERS OF DECEPTION

The multi-layered deception plan included not only surreptitiously recording the private conversations of the prisoners but the formal interrogations. The main reasons for making so much of the camp as an interrogation centre was all part of MI19's complex gambit. German prisoners expected to be interrogated after capture, and MI19 believed that if the PoWs underwent extensive interrogation they would not suspect their conversations were being bugged. The interrogation rooms were "miked" back to the M Room where the listeners monitored and recorded information which the interrogation officer was gaining from a particular PoW. Often the interrogation officer could not take notes during interrogation without running the risk of the prisoner clamming up. A fairly relaxed interrogation was deemed to enable the prisoner to feel less inhibited. At their sets in the M Room the listeners recorded aspects of the interrogation which they had been primed to listen for.

There was yet another dimension to this scheme. Having heard the interrogation interview, the listener then knew what was likely to come up in conversation once the prisoner returned to his cell. 'All prisoners were interrogated several times,' says Fritz, 'always by officers not working in our monitoring section. We never dealt with any of them face-to-face. Their reaction to interrogation was often particularly fruitful. They would tell their cell-mate what they had been asked about, what they had managed to conceal from the interrogating officer and how much we (the British) already knew.' The listeners were briefed in advance about the kind of information that MI19 needed. They had to be able to pick out certain topics to record, including a knowledge of military, U-boat and Luftwaffe terminology. Listener Peter Hart (born Peter Klaus Herz, 1914), who transferred to the Intelligence Corps in July 1944, comments in his memoirs *Journey to Freedom* about the skills needed by the listeners to do their job:

> 'Not only was it necessary to have a complete mastery of the German language, but often prisoners coming from regions where dialects were spoken, were extremely difficult to understand, unless one knew the dialect well. In addition, we not only had to be knowledgeable about the whole arsenal of German weapons in all three services – Army, Navy and Luftwaffe, but also know about the ranks of personnel, including the infamous SS. Furthermore we had to be well informed about what was going on militarily and look out for any gossip and information which our High Command wanted to pick up.'

Occasionally prisoners were brought in who were particularly tight-lipped. In one incident the secret listener discovered from eavesdropping on the conversations of a U-boat crew that they were extremely frightened, with something on their conscience. What emerged from the M Room transcripts was that they had sunk a ship off Africa and machine gunned the survivors. Primed with this information from the M Room, interrogators staged a 'court of enquiry' charged with looking into war crimes. The crew was left in no doubt that if they did not tell all they knew, they would be handed over for war crimes trials. A result was achieved and the men talked.

In November 1943 Fritz Lustig received promotion. As Company Sergeant-Major (CSM) or Warrant Officer 2nd Class (WOII), he could wear a badge with a crown on the lower half of the sleeve. It was a proud moment. He had become the senior rank in the Sergeants Mess, and by virtue of that, he became President Sergeants Mess. As such he was given responsibilities for everything that happened in the Mess and also put in charge of running a squad of listeners at the third centre at Wilton Park. Fritz Lustig transferred there with four other émigré listeners: George Pulay, Heilbronn, Douglas (originally Korn, called "Konny") and Peter Land. Some of the M Room operators were Italian-speakers whose brief was to listen into the high-ranking Italian prisoners. The Italian Generals were given free range of the grounds outside the White House at Wilton Park. 'If we passed one of them, we had to salute them – which we rather resented,' says Fritz.

Music continued to play an important role in boosting morale in two camps. Having been reunited with his cello Fritz was persuaded to play in the camp band for a concert, alongside non-intelligence staff, to perform a few solo items. Instruments in the band included two trumpets, one clarinet, a guitar or banjo, piano, double bass, percussion and one violin. Their music consisted of around 80% popular hits. For Fritz it provided a leisure activity during the hours out of the M Room. Kendrick, himself a gifted pianist, approached Fritz after the concert and thanked him for his excellent solo performance. Then a dance in the Sergeants Mess that Christmas would change Fritz's life.

## WOMEN IN MI19

In discussion with intelligence chiefs Kendrick received authorization to recruit ATS girls into his unit, especially enlisting the language expertise of German-speaking émigré women. The volume of clerical and interpretive duties at Latimer House made it essential to bring them into the Camp. One of the women was Gerda Engel, a German-Jewish refugee born in Breslau in March 1921. Her father Richard was a dentist and forced to flee after Jews were no longer allowed to hold public office or professional jobs in the Nazi regime. The family arrived in England in 1935. During the war she was drafted into the British forces and was sent to Latimer House.

Susan Cohn (b. Breslau, 1921), a friend of the Engel family, arrived at Latimer House in December 1943. She had emigrated to England on a domestic permit in July 1939 and obtained work in North London. On the day war broke out her employer dismissed her, not wanting a 'German' living in her house, so Susan joined the Engel family. The dentist-father employed her as a domestic and then trained her as a chair assistant in his practice. In 1943 Susan was called up for war work and chose to join the ATS. Her first posting was to Fenham Barracks in Newcastle-upon-Tyne to train in a platoon of other Continental ATS girls. After initial training she was assigned as a dental orderly. Later Susan was sent to a military hospital in York for four weeks training because the British forces no longer needed female dental orderlies. Then she was posted to Nottingham for three months where her main job was de-lousing ATS girls. Whilst on leave in London she happened to meet another émigré ATS girl whom she knew from Breslau. Her acquaintance was a Sergeant and attached to the Intelligence Corps, and she put forward Susan's name for transfer to her unit.

In December 1943 Susan was invited for a selection interview at the War Office where she underwent various tests. Nothing further was heard, then four weeks later she received a letter for transfer to Latimer House to join Kendrick's unit. She recalls:

'It was all very exciting. I had a railway ticket to Chalfont and Latimer Station and was told that I would be met there. A very smart Naval officer and his driver waited for me in a jeep outside.

As I got into the car the driver said to me, "I bet you a packet of cigarettes that you'll be a Sergeant by tonight." I didn't believe him. That evening I was unexpectedly promoted to Sergeant and I owed him a packet of cigarettes!'

Susan was allocated to a typing pool, but since her typing was rather poor she soon found herself transferred to a department where she checked prisoners' documents. The work was highly classified and she spoke to no one else in the camp about it. Neither did she have any idea what the other intelligence staff were doing there. Susan was surprised to come across the papers of her former English teacher from Breslau who she knew was not a Nazi. He was being held in the camp. 'I put in a good word for him,' she says, 'and he was soon transferred.'

That Christmas of 1943 saw several festive activities amongst the staff. Fritz went back to his old camp, Latimer House, for one of the Christmas parties. He noticed a number of new members of staff, amongst them émigré women in the ATS. Fritz remembers the first time he met Susan: 'The ATS girls were allowed to wear civvies (civilian clothes) at parties. At the Christmas party Susan was wearing a red dress with zebras pattern on it. I had a couple of dances with her, but she made no lasting impression on me whatever, either positive or negative.'

Wartime or not, Christmas celebrations took centre stage during times off. In the days leading up to Christmas Fritz carried on with the preparations. During a trip to London he found coloured papers strips – at a time when paper products were in extremely short supply. He stuck the strips together to make paper chains which he strung across the room in all directions. He also bought a small Christmas tree and improvised by decorating it with a few paper chains and some cotton wool balls. Holly branches were nailed to the walls and fastened to the table cloth with pins.

A dozen candles were stuck into potatoes cut in half and the whole potato/candle decoration covered in coloured paper. Army custom dictated that officers visited the Sergeants Mess on Christmas morning to wish its occupants the compliments of the season, and vice versa. Officers did not all call in at the same time, but singly or in small groups. Fritz officially hosted it: 'it was my duty to offer them drinks and of course drink with them. By the end of Christmas morning I was a little bit tipsy.'

The party in the Mess finally finished at 5a.m. Fritz and his colleagues felt it prudent to clear up afterwards. He finally turned into bed at 6a.m, with not much sleep because he started duty in the M Room at 9am. In the first post-Christmas letter Fritz told his parents that it had been the best Christmas since leaving Germany and joining the army.

Whilst at Latimer House Susan struck up a friendship with an English-born WAAF [Women's Auxiliary Air Force], Elisabeth Bruegger (sister of Lord Rees-Mogg). When interviewed in 2011, Elisabeth spoke about her secretarial work for Flight-Lieutenant Felkin in Air Intelligence and particular clandestine wartime missions which have never come to light in intelligence documents. It related to the courage of Dutchmen of the Resistance Movement who risked their lives to row the English Channel at night bearing crucial information for the British about German battle positions and military manoeuvres. Their reports were brought post-haste by bikers and couriers to Kendrick's centre and used by MI19.

In early 1944 Fritz received information that two ATS girls were being transferred from Latimer House to Wilton Park. The news was initially not well-received by Fritz because the absence of girls had contributed to a more 'peaceful' atmosphere in the Mess. In March SQMS (Staff Quartermaster Sergeant) Doreen Wilkinson and Sgt Susan Cohn arrived amidst rumours that a certain gentleman in the camp had a negative attitude towards their arrival. They were determined to prove him wrong. Fritz soon discovered that they were pleasant and their presence had no negative influence on the atmosphere in the Mess.

Susan and Doreen attended the Camp concert mentioned before, and Susan commented, 'We thought Fritz looked rather sullen and depressed and agreed that he needed cheering up. We invited him out for a drink with his friend and colleague George Pulay. And that was the start of the romance between Fritz and myself.'

## JOINT INTELLIGENCE WITH THE AMERICANS

Towards the end of 1942 MI19 began to forge a closer working relationship with the Americans. Kendrick travelled to New York on behalf of British Intelligence to liaise over matters of intelligence and the training of US intelligence officers. It is highly probable that while in New York he also visited the SIS station there, headed by Stephenson with Kim Philby on the staff. Philby later turned out to be a double agent who had been betraying secrets to the Russians and in 1963 defected to Russia, turning out to be one of MI6's most prominent and high profile embarrassments.

An important contingent of American interrogators was established at Latimer House and Wilton Park and copies of all transcripts emanating from the M Room were circulated with American Intelligence. At Latimer House Kendrick oversaw the training of American personnel for the newly-formed OSS (Office of Strategic Services – the forerunner of the CIA). This placed him in a highly trusted position not only vis-à-vis American Intelligence, but also Anglo-American relations; a contribution for which he would later be rewarded by the White House. Apart from the permanent American presence at Latimer House, other personnel passed through for special intelligence training for anything from 2 weeks to 2 months. In addition US Field Interrogation teams also worked alongside Kendrick's interrogators.

In March 1943 Donald Burkewood Welbourn RNVR joined the Naval intelligence team at Latimer House as an interrogator, on the personal recommendation of Commander C. F. Tower, a brilliant officer in charge of the German section in the Naval Intelligence Department at the Admiralty. In his unpublished memoirs now at the Imperial War Museum, Welbourn provides some rare details about the Naval intelligence work at Kendrick's sites. The Naval Section had eight interrogators, one of whom was an American interrogating officer who had been seconded to the unit. There were also WREN officers who spoke fluent German and knew as much about the German Navy as the interrogators. Welbourn also notes the presence of M Room operators who were: 'officers and sergeants who for the most part were extremely well-educated German-Jewish refugees.' The importance of the M Room work above interrogation techniques is aptly highlighted by Welbourn. One of his colleagues, Dick Wetherby, had joined MI19 after a recent spell at sea. Welbourn wrote:

'He [Wetherby] finally drove home to those in authority, who did not believe it, that the old military doctrine that the way to get information from PoWs is to interrogate them the moment they are captured, can be utter and dangerous rubbish. He was a brilliant interrogator, completely primed with all the background needed; but when his destroyer sank a U-boat, and the crew was hauled in over the side, he got nothing of value out of them. Within a couple of days of the men arriving with us, put into cells fitted with microphones, and systematically interrogated, we had most of the story of that U-boat, and a lot else to boot.'

When U-boat crew arrived at one of MI19's centres they were first stripped, searched and given a bath. Welbourn comments: 'they were often in need of clean clothes, since the stench of the typical leather clothing of U-boat crew, compounded of sweat, diesel oil and many other things, has a pungency which does not commend itself. An interrogator would be present, since a lot could be learned at this stage; nothing but German coins in the pockets suggested a boat straight from Germany. Letters from home, condoms, notebooks, all added scraps of information about the man and his boat.' Once the crews had been given clean clothes and civilian rations, they were put in a cell with another mate. A while later they were interrogated. The time between first being in the cell and their interrogation was a crucial period when M Room operators listened into the conversations for idle chatter. This careless talk gave the interrogators a head start. 'If, when a man came in for interrogation,' commented Welbourn, 'we could start by giving him the number, and sometimes the nickname of his boat, with the captain's name, his base and a pretty good description of where she had been before, he might think that we already knew so much that the effort of not talking was not worth while.'

## ENTERTAINING THE TOP BRASS

While the listeners worked methodically behind the walls of the M Room, part of Kendrick's duties involved the traditional inter-personal aspect of intelligence work – throwing luncheon parties and dinners. Human intelligence was as vital to fitting the pieces into the jigsaw as overseeing reports and making operational decisions. At his headquarters at Latimer House he worked at the highest level with British Intelligence chiefs from numerous government departments. Outward-going, but a man who commanded respect, Kendrick's unique manner made him ideal for the delicate task of balancing the egos and agendas of the different heads of the intelligence services. He was patient, measured, competent but a good listener and communicator. His early work for SIS had often involved entertainment and thereby the subtle development of human relationships. This he was expert at. As a first-class host he could hold any room with his charisma and old-fashioned humour. In the comfortable dining room of the stately house he hosted numerous lunches for the top brass and different intelligence bosses. After eating a hearty lunch or dinner the guests gathered on that occasion retired for sherry or port in the large panelled library with its marble fireplace, soft armchairs which overlooked the lush green valley around Amersham. This timeless location became the backdrop for thrashing out new strategy, ideas and important briefings. It was every bit a scene that could come straight out of the Smoking Room of any of London's exclusive gentlemen's clubs.

On a fine evening in August 1943 Latimer House hosted a cricket tournament for MI19's Head Officer-Staff working directly under Norman Crockatt. In Kendrick's absence his deputy Major Huband ensured that the evening was a huge success. After the match a magnificent supper was 'served at a late hour', followed by games of snooker and ping-pong well into the early hours of the morning. It was all part of the etiquette of the gentlemen's club which kept the shores of Britain safe from enemy invasion. A bizarre double-life but one that went hand-in-hand with intelligence and the world of deceiving the enemy.

Always a good entertainer who could draw a laugh from the most staid of commanders, Kendrick regularly entertained the top brass of

British and American Intelligence at his centre. Letters which survive amongst his papers reveal the appreciation in which his lunches and dinners were held. These occasions were a necessary part of the 'intelligence game'. His inter-personal skills and relaxed manner wooed the top commanders into cooperating with each other and sharing wartime intelligence and strategy. That level of cooperation required dedicated hard work and could not be taken for granted. The lack of cooperation between SOE and other Special Forces which led to the doubling up and bungling of clandestine operations on the Continent, for example, highlights this point and how important Kendrick's cooperation with the three services was, because it underpinned the success of wartime intelligence.

# NINE

## ROCKET SCIENCE

THE NEW YEAR of 1943 started well for Kendrick when his services to MI19 were honoured with an OBE from the King. It recognised the success of his running of the centres, but most specially the discovery of X-Gerät and his handling of the German Generals. In a letter which survives amongst the Kendrick family papers, Norman Crockatt wrote to him personally and congratulated him on 'the best merited OBE of the war.' Crockatt went on to say that the material coming out of Kendrick's unit was of such vital importance, but also marked a credit to the staff who had worked hard and loyally to bring it about. Therefore the OBE was as much a tribute to their efforts as also 'being a personal triumph for you as their leader.' Kendrick had just returned from a trip to New York. Back in England his unit was about to discover what can be described as the most important piece of intelligence of the whole war. In early 1943 listeners at Trent Park overheard something which spun intelligence chiefs into a frenzy of activity. Generals Von Thoma and Crüwell were overheard talking in the Drawing Room about the secret rocket programme. Then on 11 March the listeners at one of Kendrick's other sites picked up a conversation between a lower rank infantry soldier (M11) and paratrooper (A77) who discussed technical details about the launch ramps (WO208/4162):

> A77: I was very amused yesterday when they [interrogation officers] showed me a drawing of the sloping ramp rocket projector

M11: That doesn't convey anything at all. I've no idea how big it really is

M77: The track along which the projectile travels was tiny, just as the projectile was. You know these heavy trench mortars, these grenades with a long wing (??) ... a projectile just like that! How I laughed ... I was quite helpless with laughter. The sloping ramp looks similar but ... quite different ... They know nothing about it, which is a relief to me

It was not yet overt enough to place British Intelligence on full alert. However, Air Intelligence was still trying to understand the nature of the Peenemünde site. Reports, maps and aerial photographs of the site can be found in a number of files at the National Archives, but most especially in AIR40/1192 and AIR40/2839. A report dated 29 April 1943 was headed 'Extract from an Interpretation Report of the New Development at Peenemünde', in which it was still not clear that Air Intelligence knew of the site's exact purpose. An extract from the report read (AIR40/1192):

'The general appearance of the factory, which is situated in a clearing in the forest, suggests that it may be employed in the manufacture of explosives... The building near the centre of the works has the appearance of a gas plant. It has a chimney and dumps of coal or coke can be seen at either end of the building ... Several low buildings in the areas 10, 11 and 12 have been erected since 15.5.42.'

The decisive moment came after listeners at Trent Park overheard a lengthy discussion on 26 May 1943 between von Arnim and a senior prisoner whose voice they could not identify (WO208/4165):

C: I wonder how the development of these rockets will turn out. You don't hear anything more about them…

A: Yes, this rocket business is all very well, there are all sorts of things, but you can't propel an aircraft all the time with it

C: No, not aircraft, bombs – they just fire rockets

A: Fire rockets?

C: Yes. I know the 'liquid rocket'. It can easily travel 200km but it has tremendous dispersal

A: That doesn't matter

C: It has a tremendous dispersal, but you need large copper boilers and precious metal for the burners and for the jets. It would be economically quite impossible to produce it in large quantities in order to keep up a continuous fire. I believe they are heated by means of pure alcohol which produces a steely blue flame 8 or 12m long which comes out at the back. The great … of liquid …

A: I have heard that they have a range of even 300km

C: They can reach 300, there's no difficulty about that. You just need to make the fuel boiler longer. I saw one which we developed some time ago and was present at the first tests. It had a range of 150 or 200km

A: How big are they?

C: They were 6m high

The hunt was on. Air Intelligence staff urgently brainstormed about possible locations in Germany where such high-tech equipment could be developed. It had to be a specialist, scientific plant by the coast. Peenemünde came up and the penny dropped. Could this explain aspects which had been a mystery when RAF pilots flew photographic missions over the site on the Northern coast of Germany the previous year? Nothing obvious had emerged when the photographs had been examined in detail and the mysterious site had been dismissed.

Back at RAF Medmenham the files containing photographs of the site at Peenemünde from 1942 were pulled from storage and re-examined in every minute detail. Looking at them again it was possible to make out the mobile rocket launchers for the powerful new V-2 rocket. Without the M Room work it is doubtful that the Allies would have realised the full significance of Peenemünde before it was too late. Could this be the greatest coup yet for MI19 in thwarting Germany's race for weapon superiority?

'The first discoveries in the M Room about Peenemünde caused great excitement,' recalls Fritz. 'It was quickly realized that a new rocket programme was underway. Picking up this kind of intelligence for the British was very important to us because it could mean the difference between winning or losing the war.'

Action amongst intelligence chiefs began to move at a pace. As a direct result of the Generals' conversation Air Intelligence chiefs acted. RAF Pilots were again sent out on secret reconnaissance missions to photograph the Peenemünde site. On 29 June Churchill's Cabinet Defence Committee met in the Cabinet War Room. After hearing evidence from scientist Professor Frederick Lindemann (advisor to British Intelligence), Churchill authorised the attack on Peenemünde. Because it was beyond British radio navigation beams Churchill told the Committee: 'we must bomb by moonlight... we must attack on the heaviest possible scale.' Air crew were briefed before leaving on their special mission – one of the most important of the war. They were told that if they failed they would repeat the raid a second night, and the following night until the job was done -

regardless of casualties.

In a meeting between various Air Intelligence chiefs at Bomber Command on 7 July it was decided that for security reasons any reference to rockets at Peenemünde was to be eliminated in any reports: 'the plant is being called an Experimental Establishment'. The target information sheet for aircrew, dated July 1943, records (AIR40/1192):

> 'The target is the Experimental Establishment at Peenemünde situated on the tongue of land on the Baltic Coast about 60 miles N.W of Stettin, engaged upon the development and production of a new form of R.D.F equipment which promises to improve greatly the German night fighter air defence organization.'

Aircrew involved in the impending mission had no idea just how significant the site was. By full moon on 17/18 August 1943, pilots of Bomber Command left their base and carried out the first attack on Peenemünde Army Research Centre in a mission codenamed *Operation Hydra* that included 324 Lancasters, 218 Halifaxes and 54 Stirlings. This was the start of a much larger Anglo-American operation codenamed *Operation Crossbow* aimed at destroying any sites connected to the V-2 programme and the production plant for hydrogen peroxide needed for the rockets. The first wave of bombers attacked the sleeping and living quarters, the second the factory workshops and the final wave the experimental station itself. The raid was a success. It delayed Hitler's rocket test launches by seven weeks. But it came at a price. Two hundred and fifteen British aircrew were killed, and forty bombers and hundreds of civilians in the nearby concentration camp Trassenheide also died. Two German V-2 rocket scientists, Dr Thiel and Chief Engineer Walther, were killed during the attack.

Over the course of the remainder of the war several Generals at Trent Park spoke about the secret weapon programme, but Bassenge and von Thoma appear to be the only two with *firsthand* knowledge of the programme. They discussed explicitly the new V-2 rocket being developed at Peenemünde – a secret weapon that could devastate England and cost the Allies the war. Little did they realise that it had all been overheard and recorded. Von Thoma had seen some of the early experiments with rocket apparatus before the war with Brauchitsch, but the whole scene had been a disaster. He claimed to know something about rockets but said that they would only go to about 10,000 metres and few would reach London. Of course he had not realized just how far the technology had advanced during the war itself. Misjudging the situation he commented to Bassenge that the rockets were 'too expensive for the game to be worth the candle.'

Bassenge told him, 'I set up a department "D" for rocket development, together with a very good engineer by the name of Bender.' He then proceeded to give technical details, referring to directional control by radio and the use of rockets to attack aircraft in formation. Von Thoma was quite scornful of the decisive effect of firing rockets on Britain and said [in translation]:

> 'If there really is something, it is only rocket stories. Of course that is rather laughable and does not decide the outcome of the war. It creates only uncomfortable disturbance here. Instead of perhaps a few aeroplanes coming over here in the evening, a rocket flies in.'

Bassenge added, 'even if all London is reduced to rubble and ashes it is unimportant for the outcome of the war because they (V-2s) can get to Glasgow or anywhere else at the time.'

Within a week of RAF attacks on Peenemünde the listeners eavesdropped on yet another conversation – this time Peenemünde is specifically mentioned. It took place between Neuffer and Bassenge:

BASSENGE: This place Peenemünde was begun at a time when I left the technical office and therefore I never went to see it

NEUFFER: But for what purpose? Hadn't we already got Rechlin?

BASSENGE: Well, Peenemünde was not built by the German Air Force [G.A.F], but by the army and we had only one section built into it by the G.A.F which attracted my interest, and that was the rocket business

The conversation rambles on but ironically at the end the Generals seem quite dismissive. Neuffer says, 'this business about a new weapon – I don't believe it. As a matter of fact – I mean as regards a new weapon – technology today is such a complicated affair – you can't just produce a new weapon out of a hat.' To which Bassenge replied, 'I consider it all bluff, nothing more.' Neuffer responded, 'Just one of those Jules Verne affairs.' To which Bassenge replied, 'Yes. In England they're joking about it.' Of course nothing was further from the truth. MI19 had taken the leaked information very seriously. On 11 September Meixner, Neuffer and Bassenge were overheard discussing the following (WO208/4166):

NEUFFER: Perhaps there really is a secret weapon or –

BASSENGE: Yes. For instance there are the liquid rockets, 5 to 6m long. They contain an explosive charge about the same as that of a good torpedo

MEIXNER: Good, but that will penetrate one block of houses at the most.

BASSENGE: No, it doesn't penetrate that either. The effect is just like a 1000kg bomb. You can fire the things and they can travel a comparatively long distance; you can use them for a sweeping fire on fleets here. The things are extremely complicated and have a frightful amount of copper and valuable metal in them... I know all about these things. I've seen them.

In another similar discussion on 26 October with Neuffer, Bassenge stated that the rockets were about 20ft in height with the explosive power of a 1,000kg bomb but were expensive. 'These things have an extremely complicated apparatus,' he said, 'a frightful lot of copper and very valuable metals inside because otherwise the jet or fuel injector (that is most certainly the most expensive and valuable steel, melts away with the colossal temperatures which are generated.' Although the rockets proved to be comparatively inaccurate, he commented that they would land somewhere within the London area. To which Neuffer responded, 'then we'd better all go out into the trench!' To the bottom of this transcript MI19 added a comment that Bassenge's experience of the secret rocket programme was somewhat dated.

The RAF continued their bombing missions of the Peenemünde site in what became known as *Operation Crossbow*. Back at Trent Park speculation about new weapon technology continued amongst the Generals into 1944. Naval Captain Meixner posed the view that the secret weapons 'may force the British to make a premature landing.' He was referring to the Second Front, an invasion of Europe, which the military men knew would come, but had no idea when and where. The defeatist camp was pretty much agreed that the rockets would not win the war for Germany and would only cause bitterness amongst the Allies. As one Colonel was noted by the listeners to say, 'if we are not in a position to hold the Russian

Front, then it is a crime to undertake something like this [the rocket programme] because the only result is that the peace terms imposed on us will be even greater.' He was harking back to what happened in the Treaty of Versailles at the end of the First World War when reparations crippled Germany.

Major-General Sattler commented to Colonel Borcherdt that he believed the V-2 was to weigh ten times more than the V-1 and that it would 'require a colossal installation to launch the larger projectile.' Such snippets of information were welcomed by British Intelligence in building up a full picture of the weapons development programme and its threat. A lengthy conversation took place between Bassenge and Kreipe on 10 June 1944, in part of which they said (WO208/4363):

KREIPE: I am very disappointed that they haven't started using the retaliation weapon yet

BASSENGE: I am interested in the rocket business. I know all about this great problem of the rockets with liquid propellant. I knew about them years ago in peace time. I was constantly at the experimental establishment at Kumersdorf (?)

KREIPE: I know nothing about the liquid propellant

BASSENGE: Rockets with a liquid propellant

KREIPE: This isn't one of them. That's a very different thing. A rocket with a very long range and very high explosive material

BASSENGE: Have you seen inside?

KREIPE: No, no. I heard that it had a very high explosive charge, but nothing about a liquid propellant

BASSENGE: They are called rockets with a liquid propellant because this high explosive stuff is a mixture of liquids in the fuse container. This basis is alcohol and a high degree oxygen carrier with the addition of barium (?) – ammonia – perchlorate and such things. The difficulty is to obtain in that short time the required amount of oxygen for those high combustion temperatures ... There is a Dr Braun – the son of Dr von Braun. His son, a very nice fellow and above all a very talented engineer, has been responsible for the development of this whole affair

British Intelligence had a clear result – not only information about the rocket programme itself but the name of one of the key engineers who was developing it. But it appears that most of the Generals in captivity did not really know quite what the V-2 was or when it was coming. Sponeck asked Choltitz on 30 August, 'surely V-2 is the flying torpedo?' Choltitz replied, 'V-2 is a gun... goes 10000m into the air...' To which Sponeck responded, 'Yes, the rocket bomb – and when is it supposed to be coming?. Choltitz told him, 'in September, but of course that is much too late. We can't fire them any longer because we haven't got the territory.'

Another brief conversation about the V-2 was also recorded at the end of August 1944, this time between Schlieben, Choltitz, Spang and Elfeldt. It is clear that the Generals were isolated from what was really happening in the war; a situation which caused them no end of frustration (WO208/4363):

SCHLIEBEN: When is the V2 coming?
CHOLTITZ: Never!
SPANG: What are those enormous constructions then, which the English are always photographing? They are those enormous great concrete constructions which appear to be future launching ramps for the V-2
CHOLTITZ: They are just the same as at Cherbourg

ELFELDT: They maintain that they found some nearly ready by the Seine

CHOLTITZ: I am absolutely certain of it

In a different conversation with Choltitz and Broich, Elfeldt said, 'the V-2 hasn't arrived because the Allies have bombed and destroyed the launching sites.' Broich had seen photographs of a huge concrete installation at Cherbourg which had been under construction for six months and still not complete. Elfeldt replied, 'no, because every time they had got to the point when the concrete was to be .... the enemy dropped a six-ton bomb and bang!'

By the autumn of 1944 as the Allies had taken France and were advancing towards Belgium and Holland, Major-General Wuelfingen was overheard talking to Heyking and Seyffardt about the building and launch sites for the V-2 at Liege. This snippet of information was priceless for British Intelligence in trying to keep ahead of the constantly moving launch sites. It enabled Air Intelligence to coordinate RAF bombing missions to take out the new sites before they became operational. Meanwhile the V-1 pilot-less flying bombs continued to rain down on towns and cities, wreaking havoc and devastation across England. The German Generals experienced the frightening effects of the VIs when one passed over Trent Park the following summer and Colonel Köhn remarked to Vice-Admiral Hennecke that it would be: 'marvellous if they [the Germans] could send over a thousand of these things at a time. Raids on the present scale were merely playing at it.'

## V1s AND V2s

References to the V-1 and V-2 kept coming in subsequent conversations of the Generals but it was not limited to them. Listeners in the M Room at

Latimer House and Wilton Park picked up references to Peenemünde, secret weapons and rockets from lower rank prisoners. On 30 July 1943 a German pilot referenced the experimental station at Peenemünde and told his cellmate: 'The experimental flights were carried out up there in the Baltic from Peenemünde.' Another conversation between two German bomber pilots came less than a week after the RAF had bombed the site. Pilot codenamed A713 asked, 'is it all complete?' His cellmate A130 replied, 'Yes, all completed … now they are going to bring out the "Peter X 2" … that is … being tried out. They have it at Peenemünde at present' (WO208/4130). On 9 November 1943 something was picked up between an infantry soldier (M313) and a member of a tank crew (M271), now in file WO208/4137:

> M271: When the new weapon is used –
> M313: For one of the things you need three or four wagons, 15 tons of explosive. It was made at Peenemünde, but they bombed Peenemünde. That was why Dr Ley said that it would take five or six weeks to get it ready. I hope I shall be in Canada then! Away from here!

At the end of the following month on 27 October two different soldiers discussed Peenemünde, one from Regimental Headquarters in Italy, the other captured in Tunisia. The conversation shows clear concern about their country firing rockets on England and the fact that they may find themselves under one of them. It also gives some operational details – of course, useful to British Military Intelligence:

M238: It's hell being a PoW and perhaps on top of it all we'll get one of these new things dropped on us

M304: The whole of the civilian population was evacuated from Rügen three years ago and from Peenemünde as well

M238: They must got ... somehow ... under cover when they set a thing like this going

M304: How do you mean? The thing is set up, it is ignited by remote control, electrically, and then it goes off

M238: They get into shelters beforehand, below ground –

M304: Well of course. They may be something ... it is ignited electrically by remote control and then it rises very slowly from the ground with mighty crashing, banging and hissing – it is frightful!

M238: And they fire over to –

M304: Over to England – they can fire it 500 km. They fire up the whole length of the Norwegian coast... It is a pretty fine apparatus, it weighs eighty tons – eighty tons – the remaining sixty-five tons are just for propellant, for the rocket force .... and fifteen tons of explosive is quite a nice lot!

On 5 March 1944 the listeners recorded an unguarded conversation between two Bomber Gunners codenamed A1441 and A1500 in which the name of Peenemünde was cited. It transpired during a lengthy conversation that both were eye-witnesses to the new technology being developed there. Only part of the transcript is reproduced here (AIR40/3093):

A1441: At Peenemünde I saw a new fighter – a turbine-fighter; is that the 'Motte' (moth)?

A1500: 'Kuckucksei' (cuckoo's egg) with a pressure cabin.

A1441: Does it jettison its undercarriage after taking off?

A1500: It has a skid.

A1441: Yes, it lands on skids.

A1500: It hasn't an undercarriage.

A.1441: The one at Peenemünde had an undercarriage. It jettisoned it immediately after take-off. It did nearly a thousand k.p.h. It flew for half an hour. First there were all sorts of rumours afloat about it. The men who fly them don't talk about them. He said it takes off once he has put out ['rausgemacht'] propellers (?).

A.1500: Then I must have seen it at our place. We were at the experimental station. It can reach a speed of sixteen hundred k.p.h.

Two days later two German Air Force personnel (one a gunner, the other a fighter pilot) made a veiled reference to the V-2. Fighter pilot of a Messerschmitt, codenamed A1499 by the British and captured in Italy in February 1944, explained to fellow airman: 'we were told that if one of those things came over here a few square … would be destroyed, and so it will be. The new weapon will decide the war. I want to get away from here. The sooner the better.'

Listener Peter Hart recalls in his autobiography *Journey into Freedom* that MI19 reports about Peenemünde 'were given top-priority, as obviously there was something afoot which looked like a last desperate measure.' The discovery of Peenemünde proved the worth of the whole MI19 operation and more than justified the huge budget being spent on the three sites. V-1s an V-2s caused utter devastation and huge loss of life in Britain's towns and cities.

## V-3 ROCKET

Never off their guard the secret listeners could take nothing for granted. The range of intelligence coming through their headphones could vary dramatically and change the course of the war. In the autumn of 1944 they uncovered references to the V-3 rocket programme. The Germans planned to have twenty-five gun installations at Mimoyecques near Calais and fire up to 300 shells an hour on London, but this never happened. The Allies put the site out of commission on 6 July 1944 when 617 Squadron of Bomber Command, the famous Dambusters, attacked with deep penetration bombs. In the end two slightly smaller V-3 guns bombarded the city of Luxembourg from December 1944 until February 1945.

After hearing V-1 and V-2 explosions near Trent Park Colonels Wilck and Wildermuth leaked the first references to the new V-3 (WO208/5018):

> WILCK: The V-3 is also expected this month. Whether there's anything in it or not, at least they still keep on achieving more and more in that line, even in our case
>
> WILDERMUTH: At any rate there must still be huge stores which we shall now fire off
>
> WILCK: Desperation measures!

General Eberbach also spoke about the V-3 to a fellow officer. A transcript of a conversation between him and Major-General Gutknecht, who had been captured at Rheims at the end of August 1944, was recorded on 1 September 1944 (WO208/4168):

> EBERBACH: Above all they are counting on the V-3
>
> GUTKNECHT: The V-2
>
> EBERBACH: No, the V-3
>
> GUTKNECHT: V-3, what's that supposed to be?

EBERBACH: The V-2 is only a small affair. It is a V-1 remotely controlled from an aircraft; and V-3 is that large rocket which flies through the stratosphere, and which is said to have several times the effect of the V-1, but apparently we need special launching ramps for it which are no longer there. They have been lost to the enemy.

Three days later he spoke again about the V-3. Within hours of the listeners recording and transcribing this conversation, Eberbach found himself in discussion with a British Army officer and asked about reprisal weapons. The officer gave no hint of how he knew about V-3s and Eberbach appeared not to be suspicious about the source. 'Have you ever heard of the V-3?' the British Army officer asked.

EBERBACH: Yes, there was talk about the V-2 and the V-3. V-2 is supposed to be the remote controlled aircraft filled with explosives which is controlled from another aircraft. And then V-3 was supposed to be that rocket business which is supposed to climb very high, right into the stratosphere, and then also to be controlled some way. I don't know any more about it

BAO: How is it supposed to be controlled, by a pilot?

EBERBACH: No, by wireless or something

In a separate interview on the subject Eberbach told an interrogation officer that he had as much knowledge of the reprisal weapons as an average soldier. He stated that he thought the V-3 was a long-range radio-controlled rocket which had a longer range than the V-1 and could be fired at England from West Germany. The only difficulty in Eberbach's opinion was that it needed the necessary firing ramps which was a challenge. With uninterrupted and undetected work day and night, Eberbach told the interrogation officer that it was possible to complete such a ramp in eight days – by which time he felt it would be too late. When this information reached the ears of MI19 chiefs, and if it was true, then Hitler could fire this deadly weapon from within Germany with no hope of the Allies overpowering it until the successful invasion of Germany.

Hitler's secret weapon programme had far-reaching consequences beyond anyone's imagination. It marked the beginning of rocket technology that would advance within twenty-five years to enable the Americans to land a man on the moon in 1969.

The M Room, Trent Park

Listener George Pulay

Colonel Thomas Joseph Kendrick, OBE
Commandant

Listener Fritz Lustig

The White House, Wilton Park

Secret Listeners (left to right)
Lehmann, Pulay, Manners, Kaufmann,
Ganz, Rittner, Heilbron, Brodie

Personnel at Latimer House

Susan Lustig

Sketch of Kendrick by one of the Prisoners

German Generals, Trent Park

German Generals, Trent Park

# TEN

# 'OUR GUESTS'

*'If we entertain the possibility that we may lose the war, then*
*we have already lost it,'* German prisoner held by MI19

DURING 1944 AS the Allies prepared for the D-Day landings on the Normandy beaches, Kendrick knew that the number of PoWs being processed through the unit would soon increase dramatically, and with it, the volume of intelligence needing to be pieced together for the final stages of the war. German prisoners were escorted from the battlefields of North Africa, Sicily, Italy and later Normandy, to temporary holding camps before being brought to England where they passed through the 'London Cage' for processing. A series of other PoW centres called 'Cages' were situated at various locations in the south of England. It was here that PoWs were first brought under the auspices of Prisoner of War Interrogation Section (PWISH) where they were interrogated, and some 'turned' by British Intelligence into double agents. From these 'cages' particular prisoners were selected for further interrogation and observance at one of Kendrick's centres.

By 1944 over a thousand staff were deployed by Kendrick across the three centres. The day-to-day running of the camps was a logical and administrative challenge that required around 900 staff. They ranged from telephonists to typists, translators, telegraphists, switchboard-operators, bike runners, messengers, engineers and technicians. By now the M Room staff had risen to over a hundred; the majority German-speaking refugees who had fled Hitler. Fritz recalls: 'Most of our prisoners were initially either shot-down Luftwaffe-pilots or members of U-boat crews who had been rescued when their boat was sunk. There might have been a few army-prisoners captured in North Africa, but a major influx of those only started after D-Day in June 1944.' Prisoners of all ranks continued to unwittingly leak information to British Intelligence.

Crucial information continued to be forthcoming on the U-boat war, details of which enabled the Allies to keep ahead of the battle at sea. Back at Trent Park, General von Broich (codenamed 159) had given a British Army officer detailed descriptions about the U-boat shelters at St Nazaire. The U-boat pens were not visible to RAF pilots and without this conversation British Intelligence would not have found the shelters without high risk reconnaissance missions. Von Broich had visited the site himself and was able to give an extraordinary eye-witness account:

M 159: The most interesting sight later on will be these U-boat shelters at St Nazaire. There are large underground shelters there with a covering of cement the depth of this room.

BAO: Have you seen them?

M 159: Yes, they're terrific. You simply can't imagine what these vaults are like. As in an engine shed where there's a turntable in the middle and engines can go in from every direction, in the same way here there's a large basin and on all sides these –

BAO: How many U-boats can get in there at one time?

M 159: Oh, dozens of them. They just laugh at this bombing of St. Nazaire. I myself saw the effect of one of the heavy bombs on one of those things; it's made of special cement, not the normal kind, and it knocked out a piece this size.

BAO: Ten centimetres?

M 159: Yes. Let them go to St. Nazaire as much as possible, that's the very best thing; they get rid of their bombs and that's all.

It's a different matter down at Spezia, where the English have just been, that's not so pleasant, there's no (protection) there. That's a tremendous achievement (to fly) from here over the Alps to Spezia.

References to St Nazaire and Lorient came up frequently in conversations between lower ranks. These PoWs inadvertently offered details of the extent of damage to U-boat pens after Allied bombing campaigns and gave valuable eye-witness material. In one such conversation, two Naval prisoners discussed the following (WO208/4145):

> N15: At St. Nazaire everything has been damaged. Only the shelters are still standing and they have been partially damaged.
> N1584: Then it isn't a proper base any longer?
> N15: Oh yes, the base as such – the U-boat shelters are still standing, they can't destroy them. To do that they would have to fire torpedoes into them from aircraft, but they can't destroy them from above.

The same conversation revealed details about the complex living quarters in the U-boat shelters which also had female personnel: 'they were smart women and they really made the U-boat hostel look very nice and smart.' The complex 'bunkers' had a lounge, ladies' room, swimming bath, dance hall, and facilities for playing golf and billiards. Everything was catered for the men. In the evenings they went ashore to pick flowers to decorate their shelter. If beer was plentiful, they drank well into the early hours of the morning. Prisoner N15 even admitted, 'at Lorient we lived in the shelter. We had a wonderful officers' mess. The Chief Petty Officer had a mess, which made you feel you were in a country mansion.'

Snippets of tactical information continued to be gathered by the M Room operators. As Fritz himself readily admits, 'although it is not possible today to remember the vast quantities of intelligence that we gathered, we knew enough at the time to realise just how important our job was for the war.'

## NAVAL SUCCESSES

The sinking of the German battleship *Scharnhorst* in December 1943 made news in the M Room at Wilton Park where Fritz was then working. Thirty-six survivors, out of a total crew of 1,968, were held by MI19. Fritz comments, 'we were quite excited when we heard that the few survivors of the *Scharnhorst* had arrived at our unit. We felt privileged when we were told to cover the cell which was holding one of them. We were very conscious of the fact that they required special attention.'

For Fritz's Commanding Officer events came full circle. During the 1930s Kendrick's spy-ring had carried out espionage missions from Austria into Nazi Germany to penetrate the dockyard at Wilhelmshaven where the *Scharnhorst* was being constructed. As one of MI6's most senior men in Europe in the 1930s, Kendrick's agents gathered vital information on Germany's rearmament programme. For him, there must have been a great sense of satisfaction at seeing the military might of Germany being 'dismantled'. However, still out plaguing the seas was the German battleship *Tirpitz*. Two surviving Able Seamen from the *Scharnhorst* spoke about the sister battleship (AIR40/4104):

N 2145: The Tirpitz was lucky; the adhesive charges only adhered to her for a moment and then fell off again. There was too much sea-weed and too many mussels on the ship, she had been lying there too long. They (the charges) fell to the bottom of the sea, where they exploded; otherwise the Tirpitz would no longer be there, she would have been split in two.

N 2133: The whole thing is said not have been so serious. They (the English) are supposed to have come on board and (one of them) said: "I report having carried out the King of England's orders – the Tirpitz will blow up in so-and-so many minutes time. Then everybody left the quarterdeck.

N 2133: I suppose the Scharnhorst made off pretty quickly then?

N 2145: No, the Scharnhorst had been making a trial trip that night. She was sailing about in the fjord. The captain started off and suddenly got a signal reporting that the Tirpitz had suffered minor damage.

N 2133: Minor damage! When we sailed up there, we carried two hundred shipyard ….. on board. There was a repair ship already there.

The *Tirpitz* was also eventually sunk by the RAF on 12 November 1944. Other technical information was readily forthcoming from U-boat crew. Late in the war Sub-Lieutenant Striezel of U-1003 spoke to a junior Sub-Lieutenant (codenamed 42Z) about the new U-boats being developed (AIR40/3104):

STRIEZEL: The new boats (Type XXI) were supposed to have been ready by Christmas. But it didn't come off. To start with the Allies smashed half of them at Hamburg and at Bremen. There was a heavy air-raid just on the factories of Blohm & Voss and Deschimag and they smashed half of them then. Some are out – a certain number of the new boats are in use already. I had the nineteenth...There's a control position in the torpedo-room, the torpedo control position, six tubes. There are racks (Greifer) on both sides and the man who sits forward and does the setting sits right up below the conning-tower. When he calls from there it sets up an echo! In the dished bulkhead – the apparatus – the men sit forward in the torpedo-room and there's canvas between the tubes, so you can …….. nicely. There's nothing else forward of the torpedo-room. Everything is done by electric-motor, electrical installation. Flushing of the tubes done by alcohol – the torpedo is pulled out, the tube is flushed – ssht – and in it goes, loaded in. The 'Mixer' no longer dirties his hands. It's all the business of second division people, including the technical things and the torpedo things forward. There are also racks (Greifer) up here: three, six, nine, twelve, and below there are two more, fourteen, sixteen, and another six by the tubes.

42Z: My God, twenty-two (Torpedoes)!

STRIEZEL: It's a room on its own, i.e. two sections...You don't need to worry any more about periscope depth and being spotted or the 'snorter' head being located etc. Nothing like that any more. They are now working on it so that they can fire the torpedoes from 80m.

In MI19 files a sketch of Type XXI U-Boat, provided by the Admiralty's Naval Intelligence Department, was reproduced as an Appendix to the above report.

# FLIGHT OF RUDOLF HESS

It was not only battle details and technological information which interested MI19. Political comments about the Nazi hierarchy were of special interest because it gave an insight into the mind of the enemy and acted as a gauge by which to judge political events in Germany. During the war the most prized, high-ranking prisoner held by MI19, in conjunction with MI5, was Hitler's Deputy Rudolf Hess. Hess' failed solo mission to broker peace between Germany and Britain continues to be cloaked in myth and mystery. Did he come with the knowledge of Hitler? Or was he acting solely in his own capacity? Was he lured by the British Secret Service? Some theories have suggested that it was not the real Hess who later stood trial at Nuremberg, and others that Hess did not commit suicide in Spandau Prison in 1987. Whatever controversy continues to surround Hess, there is no doubt that the man who baled out of his Messerschmitt over Scotland, heading for the Duke of Hamilton's estate, was going to be of supreme interest to Britain's Secret Service. MI5 and SIS immediately became involved, and Hess came under the auspices of MI19 and two of SIS's long-standing officers – Kendrick and his colleague Frank Foley (head of the British Passport Office in Berlin in the 1930s; a cover for his SIS activities).

Hess was brought to the Tower of London for four days under heavy guard and accommodated in the Queen's House overlooking the White Tower. Kendrick left Trent Park temporarily to personally deal with Hess in the Tower. Kendrick had arranged for Mytchett Place, a secluded Georgian mansion near Aldershot, to be bugged in readiness for Hess' transfer there. On 21 May Hess was transferred to Mytchett Place under two 'minders', Kendrick and Foley. Kendrick was given a cover-name 'Colonel Wallace', possibly to avoid Hess recognizing his name from 1938 when Kendrick was very publicly thrown out of Austria as a British spy and his story covered by German newspapers. There is no evidence to suggest that during Kendrick's handling of him Hess ever recognised Kendrick's real identity as an SIS officer. Any information on the true reason behind Hess' mission had to be analysed by British Intelligence. Consequently, any reference to Hess in conversations of PoWs was recorded in the M Room. At Trent Park Generals Crüwell and Krause discussed Hess' mission (WO208/4161):

> CRÜWELL: If I were asked to meet Hess, I should decline. Please remember I am a man who was taken prisoner honourably and I would not (associate) with a man who – who – he is a traitor?
>
> KRAUSE: Has the matter been cleared up?
>
> CRÜWELL: It's quite clear to me. It was officially announced at the time 'against the Führer'; the adjutants were put under arrest because they allowed him to fly.
>
> KRAUSE: Where I was it was always said that he was a hundred per cent true, that the good of the Fatherland was his sole consideration, and that he said, 'I don't believe in this Russian business; I must try to get to England in order to save Germany by arranging peace with the British.

Cruwell believed Krause that Hess acted in good faith, but in the end Crüwell still regarded Hess as a traitor in enemy country. In another secretly recorded conversation on 19 November 1943 a captured parachutist (M350) revealed the following when questioned by a British Army officer (AIR40/3106):

> BAO: Do you think that the Führer knew about Hess's flight?

M350:  His flight was already beforehand – a lot of people were shot, one of my best friends.

BAO:  For what reason was he shot?

M350:  He was really less to blame, but to a certain extent they were all directly or indirectly involved in the flight. Hess was under surveillance.

BAO:  Before his flight?

M350:  Yes.

BAO:  A sort of prisoner?

M350:  He was a semi-prisoner

BAO:  But you think that the Führer knew that he intended to fly away?

M350:  No (?).

Another reference to Hess came in a conversation between two prisoners captured from their regiment in Tunisia in May 1943. M235 commented to his cellmate: 'at the time when Hess ran away you ought to have heard how the people of Berlin laughed, in the underground when the workmen were coming home and so on. We've got a suburb of Berlin called Hessenwinkel and they immediately named it Scotland.' Snippets like this were seized upon by British Intelligence in trying to work out whether Hess had arrived on his own initiative or whether he was part of a wider plan. Such tête-à-têtes also provided an important insight into the thinking of ordinary Germans.

Hess was not the only senior Nazi to be the subject of comment amongst the Generals. General Vierow commented to Colonel Ulrich about Hermann Goering: 'Goering is mad, he sits around at home in silk pantaloons, red morocco shoes with painted toes and a diamond-studded belt of this width with a diamond buckle; he sits there doing this (gestates) with his stomach and watches the diamonds sparkle. I've heard that from people who've been present. When his generals come to report on something or other he fetches them in a special train and shows them his collection of stones. He's mad – ill.'

Naturally, Hitler as commander-in-chief was the subject of conversations. Von Thoma and Sponeck show admiration for the British Prime Minister and contrast him with Hitler (WO208/4363):

> THOMA: Imagine, a 70 year-old man like Churchill travelling in a destroyer! He's a real soldier at heart
> SPONECK: Yes
> THOMA: He is personally appreciated everywhere. Hitler just sticks inside his fox-hole.
> SPONECK: Actually, it would be the natural action of any decent thinking man to pay an immediate visit to a bombed town, as the King does over here.
> THOMA: Whenever any ..... the Queen arrives and enquires after the pets etc. What could be more touching!
> SPONECK: If Hitler were at least to visit a divisional HQ up at the front, in order to see for himself the way the battle is being conducted. As it is, he speaks about the whole affair merely from the perspective of a runner in the Great War. One can't be a supreme commander and yet have no idea how things are going

After hearing a British broadcast of recordings of past speeches made by Hitler, Goring and Goebbels, Sponeck remarked to other senior officers that it would be fine propaganda for Churchill if his speeches of a year ago were broadcast to Germany. Sponeck expressed the opinion that British statesmen had never made 'boastful promises or talked such rubbish as their German counterparts'.

## KENDRICK'S GUESTS

Just prior to D-Day on 25 May 1944 Major-General Heinrich Kreipe was transferred to Trent Park from initial interrogation at Wilton Park. Captured in Crete on 26 April 1944, he had served as Commander of 79 Division and been transferred to Crete at the end of February 1944. The circumstances surrounding his capture were known to Kendrick who noted on Kreipe's personal file: 'He was held up at night at a cross-roads by two traffic control sentries wearing German uniform. These were British officers who had carefully planned the whole operation. They kept him in hiding in Crete for 18 days before taking him to Cairo.'

Kreipe's daring kidnap became the subject of a book and subsequent film. MI19 noted on his file that he was 'a rather unimportant and unimaginative anti-Nazi.' However he was amongst several German Generals to be entertained personally by Kendrick at his own home, Woodton, in the village of Oxshott, Surrey. His wife Norah lived there whilst her husband was based with British Intelligence. Kendrick travelled back to see her whenever he could. Norah dutifully understood that his work required her sometimes to entertain "guests". Whatever she thought, she was discreet enough not to ask questions. Their relationship of total trust meant that he could rely on her completely. Grandson Ken Walsh remembers this period of his grandfather's work: 'I have vivid memories of Kreipe being entertained at my grandfather's house in Oxshott where I lived with my mother and sister for over a year and where we also spent our school holidays. General Kreipe took a liking to me and made a little crane complete with a cab, a jib and a bucket. He was not the only General at my grandfather's house. The others were very relaxed and friendly. I suppose the idea was to bring them to a place with a family atmosphere and make them feel at home so they would open up.'

Importantly, Kendrick gained their trust and 'befriended' them as a fellow military man. Little did they suspect that he was one of MI6's most senior officers whose only interest in them was the secrets they could spill.

# ELEVEN

## SAGA OF THE GENERALS

*'We are not suffering an undeserved fate. We are being punished for
letting a national resurrection which promised so well,
go to the devil.'* Bruhn, Trent Park

ON 6 JUNE 1944 the Allies mounted the largest invasion force onto the
Normandy beaches, landing over 150,000 troops in a single day. It was a
massive operation involving Air, Naval and Army personnel. D-Day
became one of the greatest military triumphs of the Second World War.
Allied military successes brought thousands of PoWs that needed to be
processed through MI19 and with it more captured German Generals. In
total 98 German Senior officers passed through Trent Park. Amongst them
were some diverse and colourful characters that required careful handling.
Their incarceration afforded British Intelligence an important detailed
insight into the mind-set of the enemy. Those captured after D-Day
included, with place of capture in brackets: General Dietrich von Choltitz
(Paris), General Eberbach (Amiens), General Rancke (Brest), General
Vierow (Arras), General-Lieutenant Badinsky (Bailleul), General-
Lieutenant Daser (Middelburg), General-Lieutenant Elfeldt (Trun),
General-Lieutenant Heim (Boulogne), General-Lieutenant Heyking
(Mons), General-Lieutenant Menny (Maguy), General-Lieutenant Rauch
(Brest), General-Lieutenant von Schlieben (Cherbourg), General-
Lieutenant Seyffardt (Marbaix), General-Lieutenant Spang (Brest), Major-
General Eberding (Knocke), Major-General Gutknecht (Rheims), Major-
General von der Mosel (Brest), Major-General Sattler (Cherbourg), Major-

General Schramm (Creney-Troyes), Major-General Stolberg (Antwerp), Major-General Wahle (Mons), von Wülfingen (Liège), von Aulock (St Malo), Herrmann (Cherbourg), Jay (Paris), Köhn (Cherbourg), Krug (Normandy), SS Oberführer Meyer (Liège), Müller-Römer (Paris), Rohrbach (St Gabriel), Unger (Paris), Wilck (Aachen), Wildermuth (Le Havre), Vice-Admiral Schirmer (Brest), Hennecke (Cherbourg), Kähler (Brest), von Tresckow (Le Havre) and Weber (Loire).

One of the Generals to figure prominently in transcripts from Trent Park was Dietrich von Choltitz who was finally captured on 25 August 1944. During 1943 he had commanded five German divisions in the Crimea. In July 1944 he was transferred to France and then posted as Commandant of Paris. This overweight, coarse, bemonocled General with an inflated sense of his own self-importance was captured when American forces entered the French capital. Negotiations for an armistice had broken down and von Choltitz was arrested. On 27 August he was brought to Latimer House, then two days later transferred to Trent Park. Here his egotistic character played right into the hands of MI19 because he was boastful and full of himself in the presence of the other Generals and spoke too freely. He tried to ingratiate himself with his captors and appear in the best possible light. MI19 noted on his profile that he 'adopted the attitude that he had foreseen the outcome of the war because of his insight into historical necessities.'

Successful campaigns in France brought the Allies a number of German Generals. Heinrich Eberbach, General of a Panzer Division, 7th Army, was forced to surrender on 31 August 1944 after failing to withdraw in time from Amiens where his division encountered Allied tanks. Three years earlier Eberbach had served in action in the German advance on Russia and the capture of Roslawl. That winter of 1941 he had contracted an illness relating to the bladder and been forced to return to Germany. In

November 1942 he was ordered to Stalingrad, wounded and again returned to Germany. The day after capture Eberbach was brought first to Wilton Park for interrogation, where his interviews were bugged by the listeners. Five days later he was transferred to Trent Park. Eberbach proved to be another strong character with clear-cut views. He decided to join the 'Generals' revolt', and although he had supported the Nazis for a number of years he had never been a Party member. He came to recognise the Nazi regime as a criminal body to whom he no longer felt bound by his oath of allegiance. His son Lieutenant-Colonel Eberbach had also been taken prisoner. MI19 allowed him to visit his father at Trent Park and noted the son to have 'a fanatical trust in Hitler, although he admitted that he was not a 100% Nazi.'

Colonel Andreas von Aulock surrendered at St Malo on 17 August 1944. Known as the 'mad Colonel of St Malo' he was a typical, monocled, aristocratic German officer found to be pro-British and violently anti-Russian. He had a high opinion of himself and his attraction to women. MI19 recorded him to be 'an untrustworthy type' who 'trimmed his sails to the wind and only thinks of himself and his well-being.' Fifty-two year old General-Lieutenant Badinsky was also captured in France in August 1944. A professional soldier and anti-Nazi he was careful not to display his open objection to the regime. He confessed to a loathing of Himmler, called Hitler an ape and condemned Hitler's policy as disastrous. He criticized senior army command and expected Germany's complete defeat and total collapse. MI19 only held him at Trent Park until 23 September 1944.

Captured with General Rancke at Brest was Major-General Hans von der Mosel. He gave MI19 the impression that he was 100% behind the Nazi regime and demonstrated it by a clicking of the heels and a Hitler salute. Rancke had been captured in his 'bunker' and found to be in possession of a large quantity of French brandy and liqueurs and a whole dinner service. A regular soldier who had risen up through the ranks, he was described in his MI19 files as 'inordinately vain and has a most extensive knowledge of distorted history.' Ambitious, ruthless yet naïve, he was an opportunist who began to change his views with the decline of the Nazi Party and could lead an underground movement if he felt it benefited him personally. Rancke made no secret of the fact that he was determined to win the highest decorations from the Führer, which he had striven to do by recommending his subordinates for high decorations – knowing that he would then have to be awarded higher decorations than them.

Lieutenant-General Paul Seyffardt, captured on 7 September 1944 was brought to Trent Park on 21 September, having first been held at Wilton Park from 11 September. Since February 1944 he had been in command of 348 Infantry Division stationed on the coast at Calais. MI19 established that he took no active part in politics but believed that one of the big mistakes made by the German Officer Corps was to have allowed themselves to become politically subservient to the Nazi Party.

On the same day as Seyffardt's capture, SS Oberführer Meyer was taken near Liège. The thirty-four year old son of a factory worker had worked his way up the ranks of the SS and had seen active service in Romania, Greece, Holland, Belgium and France. During late 1941 he was transferred to the Russian front until a period of jaundice forced him to take some sick leave. By 1944 he commanded the 12 Panzer Division until wounded and captured by the Americans. During his incarceration at Trent Park, details of atrocities committed by him would come to light.

Lieutenant-General Otto Elfeldt, captured south of Trun at the same time as Meyer, had already stated to British interrogators his willingness to cooperate with Western Allies if Germany was defeated. An affable, happy-go-lucky warrior type with a fairly well-developed sense of humour and an easy manner, he was the first of the German Generals to give a Nazi salute on arrival at Trent Park.

Eberhard Wildermuth, who had served five years on the frontline since 1939, was appointed Commandant of Le Havre at the end of August 1944. He defended Le Havre to the last and resisted all requests by the Allies to surrender. He was wounded before finally being captured on 12 September. The 54-year old Colonel was, according to MI19, fundamentally a liberal and 'a staunch German patriot, a brave officer, and violently opposed to the present regime.' Wildermuth was eager to re-educate the young Nazis and, in his own words, 'lead them back to the truth.' He had been sounded out before the assassination attempt on Hitler and had expressed his willingness to cooperate.

On 8 September Major-General Bock von Wuelfingen decided to surrender to the Allies at Liège rather than have his men wiped out. On arrival at Trent Park he was assessed as rather egocentric and not very bright. His main interest appeared to be the survival of the German nobility. He told British Army officers that Nazi ideology was firstly against the Jews, secondly against the nobility, and thirdly, against professional officers.

November 1944 saw the capture of Major-General Bruhn who had been surrounded by American forces and captured west of Saverne whilst on reconnaissance. During his captivity he used his time to write his 'autobiography' from which MI19 was able to extract a detailed military career. By far the most intelligent of the Generals, he combined personal charm with an air of integrity. Since captivity he had time to reflect on the atrocities committed by the regime. It changed his views to see that Germany would lose the war as a result and that Nazism must be rooted out to allow 'good' Germans to put their house in order. He came firmly into the anti- Nazi camp at Trent Park and saw himself as one of the 'good'

Germans who must rebuild Germany. Like others there he was ardently anti-Communist.

A thoroughly despicable figure held at Trent Park was 50-year old Major General Paul Goerbig who was captured in Germany towards the end of the war. Notes on his personal file stated that he was 'determined to treat his captors courteously in the hope of obtaining personal advantage… He states his hobbies to be old furniture and young women.'

According to MI19 files, Lieutenant-General Heinrich Kittel was a professional soldier of exceptional intelligence who in the course of the war had been connected with most of the major political happenings in Nazi Germany. He detested the SS and a Nazi state within a state, however while in custody he was not prepared to go against his oath to Hitler or say anything which might damage the war effort and the Reich. He had 'a strong sense of humour and takes a philosophical outlook on life.' In April 1942 he received promotion to the rank of Major-General and became commandant of Stalino (Ulkraine). A few months later in August 1942 he was transferred to Rostov as commandant during a period of mass murder of Jews – something which he discussed in some detail with other Generals at Trent Park. He was on the Russian list of war criminals and held responsible for the poisoning of 18,000 Russians. These were not the only war crimes levelled against him. During his time stationed north of Dvinsk (Latvia) the SS and SD carried out mass executions of Jews in the region. Kittel denied all responsibility for any of these atrocities.

Many of the military men tried to distance themselves from their past by claiming they were only obeying orders; a defence which would re-emerge during the Nuremberg Trial. Others were not so quick to renounce their Nazi loyalties. Major General Hans von der Mosel who was captured at Brest in September 1944, gave the impression that he was '100% behind the Nazi regime and underlined this fact by a clicking of heels and a Hitler salute.'

## 20 JULY PUTSCH

In early new year of 1944 M Room operators overheard the Generals in the anti-Nazi clique debating whether they should set up their own political system at Trent Park. Sicily and Italy had already fallen the previous summer and the war was clearly not going Germany's way. Bassenge commented, 'it's quite possible that within the next few months the Nazi regime will collapse.' To which Neuffer replied, 'do you want to have a military council here? Crüwell might even collect the batmen as witnesses and set up a government.' This naturally led to discussions on what to do with the Nazi leaders back in Germany. On 15 January Cramer, Reimann and Köhncke were overheard discussing precisely that. Cramer commented, 'it is high time to get rid of these people.' They continued:

REIMANN: those hot air merchants like Hermann Goering.
CRAMER: These people must go, and that Jew-baiter too.
REIMANN: Yes, but Streicher really doesn't count any more.
CRAMER: Those people must disappear for good. They are...
REIMANN: Criminals.
CRAMER: Yes criminals. We must be governed by decent men again.

If anyone could achieve political change in Germany it was the Generals. But what exactly could be done? Cramer pointed out that they were also governed by the SS [who he termed the 'peacetime army'] and that the combined numbers of SS and police outnumbered the military. Köhncke considered it a 'very great risk.' To which Cramer replied, 'We can't get around the fact that we started it. That's the bad thing about it.' Cramer admitted: 'I too am in favour of fighting to the last ditch but I don't want to find Goebbels sitting in the last ditch. It is a pity that the idea of *fatherland* and *country* have been lost.'

In monitoring and recording these conversations, British Intelligence tried to ascertain whether the military men would rise up again after the war with their old aspirations for world domination. Reimann, Köhncke and Cramer all agreed that the First World War was 'an honourable, chivalrous one – we all knew what we were fighting for.' Cramer continued, 'in this war, when everyone is being killed, and all the things the army is made to do, the shooting of prisoners and commissars and Jews, etc, it's so vile. And it really was the limit when I came across the case of a General who was suddenly degraded to the rank of private.' Cramer's comments were quite extraordinary – he was more outraged by the downgrading of a General than the mass murder of innocent people.

Whatever the Generals' plans and speculations at Trent Park, events came to a head on 20 July. At 1800 hours a British Army officer sent for Sponeck and gave him the news that an attempt had been made on Hitler's life and it had not succeeded. The plot had been led by von Stauffenberg who had brought a small bomb in a briefcase into a meeting room with the Führer. He placed the briefcase between Hitler's legs and made an excuse to leave. Jodl had called out 'Stay here!' but Stauffenberg simply made an excuse that he had an urgent phone call to make and hadn't had breakfast. Outside the room Stauffenberg waited about 300 m away and heard the bomb blast. He didn't believe anyone could have survived it. He boarded an aircraft to Berlin where he declared the attempt had been successful without even checking to see whether it had been. In the crucial moment Hitler had moved away from the briefcase and was only slightly wounded when the devise went off.

The failed Putsch came as a total shock to Sponeck who told the British Army officer that it was a put-up job by the Nazis as an excuse for a purge of the anti-Nazi Generals. On hearing the news Admiral Hennecke declared, 'This is the beginning of the end.' He later told a British Army officer: 'there will be a blood-bath in Germany.' In a private conversation between von Broich and Sponeck, von Broich admitted to having known Stauffenberg on his staff at one time. Stauffenberg was described as a 'as a first-class man'. Broich could not understand why he had only used a small bomb and deplored the fact that he had failed in his attempt to kill Hitler.

Most of the Generals had an opinion on the failed assassination. Choltitz described the military men involved in it as 'brave and prepared to sacrifice themselves for their beliefs.' He went on to say that Providence dictated that such an attempt could never succeed, but that the conservative Officer Corps had been compelled to make it to save the face of the German Generals and officers as a whole, who had put up with so much against their better judgement. It rehabilitated the Officer Corps in the eyes of ordinary Germans who had lost faith in them. Choltitz later told a British Army officer that since Stalingrad it had been obvious to him that there would be a revolt against Hitler and that all German Generals tacitly agreed about this because 'there has been a feeling of hopelessness and helplessness among them about the conduct of the war and they no longer had any confidence in the strategical decisions of their leaders.' Choltitz described Stauffenberg as 'almost a genius.' The frustration of Bassenge, recorded in a transcript from the M Room, is felt in his comment, 'For God's sake, where is all this leading us?'

Questions were raised amongst the Generals about security surrounding Hitler. How was it possible to get the bomb so easily into his headquarters? Weren't people searched? Those closest to Hitler were trusted completely. Choltitz told von Thoma and Sponeck that in his experience he was never searched when going into the headquarters: 'I could easily have had a pistol or a small egg-hand-grenade hidden away.' Von Thoma asked, 'were you alone with him?' Choltitz replied, 'yes' (WO208/5017).

## TRAITORS?

The Generals deplored the fact that the perpetrators of the Munich Putsch had been hanged as traitors and had not been shot according to honour due to military men. Eberbach told Schramm: 'These people were not traitors. They first started to hang people in concentration camps. But those were mostly hardened criminals. Certainly officers who indulge in swindling might perhaps be put on the same level. But those officers – that should not have been done. And the worst of all is that the whole families of those officers have also been slaughtered.' Schramm expressed disbelief that the families of the officers involved in the plot had been murdered. Eberbach added, 'They have disappeared. Whether they've been executed or gassed or what I don't know. Graf von Stauffenberg's family, consisting of his wife and four children and a fifth expected is no more. I know about them because he lived in Bamberg where I live.'

Menny told Badinsky, 'it isn't nice to be hanged. However you shouldn't play with murder. They should have imprisoned Hitler; assassination isn't the right way.' Later Menny debated the situation with Liebenstein and commented, 'I admit it's damn bad to hang a Field Marshal, but on the other hand neither is it right for a Field Marshal to get rid of the Führer by murdering him.'

Liebenstein replied, 'All right, let him be shot, but to hang him – none of us can understand that.'

There was little doubt that the July Putsch affected the Senior Germans at Trent Park. It was something which General Heinrich Eberbach discussed with his son who was also a British PoW. MI19 permitted him to visit his father at Trent Park and of course their conversations were monitored by the M Room operators:

> SON: You've no idea how adversely this Stauffenberg business affected the Officer Corps. The fact that the individual soldier at the front was being killed, and that the officers at home were breaking their oath, infuriated the people. The fact that Lindemann, for example, through his own swinishness, let about 100,000 soldiers on the Eastern Front go to the devil – he let his whole front go to hell and went over to the other side with half his staff.
>
> EBERBACH: It hasn't yet been established that Lindemann went over to the other side. Nothing is known about him.

How did the secret listeners react to the news of the attempt on Hitler's life? Fritz Lustig says, 'we heard on the radio that same evening and that the plot had failed. By all accounts Hitler was still alive and well. It may seem a strange reaction, but I was pleased that the plot had not succeeded because most of the names of the conspirators indicated that they belonged to the Prussian aristocracy and were high-ranking army officers. I figured that not much would change for the better in Germany if that particular class were to make peace with the Allies and then rule the country. No doubt millions of lives would have been saved if the war had ended in July 1944 rather than in May 1945, but how would the political situation in Germany have developed, and would it have led to democracy?'

Over the summer of 1944 some of the Generals were due to be transferred to camps in America. One of them was General Crüwell who

185

expressed considerable surprise and displeasure that he was to be amongst them. He met with the Commandant and Lord Aberfeldy and implored them that he saw himself as a British prisoner. He hastened to defend himself at the same time against rumours at the time of his capture near Cairo and stated that he was not responsible for massacres in the neighbourhood of Krajujevac. His protestations led nowhere. Frustrations still ran high when later he conversed with Egersdorf. The listeners recorded Crüwell telling Egersdorf that he was being shipped to America to make room for what he termed 'the Free German Movement' in the camp under von Thoma's leadership. For the duration of his time at Trent Park, Crüwell had led the pro-Nazis. He expressed disappointment to Egersdorf that all efforts to feign illness had been in vain. Von Arnim and Bassenge later joined the conversation.

'It is contrary to the Geneva Convention to send me to America,' moaned Crüwell. 'I'm not an American prisoner.'

Von Arnim seemed none too bothered by Crüwell's imminent transfer and said to him, 'Well, I have no objection to the arrangement. It will be a change for you. The English have no say in the matter. They have to dance to the American tune.' At this point Bassenge added his contribution, saying: 'there's no point in protesting. Prisoners-of-war taken by Germany's allies are handed over to the Germans.' It was certainly rich of Crüwell to invoke the Geneva Convention when the Nazi Regime, including its military commanders and Generals, had completely broken the Convention. With the departure of Crüwell, his worst fears were confirmed when anti-Nazi von Thoma became new camp leader. Von Thoma seemed quite amused by the turn of events and told the other Generals that he didn't plan to change anything. He told Bassenge, 'I'm rather surprised still to be here. But then, it must be a matter of prestige.'

Towards the end of July, on 28<sup>th</sup>, Colonel Lynch visited Trent Park and met with von Thoma as new camp leader. He explained to von Thoma that it had been proposed to open a benevolent fund for wounded German PoWs. He asked von Thoma whether he and the other Generals would contribute to it. After the visit von Thoma discussed the proposal with Bassenge and told him that such a fund was really Germany's own business. However he was prepared to give a lump sum, maybe in instalments, but he was not prepared to become a regular subscriber. The following morning Capt Hamley, the camp interpreter, had an interview with Bassenge in which he explained that the sum of £100 had been suggested as appropriate for the PoW Benevolent Fund. Bassenge thought the sum rather large but put forward the idea that inmates should contribute a percentage of their earnings depending on their rank. He suggested that Generals give 50 shillings, Colonels 15 shillings or £1 and orderlies 1 shilling each. The meeting concluded with him strongly making clear that all German prisoners being held in Britain should contribute.

## PROMOTION

At the beginning of August 1944, as the Allies made successful advances through France, Fritz received a telephone call from Lieut. Col. Cassels, officer-in-charge of the M Room. Cassels began by stating that Fritz was improperly dressed and Fritz did not let on, but he knew this phrase to be a jocular way of informing someone of their promotion.

'How is that, Sir?' said Fritz.

'Well, Lustig, I understand that you still have a crown on your sleeve,' said Cassels, 'although now you are a RSM!'

Fritz had been promoted to Regimental Sergeant Major or Warrant Officer First Class (WO1), the badge of which was a coat-of-arms. He was extremely proud because this was the most senior non-commissioned rank:

> 'I dutifully thanked the Colonel for this gratifying piece of news, and waited for that day's Orders to appear, where I could read in black-on-white that I had indeed reached this pinnacle of my military career.' Promotion brought with it certain privileges. He was entitled to be addressed by officers as "Mr Lustig" rather than by rank and surname and permitted to wear a much smarter officer's beret and raincoat. Since the raincoat had no rank-insignia, it sometimes happened on leave in London that duty-conscious soldiers mistakenly saluted him as an officer. Because that was not the case, army regulations stipulated that he was not permitted to return the salute. 'A situation which made me look very rude.'

The other privilege accorded to Fritz as WO1 was his entitlement to a batman, like any officer rank; effectively a soldier who acted like a personal servant to make his bed, polish his boots and wake him in the morning.

The romance between Fritz and Susan blossomed and they became secretly engaged. Putting the relationship on a more permanent basis meant introducing each other to their friends and family, but their intention to get married was not yet mentioned to anyone. In November Fritz was transferred back to the M Room at Latimer House with the consequence that he was no longer in the same camp as his fiancée. A small army car ran a shuttle service between the two camps and Fritz was able to visit Susan on their days off. They also sent each other notes via the regular despatch rider. It made their separation bearable. That Christmas they finally made public their engagement to just their families.

# SENIOR GERMAN OFFICERS CAPTURED IN 1945

By spring 1945 Allied forces had liberated Belgium and Holland and were heading for the invasion of Germany. Von der Heydte was brought to Trent Park in February, where later he would be secretly recorded, talking about war crimes to the other Generals. Thirty-seven year old von der Heydte was a professional soldier, a Catholic, whose home was the splendid castle *Schloss Egglkofen* in Upper Bavaria. Originally an enthusiastic Nazi, he became disillusioned in 1943/4 and turned anti-Nazi. He genuinely wished to cooperate with the British to bring an end to the war and gave interrogation officers a significant amount of information about German paratroops in the Ardennes counter-attack. He provided details on the failed July assassination on Hitler and even went so far as to sketch a plan for an Allied airborne landing in North-West Germany.

During the war the most senior German military officer to be held at Trent Park was 69 year-old Field Marshal Gerd von Rundstedt, Hitler's Commander-in-Chief in the West. He was captured by the First French Army on 1 May 1945 in Bad Tölz. The previous year he had presided over the Court of Honour which had tried officers involved in the failed 20th July Putsch. At that time he was the most senior officer in the German Army until replaced by Model and Kesselring in 1945. On 5 July von Rundstedt arrived first at Wilton Park where he was held for a month until his transfer to Trent Park on 8 August. British Army officers found him the product of courtliness itself and willing to give information. His name was often canvassed by Senior German officers as a possible leader of an anti-Nazi movement to bring an end to the war in the West, but they finally concluded that he was too old and lacking in purpose. In turn he told them that he could never contemplate such a move, which he considered 'high treason'. On VJ Day he unexpectedly sought out British Army officers to offer his congratulations on 'a great victory'. During 1946 von Rundstedt was held in a cell at Nuremberg Prison as one of the key witnesses with the other military men.

General Günther Blumentritt's personal file contains little comment from MI19, except that he is described as 'a regular, friendly Bavarian infantry officer'. Captured at Hohenaspe on 2 May, just days before Germany's unconditional surrender, he cooperated with Allied forces after capitulation. He arrived at Wilton Park on 1 June and then transferred to Trent Park on 8 August. Before promotion to rank of General, he had served as Chief of Staff to Field Marshal Rundstedt and then von Kluge. During the Nuremberg Trial Blumentritt was held in the prison as a key witness at the same time as von Rundstedt.

SS Obergruppenführer General der Waffen SS Maximilian von Herff was captured at Flensburg on 9 May. MI19 found him cooperative but fellow PoWs described him as a shady character and an opportunist. Although he protested his innocence they failed to believe him, saying that a man in his influential position could only get there under compulsion and ambition.

Another General to arrive at the end of the war was Franz Halder, Chief of the German General Staff from 1938-1942 and later also held as a witness at Nuremberg during the trial. He was captured just days before the German surrender in May 1945 and eventually escorted to England. At Trent Park his fellow officers described the 61-year old General as 'the most capable General Staff Officer produced by the post-1919 German Army'. Halder gave the impression of 'a mild, inoffensive and exact civil servant... an exceptionally lucid brain and great hidden reserves of strength'.

Fifty-four year old General Karl Bodenschatz, formerly head of the Personal Ministry of the Supreme Command of the German Air Force and

Chief of Staff to Hermann Goering, had acted as liaison officer between Goering and Hitler's headquarters. With a reputation for being a complete Nazi, his high-level contact with the Nazi leaders made him unpopular amongst officers in the German Air Force. Bodenschatz sustained serious injuries during the assassination attempt on Hitler's life in July 1944.

Amongst the Generals Alexander von Falkenhausen, an infantry General, was respected by the other PoWs for his sense of fairness, uprightness and moderation. He was even seen as a possible negotiator in post-war Germany or even a Prime Minister acceptable to the Allies.

Arriving at Trent Park at the end of May was Lieutenant-General Feuchtinger who had been condemned to death in Germany in March 1945 for allegedly being engaged in misappropriation and looting. He was released on the personal intervention of Hitler. While in British custody he tried to portray himself as an anti-Nazi but MI19 saw through his façade and commented that he was 'in reality a whole-hearted supporter of the Nazi regime.' His quick promotion in the German army supported the view that he was an ardent Nazi. As part-owner of a publishing house in Leipzig he tried to ingratiate himself with British Army officers with a view to a role in post-war Germany.

Thirty-three year old Austrian Commander of a Fighter Unit Johann Kogler had ninety wartime flights to his name and four victories to his credit:

'His native charm as an Austrian gave place to the studied boorishness of a would-be Prussian. When it suits him, he can still be as personally charming as he is politically reprehensible. His morale and security were both initially exceptional but his Prussian personality, artificially conditioned in resentment and inherently "phoney", was fertile ground for doubts springing up with realism of the true facts. The bluster is gone and the conceited and very "German" German has become a comparatively reasonable Austrian with nascent enthusiasm for Austrian nationalism.'

British minders didn't fail to notice that on first arriving in the dining room at Trent Park Kogler gave a Nazi salute, which Major-General Ullersperger returned with enthusiasm.

One high-ranking German prisoner who appears not to have been held at Trent Park was General Field Marshal Busch. It is believed that he spent some time at Wilton Park before being transferred to a camp near Aldershot where he died on 15 July 1945. No cause of death has been found amongst MI19 files, nor a personal file for him, which is odd given his high-ranking status. However scant details of his funeral appear in a General Report in WO208/5622. Six German Generals from Trent Park were permitted to attend the funeral, accompanied by the Camp Commandant, along with Captain Lang who was the British Intelligence Liaison Officer in charge of the prisoners at Wilton Park. Prior to the funeral the Generals had submitted a number of requests about funeral arrangements to Captain Lang who refused to be drawn in and told them that he would refer matters to a higher authority, i.e. the War Office. The Generals therefore assumed that any decisions passed back to them by Lang had actually come from the War Office. It demonstrates that, although the Generals believed they were pulling the strings and had control, the British in reality only allowed things to go their way.

## HITLER'S SUICIDE

By April 1945 Hitler had retreated to his bunker in Berlin for the final battle. Less than two months earlier, on 18 March, Albert Speer had written to him that the war was militarily and economically lost, and beseeched his leader not to take Germany to total destruction. But Hitler's mind was made up. He told those around him in the bunker: 'if the war is lost, the nation will also perish. The fate is inevitable ... the nation has proved itself weak and the future belongs solely to the stronger Eastern nation.' On 20 April, what turned out to be Hitler's last birthday, Goebbels broadcast to the German nation to 'blindly follow their Führer and the stars.' Three days later Hitler ordered the following announcement to be made: 'The Führer is in Berlin, the Führer will not leave Berlin, the Führer will defend Berlin to the last.' On 30 April, rather than surrender in the besieged city, Hitler and his new wife Eva Braun committed suicide in the bunker.

Whether the German Generals held at Trent Park ever foresaw that Hitler would take his own life was not clear. However, as Germany's end days approached, Major-General Franz speculated to Goerbig and König about the Nazi leaders' chances of escape and commented: 'I wouldn't put it past Hitler, now that the whole affair has collapsed, to turn up in Copenhagen or somewhere and surrender to the authorities.' However the Generals did, naturally, react to news of Hitler's death. Interestingly their attentions turned, not to mourning their leader, but immediately focused on the suitability or otherwise of his successor Admiral Doenitz. They did not react at all passionately to the death of their leader. They thought only of themselves and their own future.

News of Hitler's death came to the secret listeners in the usual way during wartime – via radio broadcasts and newspaper reports. Although there were no celebrations amongst the listeners at any of Kendrick's centres, this was what Fritz and the other émigrés listeners had waited for. Hitler was dead. The man who had had singled out them and their people for annihilation was himself dead, which meant the total defeat of Nazism.

Fritz comments: 'we felt instinctively that Hitler would not allow himself to be captured by the Allies. In that sense his suicide came as no great shock. For days prior, everything had been pointing at Soviet forces overwhelming Berlin's defences. We were realistic about the end game. At last Hitler got his come-uppance.'

Germany's complete and total defeat was imminent. Kendrick must have felt a sense of satisfaction as he knew that finally after thirteen long years of Hitler's autocratic power in Germany, which he himself had been tracking for SIS, Hitler was gone and the final nails were being hammered into the coffin of Nazism. Kendrick's three wartimes centres had achieved incredible intelligence results for the Allied intelligence services. Norman Crockatt wrote to him: '*You have done a Herculean task, and I doubt if anyone else could have carried it through. It would be an impertinence were I to thank you for your contribution to the war effort up to-date: a grateful country ought to do that, but I don't suppose they will.*'

# TWELVE

## GENERALS, WAR CRIMES AND THE HOLOCAUST

*'The worst job I ever carried out – which however I carried out
with great consistency – was the liquidation of the Jews.'*

Choltitz to Thoma

The flip side of the farcical life and political power-struggles of the
Generals had a deeply dark and disturbing aspect. Early on in their private
conversations details began to emerge about widespread atrocities and
genocide against Russians and Europe's Jews. The M Room listeners
recorded conversations which revealed for the first time that Germany's
military men not only knew about the crimes committed, but were
complicit with them. Over the last seventy years a great deal of debate and
counter-argument has taken place about how much was known about
Hitler's Final Solution and the death camps. What did the various ranks of
the German armed forces know about the atrocities and genocide? Did they
have a part in it or were they innocent as claimed? From transcripts of
conversations at Trent Park, Latimer House and Wilton Park provided by
the M Room's secret listeners it is now possible to provide answers. The
files reveal that widespread knowledge and details of war crimes and
atrocities were known not only to the German Generals but also lower
ranks from across the three services of German Army, Navy and Air Force.

It is also possible to establish exactly what information was picked
up by British Intelligence and how early knowledge of war crimes and
mass murder was acquired. Knowledge of the crimes against Poles and

Russians was known to British Intelligence from the early days of the war since 1940. British Intelligence also knew from a number of other sources what was happening to Europe's Jews. However, not only did the conversations provide evidence of the numbers of deaths and places of extermination, but often precise and explicit details of the methods used by the Nazi killing machine. Gathering intelligence moved beyond the realm of political judgment and military secrets to the heart of Hitler's chilling annihilation programme for the Jews of Europe. The volume and length of conversations about atrocities means that it is not practical to reproduce them all in this book, but only a selection.

At Trent Park the Generals became concerned about the possible consequences of the brutality of the regime, and whether they themselves would be implicated in war crimes or called to testify as witnesses at the upcoming war crimes trials. Their conversations show that they tried to distance themselves from their past and agreed on a common strategy to say that they were 'only obeying orders'.

Concern at the events unfolding in Poland and Nazi-occupied areas with regard to the fate of Jews received the full attention of Parliament when, on 17 December 1942, Anthony Eden read the Allied Declaration to the House of Commons. This encompassed the condemnation of other nations, including the United States and the Soviet Union as well as the governments-in-exile of Belgium, Greece, Holland, Czechoslovakia, Poland, Yugoslavia and Norway in a condemnation 'in the strongest possible terms of this bestial policy of cold-blooded extermination... None of those taken away are ever heard of again. The infirm are left to die of exposure and starvation or are deliberately massacred in mass executions.' In reference to the deportation of Jews, the Declaration pulled no punches, and Eden read to a shocked chamber of MPs: 'I regret to inform the House that reliable reports have recently reached His Majesty's government regarding the barbarous and inhuman treatment to which Jews are being subjected in German-occupied Europe.'

William Cluse, a Labour MP, asked the Speaker of the House if MPs could stand in silence to show abhorrence for 'disgusting barbarism'. The House rose to its feet and a two-minute silence followed for the victims of Nazi atrocities. Meanwhile at London's Wigmore Hall, the Women's International Zionist Organization was being addressed by Churchill's wife. She referred to Hitler's 'satanic design to exterminate the Jewish people in Europe.' In a moment of solidarity she told the female audience: 'I wish to associate with you in all your grief, and I pray your meeting may help to keep the attention of the British people focussed upon the terrible events which have occurred and are impending in Nazi Europe.'

## THE EVIDENCE

The Generals realised that as the Allies advanced and made gains from Nazi-occupied territories, it was only a matter of time before they would reach areas where mass atrocities had been committed – and not only in Germany. Shortly after Neuffer and Bassenge arrived at Trent Park they were overheard saying on 10 July 1943 (WO208/4165):

> NEUFFER: What will they say when they find our graves in Poland? The OGPU [Russian Intelligence] can't have done anything worse than that. I myself have seen a convoy at Ludowice near Minsk. I must say it was frightful, a horrible sight. There were lorries full of men, women and children – quite small children. It is ghastly, this picture. The women, the little children who were, of course, absolutely unsuspecting – frightful! Of course, I didn't

watch while they were being murdered. German police stood about with tommy-guns, and – do you know what they had there? Lithuanians, or fellows like that, in the brown uniform, did it. The German Jews were also sent to the Minsk district and were gradually killed off ...

In a conversation on 19 December 1943, after hearing the BBC Midnight news in German, Neuffer and Bassenge had the following discourse (WO208/4167):

BASSENGE: They dished up the mass executions of Jews in Poland. They estimate here that altogether five million Jews – Polish, Bulgarian, Dutch, Danish and Norwegian – have been massacred.

NEUFFER: Really? Not counting the German ones?

BASSENGE: Including the German Jews, during the whole time. They furnished evidence that an enormous number from camp so-and-so between such-and-such a date, fifteen thousand here, eighteen thousand there, twelve thousand there, six thousand and so on – I must say that if 10 per cent of it is correct, then one ought to –

NEUFFER: I should have thought about three million

BASSENGE: You know, it really is a disgrace

Copies of such transcripts about war crimes were sent by Kendrick to a number of different government departments. After Neuffer's conversation with Bassenge (above), Cavendish Bentinck of the Foreign Office wrote to Norman Crockatt, the head of MI9, with a very specific request (WO208/5622):

*'I notice that Generals Neuffer and Bassenge are disquieted at the prospect of the Russians reaching places where the Germans carried out large scale liquidation of Jews, Poles and Russians. We [at Foreign Office] should be grateful if you would try to find out from your guest by the various means at your disposal exactly where these places are. We can then give the Russians some spots to carry out exhumations, and shall perhaps hear less about Katyn, which has begun to pall.'*

The information given up in bugged conversations frequently became more graphic. In a different dialogue Felbert asked Kittel whether he knew of places where Jews had been taken away. Kittel answered, yes. Felbert asked whether it was carried out systematically. Kittel again replied, yes. The conversation continued:

FELBERT: Women and children – everybody?

KITTEL: Everybody. Horrible!

FELBERT: Were they loaded into trains?

KITTEL: If only they had been loaded into trains! The things I've experienced! For instance in Latvia, near Dvinsk, there were mass executions of Jews carried out by the SS or Security Service. There were about fifteen Security Service men and perhaps sixty Latvians who are known to be the most brutal people in the world. I was lying in bed early one Sunday morning when I kept on hearing two salvoes followed by small arms fire. I got up and went out and asked: 'What's all this shooting?' The orderly said to me: 'You ought to go over there, Sir, you'll see something.' I only went fairly near and that was enough for me. Three hundred men had been driven out of Dvinsk; they dug a trench – men and women dug a communal grave and then marched home. The next day along they came again – men, women and children – they were counted off and stripped naked; the executioners first laid all the clothes in one pile. Then twenty women had to take up their position – naked – on the edge of the trench, they were shot and fell down into it.

FELBERT: How was it done?

KITTEL: They faced the trench and then twenty Latvians came up behind and simply fired once through the back of their heads. There was a sort of step in the trench, so that they stood rather lower than the Latvians, who stood up on the edge and simply shot them through the head, and they fell down forwards into the trench. After that came twenty men and they were killed by a salvo in just the same way. Someone gave the command and the twenty fell into the trench like ninepins. Then came the worst thing of all. I went away and said; 'I'm going to do something about this.' I got into my car and went to this Security Service man and said: 'Once and for all, I forbid these executions outside, where people can look on. If you shoot people in the wood or somewhere where no one can see, that's your own affair. But I absolutely forbid another day's shooting there. We draw our drinking water from deep springs; we're getting nothing but corpse water there.' It was the Mescheps spa where I was; it lies to the north of Dvinsk.

FELBERT: What did they do to the children?

KITTEL: (*very excited*): They seized three-year old children by their hair, held them up and shot them with a pistol and then threw them in. I saw that for myself. One could watch it; the SD had roped the area off and the people were standing watching from about 300m off. The Latvians and the German soldiers were just standing there, looking in.

Felbert proceeded to ask Kittel what kind of people the SD were – all Germans wearing the SD uniform with black flashes on which was written 'Sonder-Dienst,' replied Kittel. The orders were given by Germans and executed by Latvians. He continued: 'the Jews were brought in and were then robbed. There was a terrific bitterness against the Jews at Dvinsk, and the people simply gave vent to their rage.'

Information was forthcoming about methods used in the killing of Jews before the gas chambers were built in concentration camps. A conversation between prisoners Cramer and Könncke revealed the Nazi regime's use of mobile gas cars (WO208/4167):

KÖNNCKE: Would you ever have thought it possible, sir, that the German people would fit up gas cars in order to kill people?
CRAMER: I didn't believe that at first either, but one must believe it now, it is true.
KÖNNCKE: I mean to say, I would never have believed it if it had been in an English newspaper, but I was told about it hundreds of times in Germany. I never believed it, but now I must believe it.
CRAMER: It's true. I often heard it in Germany too and I always said to myself: "Oh, these SS are so depraved."
KÖNNCKE: Depraved or not, the mere fact that something like that is possible –
CRAMER: Yes, that's what I'm saying, I'm quite horrified.
KÖNNCKE: And that we drive all people off somewhere and make them get out, and stand about in a temperature of minus 40°C and freeze to death, and that in the fifth year of war we are accused

of tearing one-year-old children away from their mothers and sending them to Germany – Jewish children and so on!

CRAMER: As a decent human being I simply can't believe that.

KÖNNCKE: All I mean by that is, that we have seen so much that we are bound to believe anything.

Another transcript from the M Room recorded a comment by Rothkirch to Choltitz: 'Of course masses of people were shot at Lvov. Thousands of them! First the Jews, then Poles who were also shot in thousands, non-Jews, the whole aristocracy and great landed proprietors and masses of students. It's all very difficult.' Choltitz responded with two words: 'How dreadful!'

In a different conversation Rothkirch talked to Ramcke about all the 'gassing institutions' being in Poland, near Lvov. He admitted that the gassings were by no means the worst and that he had been interrogated about them by British officers at Trent Park. Rothkirch denied responsibility for the gassings but showed that he had done nothing to prevent them either. In fact his anti-Semitism rather welcomed the killings. Ramcke asked him, 'What happened?' The following conversation ensued:

ROTHKIRCH: To start with the people dug their own graves, then ten Jews took up their position by them and then the firing squad arrived with tommy-guns and shot them down, they fell into the grave. Then came the next lot and they too were paraded in front of them and fell into the grave and the rest waited a bit until they were shot. Thousands of people were shot. Afterwards they gave that up and gassed them. Many of them weren't dead and a layer of earth was shovelled on in between. They had packers there who packed the bodies in, because they fell in too soon. The SS did that, they were the people who packed the corpses in.

RAMCKE: Were they 'Waffen-SS'? What did the Security Police do?

ROTHKIRCH: I believe they were Security Police.

RAMCKE: Where were they recruited from?

ROTHKIRCH: I can't tell you that. They were typical – they were SS men. There are photographs in this newspaper, you can see them... The SS leader wrote that he had shot the children himself – women were shot as well – because it was so repulsive; they didn't always die immediately; he actually *wrote* that. I have the thing at home. He described how he grasped the children by the neck and shot them with his revolver because that way he had the greatest certainty of their dying instantaneously... A year ago I was in charge of the guerrilla school where men were being trained in guerrilla warfare; I went on an exercise with them one day and I said: 'Direction of march is that hill up there.' The directors of the school then said to me: 'That's not a very good idea, sir, as they are just burning Jews up there.' I said: 'What do you mean? Burning Jews? But there aren't any Jews anymore.' 'Yes, that's the place where they were always shot and now they are all being disinterred again, soaked with petrol and burnt so that their bodies shan't be discovered.' 'That's a dreadful job. There's certain to be a lot of loose talk about it afterwards.' 'Well, the men who are doing the job will be shot directly afterwards and burnt with them.' The whole thing sounds just like a fairy story.

RAMCKE: From the inferno

ROTHKIRCH: Yes, I was at Kunto, I wanted to take some

photographs – that's my only hobby – and I knew an SS leader there quite well and I was talking to him about this and that's when he said: 'Would you like to photograph a shooting?' I said: 'No, the very idea is repugnant to me.' 'Well, I mean, it makes no difference to us, they are always shot in the morning, but if you like we still have some and we can shoot them in the afternoon sometime.' You can't imagine how these men have become completely brutalised. Just think of it – some of these Jews got away and will keep talking about it. And the craziest thing of all: how is it possible for pictures to get into the press? For there are pictures in this paper. They even filmed it and the films, of course, have got abroad. It always leaks out somehow. In Lvov, just like people catching fish with a net, ten SS men would walk along the street and simply grab any Jews who happened to be walking along. If you happened to look Jewish, you were just added to their catch (*laughs*).

Listening to German radio broadcasts was encouraged by MI19 because it was bound to stimulate discussion afterwards. That is exactly what happened. After one particular German radio broadcast in which a German Army officer mentioned atrocities in Russia, Generals Choltitz, Rothkirch and Broich spoke in detail about what they knew of them. Broich admitted, 'We shot women as if they had been cattle.' The conversation continued (WO208/4177):

BROICH: I was at Zhitomir the day after it happened, while
moving forward when the second offensive was about to start. The
Kommandant, a Colonel Monich [?] happened to be there and
he said, quite appalled: "We might drive out afterwards; there is a

large quarry where ten thousand men, women and children were shot yesterday." They were all still lying in the quarry. We drove out on purpose to see it. The most bestial thing I ever saw.

CHOLTITZ: One day after Sebastopol had fallen – whilst I was on my way back to Berlin – I flew back with the Chief of Staff, the CO of the airfield was coming up to me, when we heard shots. I asked whether a firing practice was on. He answered: "Good Lord, I'm not supposed to tell, but they've been shooting Jews here for days now."

BROICH: The most ridiculous story is the one Wildermuth (PoW) tells about Croatia when he was there. Some incident had happened in a factory somewhere or other; maybe someone was shot; in any case nothing of any importance. The 'Bataillonskommandeur' had the six hundred workers shot, including the German foreman, without establishing their identity.

CHOLTITZ: The Führer gave orders, shouting at me furiously, that a report be sent him every day in which at least a thousand Jews were shot.'

ROTHKIRCH: Only in Germany, or where?

CHOLTITZ: No – everywhere. I presumed he meant Poland. 36,000 Jews from Sebastopol were shot.

Von Thoma told Crüwell that he would not have believed the atrocities if he had not experienced them with his own eyes:

THOMA: I don't think I should have believed it either, if I hadn't actually seen it. I made two written reports about it. I feel that no one can accuse me of having been in any way responsible for it.

CRUWELL: What did you report in writing?

205

THOMA: The atrocities perpetrated by the SS and the shootings and the mass executions at PSKIP [?] and at Minsk – two pages of typescript which I sent to the OKW. I received no reply. I established that no soldiers were ever involved, only a special detachment of the SS. They introduced the name "Rollkommando." It's no good denying it. Of course, these people have become completely brutalised by months of such conduct.

CRUWELL: I am the last to want to defend such atrocities but, taking the broad view, you must admit that we were bound to take the most incredibly severe measures to combat the illegal guerrilla warfare in those vast territories.

THOMA: Yes, but the women had nothing whatever to do with it. Orders were actually given that all Jews were (to be cleared out of) the occupied territories – that is the great idea, but, of course, there are so many in the east that you don't know where to start.

Vierow and Gutknecht both recounted their experiences of atrocities to Eberbach, Schramm and Ulrich in the following conversation. The latter seemed genuinely ignorant of some incidents. Vierow spoke about intervening and moving the prisoners into two trucks, but he did not stop the killings (WO208/4363):

VIEROW: They put one hundred people into a truck. Those were the political prisoners. One hundred people crammed into one track! They couldn't do anything but stand!
EBERBACH: Were they French people?
VIEROW: All sorts, there were Russians among them, French, English and Americans. When I heard that I intervened, thank God, and put them into two trucks, fifty men in each. That was not

so bad. They couldn't fall down, they were so closely packed. They travelled for days, for ten days on account of the state of the railways at that time.

GUTKNECHT: At Antwerp I myself experienced the way all the Jews were taken away that winter. They had to report every day that they were still there and then they were sent away. That was done in those cars with furniture vans attached. Only a few survivors arrived. The general public will have to pay for things like that.

There was not a single day when the Generals were not monitored by the M Room. On New Year's Day 1944 the listeners picked up a conversation between Krause and Broich (WO208/4167):

'Villages were immediately razed to the ground and everybody – men women and children were herded together and slaughtered. The Regiment commander, Bruckelmann, told me about it too. He told me once how horrible it was. They were driven into a pen and then the order was given: "Fire on them!" Of course there was a terrible screaming as they fell – the children too – and of course they weren't killed outright. Then an officer had to go along and put a bullet through their heads. Another time they dragged them all into the church and took them out singly. They always shot them in threes. The ones inside could hear this and barricaded themselves in and put up resistance; then they had to burn the church down because they couldn't get in. He said this massacring was horrible.'

# ADMISSION OF GUILT

Transcripts reveal that the Generals not only spoke in detail about atrocities but admitted their own guilt to each other. For historians today these transcriptions are hugely significant because they dispel the view that the Wehrmacht [German Army] played no part in war crimes and the Holocaust. In a private conversation recorded on 29 August 1944 Choltitz candidly confessed to Thoma: 'The worst job I ever carried out – which however I carried out with great consistency – was the liquidation of the Jews. I carried out this order *down to the very last detail.*' Thoma's reply laid the blame on Hitler for issuing the orders, then sniggered, 'Ha! Ha! Ha! It's a good thing that you can now produce such unimpeachable proofs.' Even Thoma's laughter was written into the transcript of the secret recording.

In October 1944 the listeners picked up another frank admission from Choltitz: 'We all share the guilt. We went along with everything, and we half-took the Nazis seriously, instead of saying "to hell with you and your stupid nonsense". I misled my soldiers into believing this rubbish. I feel utterly ashamed of myself.' It begs the question – why did Choltitz not have a moral conscience about the crimes before? It was all very well expressing guilt afterwards when his fate was uncertain and he could face charges of war crimes. But von Choltitz was not the only Senior German Officer to admit to war crimes. The listeners picked up a conversation earlier in the year between Thoma and Liebenstein in which Liebenstein said: 'we once shot forty thousand Poles in a concentration camp.' Thoma replied, 'out at Dachau in 1940 were a great part of the Polish intelligentsia, university professors, doctors, lawyers – that's the pathological part of it, this mania.'

On another occasion von der Heydte confessed to Meyer that he had once had a PoW shot in Normandy because he had been forced to swim a river and he did not wish to take the prisoner with him. In a conversation in January 1944 Neuffer and Bassenge discussed crimes committed by the German Army. Bassenge told Neuffer that the Göring Regiment was a wild lot. 'I know officially,' Bassenge said, 'because part of the paratroops were formed from the Göring Regiment.'

'Did they commit murders?' asked Neuffer.

'Yes,' replied Bassenge, 'they secretly condemned and murdered people in the barracks and the officers took part.'

## ATROCITIES IN POLAND AND RUSSIA

The programme of persecution and mass murder applied also to the Russians. At Trent Park Generals Neuffer and Reimann spoke about the maltreatment of captured Russians which had allegedly taken place on the orders of Hitler. Neuffer referred to 'ditches by the side of the road full of shot Russians.'

> NEUFFER: In 1941 the Führer issued an order to the effect that as few Russian prisoners as possible were to be left alive and as many as possible killed.
>
> REIMANN: What barbarians!
>
> NEUFFER: That transporting of the Russians to the rear from Vyasma was a ghastly business!
>
> REIMANN: It was really gruesome. I was present when they were being transported from Korosten to just outside Lvov. They were driven like cattle from the trucks to the drinking troughs and bludgeoned to keep their ranks. There were troughs at the stations; they rushed to them and drank like beasts; after that they were

given just a bit of something to eat. Then they were again driven into the wagons. There were sixty or seventy men in one cattle truck! Each time the train halted ten of them were taken out dead: they had suffocated for lack of oxygen... At the stations the prisoners peered out of the narrow openings and shouted in Russian to the Russians standing there: "Bread! And God will bless you," etc. They threw out their old shirts, their last pairs of stockings and shoes from the trucks, and children came up and brought them pumpkins to eat. They threw the pumpkins in, and then all you heard was a terrific din like the roaring of wild animals in the trucks. They were probably killing each other. That finished me.'

Even after the passage of time of some seventy years, passages like these are still chilling. Honest, eye-witness descriptions of the last moments of Russian prisoners, and how they met their death.

What is becoming apparent from the transcripts is that the Generals had widespread knowledge of massacres being committed by the Nazi regime. In some cases, they themselves were complicit in them. But what exactly was known about the concentration camps? In this respect a conversation between six Generals in May 1945 proved revealing (WO208/4178):

DITTMAR [*re concentration camps*]: What did we know about them?
SCHLIEBEN: Everybody knew that dreadful things happened in them – not exactly what, but just that dreadful things happened – every one of us knew that as far back as '35.
DITTMAR: To Germans?

BROICH: Primarily to Germans.

ELFELDT: We knew (what happened) in Poland to the hundreds and thousands of Jews who, as time went by, disappeared, were sent away from Germany and who after '39 were said to be accommodated in ghettos and settlements in Poland – we were told that.

SCHLIEBEN: They all disappeared.

ELFELDT: Whoever got to know that millions of these people – as the Russians now assert – perished or were burnt in Auschwitz and whatever these small places are called?

BROICH: Certainly none of us.

ELFELDT: We heard about Auschwitz when we were in Poland

BROICH: I visited Dachau personally in '37. The commandant of the camp said to us: 'If I had to spend a year here, I should throw myself on the electric wire. I couldn't stand it for longer than a year – nobody could.'

HOLSTE: Some people stood it for twelve years.

BROICH: We were quite convinced that we were only shown what we were supposed to see. I went there with the hereditary Prince of Waldeck, that swine; he had two camps under his control. We spent six hours there and afterwards were absolutely overcome by what we had seen, although we did not see any of the tortures we have heard about lately.

Dittmar said that he did not hear the name Auschwitz until he went to Paris. And Thoma replied: 'That's how they led the people up the garden path.' Senior German officers like Lieutenant-General Feuchtinger, who was captured in Hamburg on 3 May 1945, had not previously believed it possible for mass shootings in the thousands to have been carried out until he visited Pinsk where 'the previous year there had still been 25,000 Jews living there and within three days these 25,000 Jews were fetched out, formed up on the edge of a wood or in a meadow – they had been made to dig their own graves beforehand – and then every single one of them from the oldest grey-beard down to the new-born infant was shot by a police squad.' It was the first time Feuchtinger had heard about mass executions.

In some comments by the Generals it became apparent that ordinary Germans knew much more about what was going on than they were prepared to admit to the Allies after the war (WO208/4177):

HEYDTE: There's another camp which is even worse than Lublin. It's in Czechoslovakia. Half-a-million people have been put to death there for *certain*. I know that *all* the Jews from Bavaria were taken there. Yet the camp never became over-crowded.

WILDERMUTH: Yes, I've heard of that too.

HEYDTE: But I don't only know that all the Jews from Bavaria were taken there, I know that all the Jews from Austria were taken there, and still the camp wasn't over-crowded.

WILDERMUTH: From all over Germany. It appears that most of the Jews from Germany were either sent to Lublin or to that place.

HEYDTE: I was also told that the Jews are simply gassed in a gas-chamber there. They gassed mental defectives too.

WILDERMUTH: Yes, I know. I got to know that for a fact in the case of Nuremberg. My brother is a doctor at an institution there. I've seen one of those transports myself. The people knew where they were being taken.

The Generals unwittingly revealed how far Hitler was prepared to go in creating his pure Aryan race. Those who did not fit the Nazi ideal of racial perfection were also singled out for annihilation. That included the elderly and insane. Wildermuth, Broich, Elfeldt and Wahle had an intense discussion about it. Wildermuth stated evidence at his disposal led him to estimate that '70,000 to 80,000 mental defectives had been put to death.' The treatment of the aged was also discussed and how people over the age of 70 were no longer being accepted for admission into hospital. Broich commented that some operations were still being performed on the elderly but they had to return home straight afterwards. This was in the spring of 1942. Seyffardt seemed to know about the 'liquidation of the insane'. Listeners overheard him telling other Generals: 'There was a provincial lunatic asylum near Baden-Baden where there were harmless lunatics who worked in the vineyards, but who were no use for anything else. Then one day they all suddenly died. Then, after they had turned it into a hospital for people who had limbs amputated, they put up a huge notice board: *From lunatic asylum to a home for cripples – Adolf Hitler.*'

As the reality of defeat finally sank in, the Generals became quite philosophical about the atrocities. Bruhn commented, 'Have we deserved victory or not? No, not after what we've done. After the amount of human blood we've shed knowingly and as a result of our delusions and also partly instigated by the lust of blood and other qualities, I now realise we have deserved defeat. We've deserved our fate.'

# THIRTEEN

## 'ONLY OBEYING ORDERS'

*'All that is needed for evil to triumph is for good men to do nothing'*
Edmund Burke

DISCUSSION ABOUT WAR crimes and the mass murder of Jews was not limited to conversations amongst the German Generals. References were picked up as early as 1940 and 1941, although not necessarily in the same graphic detail as later. One particular important testimony came in 1941 from a 'turned' prisoner whom MI19 used as a stool-pigeon to mask as a fellow prisoner in the cells. His name has never been disclosed but he was a survivor of Belsen concentration camp where he had been incarcerated for his political views. It was from him in 1941 that MI19 got some of its firsthand eye-witness accounts. There was a shortage of good mechanics and so this inmate had been taken on as a member of staff to carry out repairs to the commandant's house. He was finally released and conscripted into the German forces, then captured by the British. MI19 Naval interrogator Donald Welbourn wrote about him in his unpublished memoirs:

> *'He was the first person to tell us about the Beast of Belsen, and of the lampshades made from tattooed human skin. The Foreign Office did not want to believe our reports. All this information came out very quickly, together with the fact that this prisoner wanted to do everything in his power to make sure that the Nazis did not win the war.'*

In his intelligence reports for 1942 Kendrick recorded that most PoWs spoke about 'the severity of German measures in Poland.' However the bulk of the detailed information on war crimes came from the bugged conversations during and after 1943 and came primarily from captured parachutists and airmen. When read alongside the transcripts from the Generals, it is apparent that MI19 amassed a substantial amount of evidence which covered most of what is known today about the Holocaust. Only sample extracts can be realistically included here. Unlike the situation of the Generals who were held at Trent Park until the end of the war, prisoners of lower rank were typically held only for a few days or a week at Latimer House and Wilton Park because the sites could not accommodate large number of prisoners at any one time – remembering that over 10,000 were processed by Kendrick's centres during the course of the war. After interrogation and bugging the cells, the lower ranks were transferred to other PoW camps across England. Therefore MI19 did not complete personal files for these prisoners, neither was there the volume of General Reports on their activities in the camp. Only the day-to-day life at Trent Park was recorded in detail. Therefore from extracts below, it is often not possible to provide a wider picture of the lower rank prisoners' military career or background.

Kendrick's colleague Felkin of Air Intelligence at Latimer House ensured also that all recordings of atrocities were kept. Amongst lower rank officers, overt details were picked up during 1942. One such example came from Luftwaffe officer Heimer:

'There was a large collecting place, the Jews were always brought out of the houses and then taken to the station. They could take food with them for two or three days, and then they were put in a long distance train with the windows and doors sealed up. And then they were taken right through to Poland, and just before they reached their destination they pumped in some sort of stuff, some sort of gas, cool gas or nitrogen gas – anyway some odourless gas. That put them all to sleep. It was nice and warm. Then they were pulled out and buried. That's what they did with thousands of Jews! (laughs)'

A young twenty-one year old seaman Horst Minnieur gave an eye-witness account of executions in Lithuania to his cellmate, a member of a U-boat crew: 'they had to strip to their shirts and the women to their vests and knickers and then they were shot by the Gestapo. All the Jews there were executed... Believe me, if you had seen it, it would have made you shudder.'

Kendrick's Summary Reports for 1943 noted that one of the German PoWs spoke about 300,000 civilians shot; another PoW that boys and girls had been killed. There was talk of 'armed conflict between the SS and members of the other armed forces because the latter would not commit atrocities.' The suffering of Jews in the Lodz ghetto was also mentioned. One PoW whose sister had worked in a hospital in Lodz spoke about the poverty and disease amongst the people, their complete disillusionment and the rigid control exercised by the SS who supervised the hospital.'

Atrocities were not limited to Poland. The situation in Russia was equally grave. There were allegations of atrocities committed by the Russians and counter-atrocities carried out by German troops. It was said that 3,000 Russians escaped from Smolensk where 'they were imprisoned under appalling conditions and that 2,500 who were recaptured were systematically shot.' The fear amongst German airmen of being captured by Russians was so intense that when the airmen were forced to make a landing behind Russian lines they endeavoured to get back to their own forces as quickly as possible.

## EVIDENCE FROM POW HAUPTMANN

German parachutist Hauptmann, who was captured in Italy on 18 October 1943, provided the most information from a single prisoner during that year about the extent of the atrocities committed by the Nazi regime. Transcripts of his conversations with a British Army officer, who is not named but was a fluent German-speaker, have survived and represent what the secret listeners recorded of the conversations between the two men. Hauptmann was given the codename M350 by MI19. An unusual comment was noted at the beginning of the Special Reports dealing with the information provided by him, which doubted the reliability of some of this: 'M350 claims to be a fugitive from justice, having shot a Nazi official in Hamburg. In interrogation he has given a certain amount of information, some of which appears to be accurate and some highly improbable. His statements should therefore be treated with reserve.'

However, with the benefit of hindsight it is now known that what Hauptmann spoke about with regard to war crimes was true. Four weeks after his capture in Italy Hauptmann was being held at Kendrick's centre and talking with a British Army officer; of course completely unaware that the conversations were being recorded. The following transcript about the treatment of incurables in Germany was dated 20 November 1943 and is in AIR40/3106. In it, Hauptmann speaks about various institutions: large orphanages, homes for women and charitable institutions run by Catholic nuns. All of them had been 'cleared out', commented Hauptmann.

'By whom?' asked the British Army officer.

'By the Nazis,' replied Hauptmann. 'They have been completely cleared out, not a soul has been left, not even staff. Everybody has disappeared.' The British Army officer naturally asked, 'Do you know where they've gone?'

'To Heaven,' answered Hauptmann (M350).

BAO: Why? Were they superfluous? Couldn't they do any war work?

M350: Hmm. In Southern Germany we had a great many institutions, including homes for cripples and so on. In Württemberg, the Black Forest and so on, there is a comparatively large amount of in-breeding and that's where the largest percentage of cripples is found. Well all these people – they (said they) got inflammation of the lungs or something and died suddenly.

BAO: Really. How did they get the people away? In trains?

M350: In omnibuses.

Two days later Hauptmann spoke to a British Army officer about Sachsenhausen and Dachau concentration camps. He told the officer that Sachsenhausen had seven to eight thousand people in it. He then carried on, 'At Dachau at times there were more – especially when the Heuberg camp was closed down there were considerably more at Dachau. The forest camp of Fuhlsbuttel was in the Hamburg area. People who were arrested up there went to that camp.'

'You say there were seven thousand at Sachsenhausen and ten thousand at Dachau?' asked the officer.

'Yes,' replied Hauptmann.

British Army officer, 'And Fuhlsbuttel?'

'About four thousand, counting the Jews,' said Hauptmann. Then the officer asked if there are only three concentration camps. To which

Hauptmann replied, 'Oh, there were a lot. Concentration camps were not the only topic of conversation. In a separate report of another conversation that day, possibly with the same officer, the listeners recorded Hauptmann talking about Hitler's use of "stud farms" to breed a pure Aryan German race. This was part of the Nazi *Lebensborn* (Spring of Life) programme to create a perfect master race. Such breeding camps or 'farms' existed across Nazi-occupied Europe. Hauptmann explained that good German girls agreed to conceive the baby of an SS officer. A few days before the girl went into labour she was taken to one of the special 'stud farms' where the baby was born. The baby was immediately surrendered to the Nazi regime and the mother never saw her child again. Hauptmann commented that 'it [the baby] is looked upon as a child of the Führer.' The British officer probed further, 'Are these SS men specially selected?'

'It's a thoroughbred stud farm,' replied Hauptmann. 'They are the military stallions. I know a BdM leader [League of German Girls] who has already presented the Führer with two children.' The conversation continued:

BAO:   Are only SS men employed as 'stallions'

M 350: Yes

BAO: Is there no 'stud fee'?

M 350: No

BAO:   Can the SS man select the girl?

M350:  Hmm. That's of no importance.

BAO:   But it might happen that a girl came forward who wasn't a bit pretty?

M350:  Yes, but that makes no difference.

Hauptmann confirmed that the girls were examined beforehand to see if they were suitable breeding stock. Asked how many children the Third

Reich had acquired through these human 'stud farms', Hauptmann was unable to give an answer. After a further brief exchange the officer prompted, 'They have this fanatical love for the Führer, and if he wants them to...'

Hauptmann replied, 'yes' as he laughed. The British Army officer asked, 'Was there a parade of 'stallions' beforehand or afterwards, in order to entice the girls?' Hauptmann laughed again. 'Unfortunately not. They are men from the Führer's bodyguard. They do that as a single line. While other men go to brothels, they go to this stud farm. There's a better selection.'

The above transcript lay in classified government files at the National Archives until 1999, unknown to historians. However, it was in the 1980s that the first details of these breeding farms became public knowledge from a different source, when some of the children who had been fathered by SS officers and had lived a life of shame and trauma, decided to reveal their shocking past. What the MI19 files demonstrate is that British Intelligence knew of the existence of 'stud farms' long before the survivors came forward. The transcripts also independently corroborate the testimonies of those women who had succumbed to the Nazi breeding programme.

There was more to come from prisoner Hauptmann. On 12 December 1943 he discussed further atrocities with a British Army officer. Again, it is not clear whether it was the same officer as before. This time Hauptmann was prompted to speak about partisans (AIR40/3106):

M350: There were all kinds of people among the partisans: Russians, Yugoslavs and Germans.
BAO: Germans too?

M350: You found rogues, criminals, vagabonds, robbers and gipsies – all sorts there. A few Greek patriots had occupied the village and were terrorising it because there was no authority or discipline. They were well armed.

BAO: Did you capture them?

M350: Yes, we encircled the village and hanged them all in turn. Those who were foreigners, were hanged straight away and the Greeks were handed over to the Greek court of justice, which was in the village, and they hanged them too, of course. We were there a few days and the people who had made off came back again from the hills with their cattle and whatever they had. Then celebration after celebration was organised, one sheep after the other was slaughtered and one cask of wine after another was brought up and we drank the wine out of great big pots.

This transcript gives an admission of guilt for the crimes committed. Such a text is important because it corrects various myths and shows historians that German airmen had as much knowledge of war crimes as Hitler's military men, and some were perpetrators too.

## PRISONER M320

On 31 October 1943 an SS officer was brought to Latimer House after capture in Italy. He was no ordinary SS officer but from one of Hitler's infamously brutal and merciless 'Death Squads' – *Einsatz-Kommando 3*, Sicherheits-Polizei [Security Police]. In a rank equivalent to Sergeant-Major, this SS Hauptscharführer came from one of the highest positions in Hitler's Secret Police. Special Reports generated from the M Room merely give him the codename M320. In an unguarded conversation with another

PoW (named M322 in the transcript), this time on 28 December 1943, the SS Hauptscharführer spoke about Auschwitz. It is one of the few mentions of the camp by name amongst MI19 files. His fellow prisoner appears not to have heard of it, but certainly knew about other camps (WO208/4137):

> M320: I know the Auschwitz concentration camp in Poland by hearsay. Actually you can see it from the train. It is a hutted camp for Jews. I heard say that there's a crematorium there, and that no one who enters the camp comes out alive.
>
> M322: I heard a lot in Vienna about Mauthausen
>
> M320: I personally haven't seen any concentration camp, apart from Auschwitz, which I saw from the train. It's not far from Cracow
>
> M322: Oh, down there
>
> M320: Yes. When you go through by train you can see it
>
> M322: Were mainly Jews sent there?
>
> M320: Yes. I should be interested to know what they have done with all the Jews in the Reich, and then the ones from Austria, since they started to get rid of the Jews. I wonder whether they've slaughtered them?

In a different conversation, this time with a British Army officer, the SS Hauptscharführer (M320) spoke freely and at great length about mass executions by firing squads in the village of Ananiew and Cherson and said that in one day as many as 5,000 Jews were shot in Cherson and four hundred in Ananiew. These were carried out under the orders of Obersturmbannführer Bersterer of Detachment 10B who had been involved in Hitler's failed Munich Putsch of November 1923. The SS Hauptscharführer explained in detail how at first the Jews had been employed by the German detachment to fetch water, chop wood and work in the kitchen while stationed in the neighbourhood of Pervomaisk. Then one day when he returned, there were a whole lot of new people and he was told that the Jews had all been rounded up and shot. The excuse given was that the Jews had shot some Germans; an allegation which the SS Hauptscharführer stated he did not believe. He had not seen these shootings himself, but he did witness shootings at Cherson. His detachment was sent as reinforcement to supervise the executions. He explained that people were first held in houses and then driven away in cars to the execution point. 'How many people were shot at a time?' asked the British officer.

M320: 'They were always shot in groups of ten.'

BAO: With tommy-guns?

M320: 'With rifles. One man to each. Ten men with rifles to ten –

BAO: 'Did they simply fall down into trenches or what?'

M320: 'Yes. They had to get down into a trench – it was a kind of anti-tank trench. It was about two and a half to three metres deep and wide as this room, we'll say. You had to shoot down at them from above.'

BAO: 'Were they all killed instantaneously?'

M320: 'Yes. There were men with tommy-guns who finished them off. The cars drove away one after the other and they could see the others being taken up and shot, and they knew that it might be their turn next. You'd see a woman holding a little child on each of her arms, and she might be pregnant as well – and there were whole families.

The killing of women and children in cold blood caused psychological problems for the firing squads and M320 told the British officer that many went mad as a result. When asked about the lunatic asylums in Russia, M320 confirmed that he had heard about them and the shooting of the inmates. He added, 'In the Reich they poisoned lunatics in some way and then burnt them. It caused a lot of bad feeling; there was a lunatic asylum in the Vorarlberg and the people there simply disappeared. I don't remember the name of the family, but one of them wanted to visit some relatives and was told they were no longer there. Then later on they received the ashes.' He had witnessed smaller executions in Russia – groups of ten or twenty people.

It is well-known today that the Nazi regime found that the method of death by shooting was causing no small amount of distress and psychological difficulty for men in the firing squads. But back in 1943 such information was only just coming out. For Hitler, there was going to be no turning back from the 'Final Solution'. M320 explained that the mass execution of Jews continued but an alternative had to be devised by the regime and this led to the use of mobile gas trucks. From the transcript of the conversation it is obvious that the British officer knew about the gas trucks and had been primed to ask more. M320 described how he had seen two of them in use at Feodosia and Sudacm and that both gas trucks were used to kill Jews. He explained how the bodies were then buried near Staryi-Krim, near Feodosia.

BAO: How many do you think were killed there?

M320: There was talk of about fifteen hundred at Feodosia.

BAO: A great many were said to have been killed at Simferopol, weren't they?

M320: They even spoke of sixteen thousand there.

Possibly because of his position in the SS death squad, MI19 held the SS Hauptscharführer longer than most prisoners (apart from the Generals). He was still being questioned by British Intelligence during 1944. On 23 February 1944 another important conversation about the gas trucks was recorded by the secret listeners. This time he spoke in graphic detail of exactly how the early Nazi killing machine worked. It happened from the time when he was a stationed at Sudak and travelled to Theodosia to collect stores. He told a British Army officer: 'I saw the gas lorry there for the first time and how the people were shoved in, and then I was interested to find out what kind of a lorry it was. It was explained to me that it was a gas lorry – that exhaust gases were used in it. There had been some talk earlier of the existence of such a lorry, but I hadn't seen it before.' The people were told some tale about being taken to another place, so they climbed into the back of the truck. 'Were they men, women and children?' asked the officer. M320 confirmed: 'Yes. Once they were inside they were shut in, the engine was turned on, and in a few minutes they are dead.'

BAO: How long does the engine run?

M320: Ten minutes, and in four, or at most five minutes, they should be dead.

BAO: What happens then?

M320: They are then driven away, buried and –

BAO: Where were they buried, do you know?

M320: Generally in anti-tank ditches.

BAO: Where were the anti-tank ditches?

M320: They were in various places. One was between Starikrim and Saaly and then there were some more in the direction of Kerch but at that time they couldn't use those because the Russians were still on the isthmus. I saw a large anti-tank ditch about 3 or 4 km away from Cherson. There was a hell of a lot of corpses there.

BAO:  When was that?

M320:  That was round about August/September, 1942. The 'Teilkommando' was then disbanded and others from 'Einsatzgruppe C' then took over the area and 'Einsatzgruppe D' moved on further...

BAO:  Did you see the interior of the lorry too?

M320:  Yes, I saw it as the people were getting in. Only a glance though, therefore I can't remember it very well.

BAO:  Do they stand up inside?

M320:  They must stand up as I didn't see any seats.

BAO:  To which unit did that lorry belong?

M320:  'Einsatzgruppe D'

BAO:  Did you have it all the time you were in that area?

M320:  The lorries arrived only after the 'Kommando' had been stationed in Theodosia. Up till then people were shot... I believe there must be four or five thousand people buried in that mass-grave at Cherson. Terrible! They were all shot, women and children, pregnant women carrying another child in their arms and leading one by the hand.

BAO:  Who shot them?

M320:  The police, the Waffen SS and also people from the Security Service. It was dreadful! There was an anti-tank ditch here and a small strip of woodland and here an open field with a road running in between. The people, who were all Jews, were taken there. They stood there and were brought up in batches of ten, ten here and ten there and so on. You can imagine the scenes.

This transcript adds further evidence about what is now known about the Holocaust and actions of the mobile death SS squads 'Einsatzgruppe C' and 'Einsatzgruppe D' that carried out mass executions, mainly of Jews in Nazi-occupied areas.

## PRISONER M363

On Christmas Day 1943 British forces captured a Lieutenant of Nebeltruppe, 56 Regt in Italy. By March 1944 he had been brought to one of Kendrick's centres and a British Army officer primed to converse with him about war crimes. The prisoner was designated M363 in Special Reports and spoke about a special SS Kommando unit at Simferopol. He revealed that the SS unit ordered Jews to hand over their belongings and were told that they were being transferred by truck to another location. In reality, he explained, they were going to be ushered into the mobile gas lorries. He continued: 'Then they all collected together at a certain place, lorries drove up and they were told to leave their things where they were and to climb into the lorry. From there they were dumped into the nearest anti-tank ditch.' He also spoke about regular forces, like the Engineers, who had been given orders to shoot all Jews in the locality of Dniepropetrowsk. One engineer had refused because he could shoot in battle but not innocent civilians. Convicts or men of rough character came forward and volunteered to carry out the shootings instead.

In some conversations the M Room listeners overheard admissions from lower ranks of crimes committed against Allied forces. One such brief conversation was recorded by them on 6 June 1944 – i.e. D-Day. The names of the PoWs are not given in the Special Report and news of D-Day and the Allied invasion of France had probably not yet reached their cells. The dialogue occurred between a Lieutenant in command of U-boat 550 and the commander of U-boat 852. The latter, a Lieutenant Commander, was captured a month earlier on 2 May 1944 and spoke to his cellmate about the killing of Naval personnel from an Allied ship after it was sunk. Was it because his conscience pricked him that he decided to admit the crime to his colleague? He told him, in translation (AIR40/3104):

> 'I searched my conscience in that moment – I mean one doesn't do that kind of thing cold-bloodedly, and I said: "It's got to be." I shall tell the IO [interrogation officer] what my attitude was, namely, that, if we had saved the crew, they would have operated against us again. I would naturally have taken the people prisoner, if it had been possible, but it wasn't possible. It's obvious that I can't drag in the High Command. I can't say we had orders.'

This transcript marks one occasion when a U-boat commander acted unilaterally and without orders from above. He could not claim to be 'obeying orders'.

## SS MUTINY

The fanatical participation of the SS and death squads in the annihilation of Jews has been well documented over the last seventy years. However, transcripts from the M Room have thrown up some hitherto unknown details about the behaviour of the SS. During early July 1943 listeners at Latimer House overheard an astonishing conversation between a British Army officer and a lower rank prisoner, a Lance Corporal, codenamed M222, who had been captured in Tunisia. Lance Corporal M222 described two separate mutinies amongst SS guards in an unnamed concentration camp prior to 1937. Nothing like this has ever come to light before and, if true, forces historians to re-evaluate previous knowledge about the SS. The two attempted mutinies occurred in the period before Hitler's formulation of the "Final Solution" and before the concentration camps in Poland were constructed. In the conversation with a British Army officer he refers to 'us' and appears to have been an eye-witness of the extraordinary things in the concentration camp. Because of the importance of this transcript, it is quoted in full below (AIR40/3106):

> BAO: What sort of people were these SS men? Had they been criminals or - ?
>
> M222: No. They were people from outside, who happened to be in the SS; they had all volunteered as guards. I have sometimes spoken to some of them. They said they didn't all get work immediately. Several were there for three or four days or a week and then went off again. Others felt really happy there.
>
> M 222: In 1936, at Easter, or I believe it was 1937, some of the guards even fired on each other.
>
> BAO: Why was that?
>
> M 222: We were told that this is what happened. There were three guard platoons with 100 men in each, making 300 in all. It was the turn of one platoon to be on guard every third day, the second had to go out with the working party, and the third was off duty. It was, so to speak, standing-by. It was resting. Round about midday shooting suddenly started: one platoon was trying to disarm the guards and let us out, but that wouldn't have succeeded in any case.

Whether there was any punishment for the shootings is not known, but the guards clearly did not succeed. M222 moved quickly to explain another similar incident that happened a year or two previously, of which he had vivid memories. There are gaps in the conversation where the listeners were unable to distinguish some of the words:

M222: Shortly before Christmas 1935 we had sixty men killed. It happened like this. It was pretty cold and had snowed a little too, and, as sometimes happens, for we only had on our thin blue uniforms ...... Everyone ...... his hands from time to time. When a sentry saw that, he said: "Come here, if you're cold!" Then he had some sort of things erected on the grass and they had to get on them with their caps off and stand at attention with their faces to the wall. In the course of time there may have been about twelve figures standing there. I don't know how it happened, but at any rate one man said: "That's too much of a good thing in this cold." Then one of the sentries said. "They are mutinying!" and as soon as he shouted: "They are mutinying!" they fired into them with their machine guns. Then the camp commandant came out. A whole number of us had been killed. You can well imagine that when you are all working bunched together one beside the other and they fire into you with machine guns, there are bound to be some killed. The camp commandant had a look at things and then he said: "The remainder will be shot." The remainder, there may have been about a hundred of them or a little more, I can't remember exactly, were to be shot too. He said it was mutiny. Anyhow more sentries came out and we went into the camp; at least we didn't go straight into the camp but remained in front of it, and then the order was given that the others were to be shot too.

At the moment the order was given to shoot the mutineers a Sturmführer

[SS lower officer rank], who was nearby and having problems with the engine of his motor-cycle, witnessed the whole happenings. He disagreed with the treatment of the guards and threatened to report it to the Führer himself. Evidently they were outside the camp:

> M222: He [the Sturmführer] said the people were to go into the camp immediately. They had no business to be out in front. Then they did let us into the camp, but we didn't hear any more about it; only we didn't get anything to eat that day.
> BAO: Where was the cemetery?
> M222: That was about 3 km away in the bog, just beside the road.
> BAO: Who took the bodies away? For instance those who were killed in the working party?
>
> M222: Usually the prisoners did that. I saw the cemetery. It was surrounded by barbed wire; you couldn't see anything except that the earth had been turned over a little there. There were no crosses or anything. If anyone was buried, it was done just before dawn.
>
> BAO: Can you estimate at all how many were shot during the time that you were there, that is, about five-and-a-half years?
>
> M 222: I should say 500-600 men not counting all those who hanged themselves. Perhaps that's an under-statement. They looked for some for days, when all the time they had hanged themselves from the hooks in the little wardrobes. Each man had a sort of small wardrobe. That happened in that particular camp and there were ten camps there altogether.

BAO: Could you reckon on 100 men a year in that camp?

M222: That's hardly enough. There certainly were more. The people never had any feelings about it or had it on their consciences. They were so utterly callous that they just said: "We are the hunters, you are our prey." Those were their actual words.

BAO: How long do these SS men remain there?

M222: They are often changed. This lot had stayed there for three months. You could really say that the people who were there were from every part of the German Reich... Then the people would be sent from this camp to another one. What they did with a number of us was that they took some out and sent the whole hut-full to another camp; and from the other camp one hutful would come over to us because the people stuck together too much, like brothers and sisters and were always trying to bribe the sentries. 95% of them were thugs. Many of them were killed; you have no idea how many SS men were shot there.

BAO: Where, in the camps?

M222: Yes.

This transcript appears to be the only conversation of its kind amongst the tens of thousands of transcripts from MI19 which were kept in government archives. It is all the more extraordinary because the British Army officer has prompted the conversation and demonstrates that British Intelligence was not only interested in military secrets but actively seeking information about the SS involvement in war crimes. From the perspective of SS history it sheds light on the fact that there were at least two SS mutinies, hitherto never recorded elsewhere, and that the SS men were shot for their actions.

As to the name of the camp, it must have been one of less than half a dozen camps which existed during this period. Recent enquiries at the archives of the Dachau and Sachsenhausen concentration camps have thrown up nothing to confirm that the mutiny took place there. It could have possibly happened at Bergen-Belsen which was built as a large military complex from 1935. The workers were housed in camps near Fallingbostel. It became a prisoner-of-war camp before being extended to be a concentration camp.

As with much of the evidence of war crimes surreptitiously gathered by MI19 between 1943 and 1945, it was possible to verify the details in the post-liberation period of the camps. There is no logical reason to doubt that the testimony of M222 was accurate. The transcript leaves a baffling mystery and only provides half the picture. It leaves unanswered questions: what provoked the first mutiny? Was there any sense amongst these SS guards that the killing of Jews and political opponents was wrong? Or did the mutiny occur for other reasons? What does emerge is that for a short time, some men of an SS battalion in a concentration camp "broke out" emotionally against the situation in which they found themselves. Where the two mutinies took place still remains an open question.

On the subject of the SS committing atrocities, further revelations came from bugged conversations in the M Room; not only from lower rank prisoners but also from an exchange between three Generals at Trent Park. Sponeck, Schlieben and Sattler spoke about how, in 1939, some military commanders in the German Army wanted to punish SS men who carried out mass killings of Jews, Poles and Russians. The suggested punishment for the perpetrators was that they should be shot. Himmler stepped in and forbade such court-martials to be convened and removed the SS from the jurisdiction of Army courts. An extract of a conversation about SS actions is reproduced here, in translation:

SATTLER: Yes, we have shot people. That began in Poland back in 1939. The SS is said to have wreaked terrible havoc.

SCHIEBEN: That was probably the reason why Blaskowitz was dismissed.

SATTLER: Yes, of course, and Kuchler, too, because he severely punished a few SS-men who had murdered people. Thereupon there was the hell of a row and after that the SS got their special court, that is, SS-men could be had up only before SS courts-martial, not ordinary service ones, whereas up to then the SS was supposed to come under the armed forces. That followed on the disgraceful behaviour of the SS in Poland, because the military authorities said: "This dirty scoundrel goes around shooting women and children; it's the death sentence for him." Then Himmler came along and said: "That's out of the question." I had actual experience of that myself.

SPONECK: But even before that business we were not allowed to take proceedings against them. I know the case of the Director of Music of the 'Leibstandarte', whom we dragged off his band-waggon, because he had shot so many Jews in a mad lust for blood. We had him brought before Hoth's court-martial. The man was immediately taken out of Hoth's jurisdiction, sent to Berlin and came back again, still as Director of Music.

SATTLER: Was that in peace-time?

SPONECK: It wasn't in peace-time; it was during the war before Warsaw.

SATTLER: Yes, that's just what I mean. The SS intervened and said: "No." like mad and the higher authorities, like Kuchler, for example – he had a row, too – stepped in and wanted to condemn the fellows to death, but the SS came along and said: "No, we have our own courts; that's out of the question." Thereupon, in spite of the fact that the SS came under the armed forces, and in war-time was actually a part of the armed forces, the SS suddenly got its special courts. Instead of getting shot, those fellows got promotion and that was the end of the matter.

The practical result of Himmler's decision meant that the SS were answerable only to special SS courts. In reality this meant that the SS perpetrators would never face trial for their crimes nor be punished. Now the infamous SS Death Squads could continue their crimes unhindered throughout the war with no effective opposition.

## REACTION OF THE LISTENERS

For one group working at MI19, overhearing such details of atrocities must have been particularly painful and heart-wrenching. How did the secret listeners, the majority Jewish émigrés, react to overhearing such admission of war crimes against their own people?

Many had left families behind in Nazi Germany and spent the war years worrying about their fate. When they eavesdropped on the conversations about mass shootings of Jews into shallow-dug pits in Russia, Poland or Latvia, they could have been overhearing descriptions of the murder of their own parents, sister, brothers and friends. For them this must have been one of the most difficult parts of their work. Listener Peter Hart spoke about it in his memoirs and specifically overheard what went on in Buchenwald concentration camp:

'We came across many a horror story. One of the worst that I can remember was when we heard from a prisoner that the wife of the Commandant in an extermination camp, had her lampshades made from human skins taken from the inmates, selected before they were put to death, because of their attractive tattoos. We had this confirmed more than once... We also heard gruesome stories from prisoners who had been employed in extermination camps. There was absolutely no doubt that these were true stories from the people who had actually seen what was going on... Some of the worst reports from the extermination camps which shocked us most, were those which described the callous use made of victims' bodies after they were gassed.'

Later during the Nuremberg Trial the shrunken heads of prisoners and the lampshades made from their skin were used a key evidence for the horrors committed at Buchenwald. When asked today about the atrocities, Fritz Lustig replied:

'We all tried to be professional in our approach to hearing PoWs discussing war crimes, which meant that irrespective of the personal circumstances of our own families we tried not to become emotionally involved in what we were hearing. By 1943 we already knew what was going on in Eastern Europe and therefore it was not such a shock to us. We knew the terrible truth which the world would see in all its horror after the camps were liberated at the end of the war. Because we were told to keep the cut records of any war crimes, there was the expectation that justice would eventually be done.'

Fritz was one of the lucky ones not to lose a single member of his family in the Holocaust. For other listeners the awful truth was revealed after the liberation of the camps. Within the confines of the basement of Trent Park in the M Room, listener Peter Ganz heard the admissions of guilt by the Generals and details of war crimes against the Jewish people. That included his own family. On a personal level it must have been extremely difficult for him and fellow listeners to hear and record the accounts from the lips of Hitler's top military men. Nothing could bring back those family members who had been murdered and after the war Ganz learned the terrible truth that his grandfather had been murdered in Auschwitz in 1944.

For other listeners there was some hope in these dark days. After the war listener Rudi Oppenheimer learned that his niece Eve, the daughter of his elder brother Hans, had survived Belsen, together with her brothers Paul and Rudi. The latter both came to England under their own steam a short time later. Because Eve was too young – she was under five – that autumn of 1945 her uncle Rudi was granted compassionate leave and travelled to Holland, where she then was, to collect her. He brought her back to England where she still lives today. The Oppenheimer family learned that Eve's parents perished in Belsen just months before its liberation by British forces on 15 April 1945. It was to be an all too familiar story for so many of the German-speaking émigré listeners working for MI19.

# FOURTEEN

## BREAKING THE GERMAN WILL TO RESIST

*'We are disgraced for all time.'*
General Felbert to Schlieben, Trent Park

FRITZ LUSTIG WAS working in the M Room at Latimer House when he read in newspaper reports about the liberation of Belsen on 15 April. Photographs and film footage, recorded by the Allies of the emaciated survivors barely able to walk amidst piles of dead bodies, sent shockwaves throughout the world. Nothing had prepared the liberating forces for this. Fritz comments: 'when I saw film footage of Belsen for the first time I was deeply shocked at the emaciated survivors and heaps of naked dead bodies lying around. Although coming from Nazi Germany I had known about concentration camps, I was not prepared for this. Seeing the extent of the Nazi disregard for human life raised questions about how such unspeakable acts could have been committed in the civilized country of my birth.' Earlier that month American forces had entered Buchenwald concentration camp, the first of the death camps to be liberated by them, and similar horrific scenes had confronted the soldiers there. Copies of the film footage were sent to British and American intelligence services, and that included Kendrick and his American counterparts at MI19.

MI19 decided that the German Generals should be shown both film and photographs of the camps. Their reaction to what they saw would be secretly monitored from the M Room. The listeners were again instructed to keep 'cut' records of any admissions of war crimes during these particular conversations. The release of visual material pertaining to concentration camps was carefully staged by British Intelligence. First, copies of black and white photographs of Belsen, Buchenwald and Dachau were circulated alongside copies of the forthcoming White Paper on Buchenwald. This provoked some broad comments by the Generals. Goerbig, for example, expressed to Franz his belief that many of the photographs had probably been faked. In another discussion Felbert admitted to Schlieben, 'We are disgraced for all time.'

Amongst some there was disbelief. In a different conversation Franz said to Konig: 'I freely admit that the worst outrages have been committed in the camps – that's beyond doubt – but I can't imagine that the bodies were left lying about like that. I don't know how far away from the town the Dachau camp was, but, if thirty or forty bodies are left lying out in the sun for three or four days, it would make such a stench that they couldn't stand it in the town.' Franz went on to say that he believed the Generals were being subjected to enemy propaganda 'with the same crafty methods' as Goebbels had used on the German people. Konig then pointed out that they were being treated much better than if Germany had been the victor. Franz responded by saying: 'The victorious country has a perfect right to carry on as they are doing. Our behaviour would have borne no comparison. We are at least comparatively lucky to have landed up in our present conditions than if we were now English officers in German hands after a German victory.' In a similar vein Broich commented to Wildermuth that the camp stories, whether true or not, were the best possible propaganda for the Allies. Wildermuth responded that it released the Allies from all responsibilities towards the Germans.

In a conversation secretly recorded between von der Heydte and a British Army officer, von der Heydte commented that it was useless for the Senior German officers to deny knowledge of the camps because 'practically every German suspected that that sort of thing went on.' He commented that Goebbels had been so successful in his propaganda to make inmates in the concentration camps look sub-human that the German people did not care what happened to Jews. Von der Heydte feared that even the photographs taken at the liberation of the camps would not be sufficient to convince the German people of the true horror of the situation. He appeared to be the only General at Trent Park to suggest some kind of personal recompense for the crimes committed by Germany. When speaking to General Eberbach, he stated that as Germans they were under an obligation somehow to make good what had happened in the camps. For his part he was prepared, if he got home again, to receive into his home one of the 600 concentration camp children referred to in the Press and see to the child's upbringing.

In a conversation about Buchenwald between Schlieben and Vaterrodt, Schlieben questioned whether people who had carried out such bestialities and escaped the clutches of the Allies could still be recognised as fellow Germans. Vaterrodt's only reply was to say he knew so little about it and these people must have acted to some extent under compulsion. He suggested asking fellow prisoner SS-Oberfuhrer Meyer for the true facts, but then decided that Meyer would probably not give them.

What did ordinary Germans know about the concentration camps? Bassenge, who had firsthand knowledge of atrocities (especially in Poland) told a British Army officer that not even one half of 1% of Germans knew about Buchenwald, or generally what went on inside concentration camps. He added that people living in the neighbourhood might know, but anyone who spoke about it would immediately find themselves inside. He claimed to have told his fellow Generals stories about concentration camps, but the stories were discounted as mere propaganda stories. Bassenge claimed that not more than two per cent of his hearers had any inkling of the truth.

The second stage of 'educating' the Generals about the liberation of the camps was to show them film footage. Attendance was compulsory.

Dittmar and Hoslte agreed that the film was revolting, but added a comment that there was no means of comparing it with what had happened in Russian camps. They could not understand why the SS had not destroyed all the damning evidence. Oriola and Siewert blamed Hitler for ordering the killings and continued by saying:

> SIEWERT: Still, it's no wonder those people starved; we hadn't anything left ourselves
>
> ORIOLA: Concentration camps will always remain an impossible institution, specially in countries which have a depraved government
>
> SIEWERT: It's a very effective film; it's a fine sort of recommendation from us! It really was like that, I saw it. The worst thing was that anyone could have anyone else put in such a camp without a sentence.

Later, Bruhn philosophically and truthfully commented to Schlieben: 'I believe that when the policy of extermination overtakes us, which we have actually merited by our shedding of blood, the blood of our children will have to be shed too or perhaps that of our relations.' News of the liberation of Belsen and images of the horror was soon overshadowed by the news that Hitler had committed suicide in his bunker. As noted in an earlier chapter, rather than mourning the death of their Führer, the Generals became more concerned about the balance of power shifting to Admiral Doenitz and Doenitz's suitability, or otherwise, to take over the reins of government.

## 'ONLY OBEYING ORDERS'

The Generals swiftly turned their attention to whether they would stand trial as war criminals, and this was reflected in their conversations during this period. They tried to distance themselves from their past and agreed amongst themselves that they would say that they were 'only obeying orders'. MI19's General Report recorded: 'various of the Senior Officer PoWs are expecting to be called as witnesses at the Nuremberg War Crimes trials.' Some, like Eberbach, expected to be called as a witness. In conversation with Thoma and Wildermuth, Eberbach said: 'Either they want me about the shooting of the Canadian PoW – I have already once proved to them that it happened before I went there. Or they want to interrogate me about the transfer of the police into the armed forces in connection with preparations for the war. I joined two years before the law was enacted. Or Speer has named me as a witness; I can tell only good of him.' Wildermuth advised him to say as little as possible. At which point von der Heydte interrupted: 'If I may butt in, I do not believe that it will be a staged trial.'

Eberbach was also recorded by the listeners as speaking to Lieutenant-General Heim, von der Heydte and Wildermuth about the duties and obligation of a witness. He argued that a witness gave evidence under oath. Wildermuth commented that it would not be in order to shake hands with any of the accused whom they knew. He further advised Eberbach 'not to remember' if he was in doubt as to the implications of any given answer. In a different discussion Elfeldt expressed the opinion to von der Heydte that all Senior Officers would be tried by the Allies in due course. They both agreed that the British and Americans wanted to annihilate the German military and academic classes. They also agreed in condemning Hitler's use of gas chambers but stated that, in their view, the Germans had already been sufficiently punished. Elfeldt together with Heim stated that too much fuss was being made about German maltreatment of Jews: 'after all, many more Germans died in this war than

Jews died in gas chambers.'

There was now plenty to occupy the Generals' time. They reacted to news that General-Field Marshal Rundstedt was to be put on trial as a war criminal, so too General Dostler who was wanted by the French. General Blumentritt engaged much of his time, with von der Heydte's assistance, marshalling evidence and arguments to be used in defence of his former chief, should the occasion arise. Meanwhile another alleged war criminal and Trent Park captive, SS-Oberführer Meyer, had requested von der Heydte to undertake his defence before a war crimes tribunal. Von der Heydte refused and gave his reasons:

> 'He [Meyer] is charged with the fact that PoWs were shot in front of his position. Two cases are particularly serious – in the first nine were shot 200m from his battle HQ and they're quite right in maintaining that it is incredible that he knew nothing of it or that there was anything unusual about it. I've taken good care not to define my attitude regarding the matter. Of course, as a regimental commander I can well imagine that, in the heat of battle, I might not know what was going on 200m in front of my battle HQ – I've other things to do and think about. But that there were many cases of shootings of PoWs – that PoWs were shot – is incontestable. It has been ascertained who shot them and the people involved are, of course, falling back on the excuse of orders received from Meyer.'

Kittel was in doubt that he would be named as a war criminal. His explanation: '18,000 Jews were killed at Rostov. Of course I had nothing to do with the whole affair! But it is down on my account because I was the only known General there.' Eberbach asked: 'who is really responsible for the affair? There's no doubt at all that the Führer knew all about this massacre of the Jews.' In typical fashion, Kittel blamed the Jews and replied: 'Well, those Jews were the pest of the east! They should have been driven into one area and employed on some useful occupation.' He added that he was going to hold his tongue about the things he knew until he was called to give evidence:

'After the fall of Rostov the Russians accused me, in a great official solemn declaration on the radio, of having poisoned 18,000 Russians. As regards that I can only say: until then I knew nothing whatsoever about the whole affair in which so many people were killed, and was actually not under the impression either that so many people had been removed from there. They were probably carried off. I don't know. Anyhow, I'm certainly one of the best nominees for a war criminal – although there are quite a number of them. Wildermuth also told me in the strictest secrecy that he has signed about forty sentences of death in his official capacity as Field Commander. Yes, I have some anxiety on that score!'

In the apologia which followed, while admitting that atrocities had taken place, Kittel pleaded his own helplessness in view of the attitude adopted by higher authority: 'I deprived the Security Service people of every possibility of maltreating the population, but I could not overcome the fact that my own superiors made arrangements with the Police General which simply knocked me off my feet.'

Such discussions intensified after SS Oberführer Meyer had been notified that he was to appear before a War Crimes Court of Enquiry. Camp Leader Bassenge notified Meyer that he would be transferred at midday to London in readiness for a court appearance at 8.30am the following morning. Meyer told Eberbach: ' He [Bassenge] didn't know what it was all about. It's quite possible that it is in connection with that question I raised some time ago. I can't imagine what else it could be, as otherwise they wouldn't have given me two days' notice. They'd simply have packed me off and taken me away from this camp.'

'Court of Enquiry?' asked Eberbach with some surprise in his voice.

'That's what he said,' replied Meyer. 'Well, the newspapers say an investigation commission is already busy picking out people from camps who are to be charged as war criminals,' retorted Eberbach.

On his return from the Court of Enquiry, Meyer was full of it. 'They wanted me to answer 'yes' or 'no' to their questions,' he told Elfeldt, Kittel and Kogler, as if staging the whole occasion again. 'Did they tell you who accused you?' Elfeldt asked. 'Yes, they never stopped doing that,' replied Meyer. The questioning of Meyer by fellow officers continued, all meticulously recorded in the M Room:

KITTEL: Did they first tell you the charges under which you were accused?
MEYER: No
KITTEL: When being questioned, you should first say: "I should like to know why I'm here and I request that the order for committal be read to me."
KOGLER: It's no use, Sir.
KITTEL: There is some sense in everything, my friend. If you just stand there shaking in your shoes, that's no good either! Whenever you are dealing with lawyers there are only two possibilities: one is to lay all your cards on the table and say: "Do with me whatever you like," or else stand your ground and fight it out point by point.
KOGLER: I'm at their mercy anyhow – they can do as they like

with me in any case. Its' all just pretence!

KITTEL: Right down to your skin and your honour! You can't do more than that! On the strength of your obligation as an officer you need to be released from your oath of secrecy by the German Government, and unless you are released, there is no use in torturing you. That's a point of view for you!

With some frustration Kittel added curtly, 'I gave the order for the shooting of Russians, allegedly. I gave the order myself – allegedly.' Elfeldt feared the Russians would take the army list from a particular date and ask for the people they wanted. Kittel replied, 'they can wipe out the whole of the Officer Corps, it won't matter to them. Then that will be the end of us, but at least the others have the satisfaction of knowing that they have all kinds of unsavoury matters in their own records.' He had worked out his response to an official Court of Enquiry. He would dispute the legality of the court and plead to be heard only in a German court. He ended by saying: ' the Allied courts can do what they like with me, but I am under no obligation to say anything more than appears in my pay book.'

Later in a separate conversation Kittel pleaded: 'in my opinion we are obliged, whenever it concerns matters which might be harmful to the German Reich, – and they will be harmful – to say: "I'm sorry, I know nothing about this affair. I shall answer whatever questions you put to me if a representative of the German Government is present and I have his consent to do so." He then told fellow officers: 'You are under an obligation of silence.'

With the impending defeat of Nazi Germany, MI19 and Chiefs of Staff had already mulled over plans to use the German Generals belonging to the anti-Nazi clique at Trent Park. A report from the Director of

Military Intelligence to Major-General Strong (overseeing military intelligence in Europe under a unit called G-2) said: 'this plan calls for efforts to be made to persuade the captured German Generals to help by broadcasting to the German people, or by working in the fighting line.' Could the Generals be persuaded to broadcast to the German nation and bring an end to the war? Did they have that kind of authority? And if so, would they agree to this new plan? Lord Aberfeldy submitted a list to Lt Col. Rawlinson at the Directorate of Military Intelligence, listing the names of Senior German officers who he felt would cooperate. On the list were von Thoma, Broich, Neuffer, Bassenge, Reimann, Schlieben, Elfeldt, Eberbach, Wahle, Heim, Wilck, Wildermuth, Daser, Felbert, Bruhn, Vaterrodt, Schaeffer, von der Heydte and Rothkirch. A copy was sent to Kendrick at Latimer House.

Having received a telegram of approval from intelligence chiefs in America, British Intelligence was given the all-clear to negotiate with particular German Generals, but it needed a high-ranking British commander whose status would appeal to their egos. The German Generals must be convinced that they were talking to an officer their equal. It was therefore decided to dispatch General Officer Commander-in-Chief Sir Andrew Thorne.

Thorne arrived at Trent Park on 3 April, where he met with Eberbach, Bassenge and Wildermuth. The three German Generals had been chosen as the deputation by the German Senior officers themselves. Thorne started by assuring the Generals that any discussion between them would remain secret. He also told them that he was acting on instructions from American General Eisenhower. Thorne explained that the purpose of his visit was to 'enlist their cooperation in putting an end to the senseless slaughter and annihilation that was taking place at a time when there could be no other possible outcome of the war but the defeat of Germany.' For this purpose Thorne promised them the radio networks of the British Empire and America would be at their disposal to make a historic broadcast asking their nation to surrender. The Generals made several points in response: first, they recognised the inevitable defeat of their country and they would do all in their power to avert unnecessary bloodshed. However their hands were tied because of reprisals that would be taken against their own families – therefore they could not agree to their names being used publicly. Second, they argued that the military men with the real power (Kluge, Rundstedt and Kesselring) were not behind barbed wire. Thirdly, they feared that German soldiers may be held as prisoners for years, with some even being deported to Russia. Seeing how brutally the Russians treated PoWs, they argued that German soldiers would rather die in battle than face the prospect of being a PoW in Russian hands. Finally, in a clever negotiating tactic, the Generals suggested that if the German Army could seize executive power from the present German government, they would allow the Allied armies to march through Germany. Thorne left that day with the Generals still mulling over their final decision, a decision which would be relayed to intelligence chiefs via the 'welfare officer', Lord Aberfeldy.

The following day at dinner General von Thoma made an announcement to the other Generals. His speech was recorded via the bugging devices hidden in various places in the dining room and later transcribed by the listeners. A hushed room turned its attention to Thoma who said:

'Gentlemen, I have the following announcement to make because I consider it right that you should all be in the picture. The Camp Commandant approached me requesting that General Eberbach, General Bassenge, Colonel Wildermuth and myself attend a conference on post-war questions with an English General, an emissary from General Eisenhower. I was given no further information on the subject. I asked to be excused from taking any personal part in it because I consider it wiser that I, as camp leader, should have nothing to do with it for the time being. The conference took place yesterday afternoon. They were asked to say whether they would be prepared to draw up and sign a proclamation to the Wehrmacht [German Army] to lay down its arms. The proclamation would be broadcast by means of the radio and leaflets. They turned it down with one accord. I am in complete agreement with their point of view… Our government at home must know themselves what to do in order to end the thing. That's all Gentlemen, I thank you.'

The reactions to Thoma's speech, which then ensued over the dinner table, were also recorded by the listeners. Kittel and SS Oberführer Meyer agreed that General Ramcke was the best man to speak to the German people. Across the table, Eberbach told Elfeldt that the focus should be on trying to persuade the Allies to stop using the term 'unconditional surrender' which was bad propaganda for soldiers who had been defending the Reich for six years. Elfeldt felt it would be treason to take part in any proclamation to the Wehrmacht as long as the fighting continued. Eberding thought it showed complete lack of character if they took part in any proclamation just to receive better treatment in captivity.

A final written decision of the German Generals concerning a wireless broadcast was given to Lord Aberfeldy within days of Thorne's meeting. A copy of their report was circulated at a meeting of the Joint Intelligence Sub-Committee in London on 11 April 1945. The report differed little from what the Generals had told Thorne. In it they said: 'An appeal from German Generals in captivity for the cessation of resistance even with the sole object of preventing further senseless destruction of the basis of German existence would – even in the present war situation – constitute an action which would not be understood by the troops in the field or by the German people.'

Furthermore, it was considered that such an appeal would bear no weight because fighting troops would refuse to accept orders from prisoners-of-war, albeit high-ranking prisoners. In the current war situation the Generals did not believe that retreating troops on the Western Front would have time to listen to wireless broadcasts, and leaflets rarely reached frontline troops. They also feared for the safety of their own families who would be subject to death threats and reprisals. Finally, on a political note, the Generals said that the Nazi Party had already begun to blame them for the defeat of Germany – their betrayal was deemed to be the cause of Germany's downfall: 'an appeal by German Generals would merely encourage a new stab-in-the-back legend, and would be laying the foundation stone for an attempt to recreate the Nazi Party.' They now admitted that the only way forward was the elimination of the men currently in power in Germany; namely the eradication of the Nazi Party. In a separate statement to Lord Aberfeldy, Bassenge said that the Generals had essentially the same aims as the Allies – to bring an early end to the war. However he wished to raise objections to Allied propaganda methods, and the conclusions which the Allies were drawing from prevailing conditions in Germany. Lord Aberfeldy appeared sympathetic to Bassenge's concerns; then filed a summary report of Bassenge's views to MI19.

British and American Intelligence departments at the very top had tried to bring a swifter end to the war. Having failed to secure the cooperation of the Generals in captivity, there was no option left – Allied forces would continue to fight and push their way through Germany until the total defeat of the regime that had wreaked death and destruction on millions of innocent victims, including their own people.

# FIFTEEN

# BRITISH INTELLIGENCE AND WAR CRIMES TRIALS

*'The records of conversations between enemy prisoners of war afford an excellent insight into the German character and the results of the Nazi regime.'* Winston Churchill

WHEN THE MOUNTAIN of evidence for war crimes and atrocities was finally presented at the Nuremberg Trial, there was one vital bulk of evidence missing – the files from the secret listeners who had bugged Nazi PoWs during the war. Information received from the bugged conversations of all ranks of German PoWs provided enough evidence to bring some Nazi war criminals to justice. Why were the files withheld?

Other important issues are also raised from the content of the M Room transcripts. The question of what British Intelligence knew about the mass killings is unambiguous. Transcripts from MI19's three sites confirm that such knowledge was early and sent by Kendrick to various government intelligence agencies and departments. Could the knowledge gained have been used to halt the atrocities? Why was British Intelligence interested in recording atrocities? As will be seen shortly, MI19 and its sister branches MI9 and MI6, fiercely protected the nation's secrets. Like the other top secret site at Bletchley Park, any possibility of leaking the original source of intelligence risked other ongoing operations. Information could only be used if it could be corroborated from another source known to the enemy. It may seem a rather simplistic response, but having particular intelligence and being able to act on it are two different things.

As already noted, M Room operators were instructed to record all reference to atrocities, mass exterminations and war crimes. The 'cut' records were to be kept indefinitely. It is possible that 70 years later these have survived in some dusty basement of a government department, but thus far it has not been possible to trace them. Why were Kendrick and his ultimate bosses at MI19 so insistent that the original records be kept? Fritz Lustig and fellow listeners were told it was for use at the war crimes trials and that made them feel that at least the war criminals would be brought to justice. It may be true that during the war MI19 chiefs believed the evidence could be used, but that such decision to release the material had been blocked as hostilities drew to a close. A very different scenario unfolded. Fritz would not find out until decades later that the transcripts were not actually used at Nuremberg or other war crimes trials. Even if he had known at the time that they were being withheld, he had signed the Official Secrets Act and was sworn to say nothing to anyone.

## M ROOM FILES AND NUREMBERG

Surviving letters from this period reveal for the first time that MI9, which had a voice on the Joint Intelligence Sub-Committee, was unyielding in its view that the source of information on war crimes and death camps which it had gathered could not be released. The reason: the secrecy of Kendrick's centres could not be compromised and bugging of prisoners was still going on well after the German surrender – both in Britain and Germany. Surviving letters and memos in MI19 files reveal that not everyone in British Intelligence agreed with the idea of withholding evidence from Nuremberg. What transpired at the end of the war was a heated debate within intelligence circles about whether or not the files could be released. Files about the war crimes which had been gathered at

Kendrick's three sites over the course of MI19's existence had been circulated to the War Office, Foreign Office, various departments of British Intelligence and American Intelligence. Extensive reports provided confirmation from a number of German PoWs about the sheer extent and detail of the atrocities. What has never come to light is the sharp exchange which took place within British Intelligence circles about not releasing evidence of war crimes from the bugged conversations. Which part of the British Secret Service made the overriding decision?

This was taken by MI9, via the Joint Intelligence Sub-Committee, and the primary reason given was that it would blow SIS methods of eavesdropping that were still in practice at the end of the war. The files would have become public property and neither MI6 nor MI9 were prepared to allow this to happen. Three surviving letters in a slim government file provide an insight into the exchange and feelings of those within the British Secret Service. The first is dated 31 October 1945, at a time when the twenty-one surviving leaders of the former Nazi government were being held at Nuremberg Prison ahead of their trial. It was written from the Military Deputy of the Military Department at J.A.G [Judge Advocate General] in Whitehall in which he expressed no objection to evidence from MI19 being used in war crimes trials as long as the methods of obtaining it are kept secret. He wrote:

'From time to time CSDIC [MI19] Reports have come into my hands where a PoW has made a statement to his fellows to the effect that he has committed a war crime. Obviously what a PoW says to another PoW is evidence against him, but I understand the DMI may take objection to members of CSDIC staff giving evidence of what they heard a prisoner-of-war say, in the circumstances. In my opinion it may in some cases be essential to call an officer of CSDIC [MI19] staff as a witness. He could say that he overheard a conversation between the PoWs and give the context of the conversation without saying how he came to overhear it. On the other hand it appears to me now obvious that the Germans were fully aware of the procedure adopted by CSDIC, and it is clear from investigation in the Dulag Luft case that the Germans employed exactly the same methods. The matter, therefore, does not appear to be so secret as it was during the war. In any event I understand that CSDIC is coming to an end and it will be no secret in the next war that such a practice was employed.'

On 16 November Lt Colonel S. Kerry of MI9 replied categorically that material from Kendrick's centres should not be disclosed under any circumstances:

'We consider as of the highest importance the avoidance of anything which could draw attention to, or make public, the methods employed at CSDIC [MI19] – this notwithstanding the fact that the Germans may have been aware of them and have in fact used similar methods themselves... It is admitted that in spite of warnings memories are short and PoWs continue to talk indiscreetly, but anything which will tend to increase security-mindedness on the part of an enemy should at all costs be avoided. This is particularly the case at the present moment when these methods are still being employed elsewhere and would presumably again feature largely in any future war. Disclosure at War Trials of methods used for securing information would inevitably lead to their becoming public property and emphasising them to the extent of making them largely valueless – and the future must be considered. It does not require much imagination to visualise the sensational Press articles to which such disclosure might well give rise. In short, what up to now has been known to comparatively few (and those mostly persons who are directly interested and are under oath of secrecy) would become common knowledge. There is, too, another aspect which must be considered. The use of this information as evidence would of necessity in many cases entail the disclosure of the names of PoWs who have been actively working for us, which we are anxious to avoid at any cost. Nor would we view with equanimity the calling as a witness of an Officer who had been employed in the particular branch concerned who would have to submit to cross-examination which might easily result in the disclosure of information which was then and still is Top Secret.'

A response to the above came in a third and final surviving letter dated 28 November; this time from a Brigadier whose signature is illegible. He strongly objected:

'I must return to the attack. It is unfortunate that war criminals should avoid the consequences of their misdeeds because evidence cannot be given of what they said quite voluntarily while a prisoner-of-war to another prisoner-of-war. If the MI [Military Intelligence] are of an opinion that it is undesirable that evidence should be given in open court, orders can be given that an application should be made to hear the evidence in camera or the names of witnesses suppressed. With regard to the 4th paragraph of MI9/19 minutes, I do not see how, even if the trial was held in open court, it would come to light that a prisoner-of-war had been actively working for us. I am quite prepared to submit each case in which I should like to use CSDIC Reports to MI9/19 with a view to seeing whether the information which is likely to be disclosed is still of a Top Secret nature. A point raised by MI9/19 that cross-examination might result in the disclosure of information which is Top Secret can be got over by the witness claiming the privilege under the Official Secrets Act. Will you please take this matter up again with DMI.'

Much of the evidence gathered on war crimes by MI19 could only be used to steer post-war investigations, but could not be used in court. In the end MI9 had its way and none of the evidence from the M Room was ever given to the legal teams and prosecutors at Nuremberg or the other war crimes tribunals. At the time Fritz Lustig and the other M Room operators were told that their material could not be used because 'the methods used to obtain it contravened the Geneva Convention.' A meeting of the Joint Intelligence Sub-Committee on 5 June 1945 confirmed otherwise. Under discussion at that meeting was whether cut records of atrocities could be played in court as evidence for war crimes. One objection raised was how almost impossible it would be to 'prove that the voice of any individual is, in fact, the voice alleged to be reproduced on the record.' The report of that day's meeting further stated:

'Even if this could be established, the basic security, from the point of view of the future, of CSDIC [MI19], methods as developed in this war must be considered. A large measure of success has been achieved by the methods we have employed, and it is the measure of success which has been attained which is of even greater security importance than the methods themselves which have actually been used. From this angle, the greater effect of playing back these records in open court, the more deeply will the future use of CSDIC's be compromised.'

However some concessions were made. 'If the records and reports were made available on a TOP SECRET basis for the purpose of briefing the cross-examiners at the trials (in order that the accused may be induced to confess or be so shaken that he is discredited), then it would appear that Security would be preserved and the main object of discrediting the accused achieved.' It was felt by members of the Joint Intelligence Sub-Committee that sufficient alternative evidence was available in sufficient quantity to bring war criminals to justice – and that included Senior German officers.

By mid-May 1945 pressure was mounting on MI19 to release files on atrocities. The matter was raised again by Cavendish-Bentinck as part of the agenda of the Joint Intelligence Sub-Committee which met on 15 May. He reported that the leaders of the German armed forces were likely to do their utmost to show that they were not guilty of atrocities, which, of course, was already known from M Room transcripts. Senior German officers at Trent Park had already denied to British Army officers any complicity in war crimes. MI14's representative on the committee said: 'I regard it as of the utmost importance that everything possible should be done to discredit the German General Staff and Officer class in such a way that they may never regain their former influence.' The Committee's Minutes concluded: 'There is abundant evidence of atrocities committed under the authority of German Armed Forces leaders in the occupied countries. It should therefore be possible to conduct an effective propaganda campaign both inside and outside Germany.' The committee believed it was not difficult in Allied propaganda to Germany to discredit the plea that Hitler alone was responsible for Germany's military failure.

Nothing can conceal the fact that ultimately some Nazi war criminals never faced trial for crimes which they admitted during captivity and under internment by MI19. It meant that the likes of SS General Kurt Meyer, commander of the 12th Panzer Division captured by the Americans near Liege in Belgium and held at Trent Park, never stood trial for some of his crimes. As one of Hitler's most decorated warlords Meyer had served in the major campaigns of the German offensive. In 1945 he was extradited to Germany from Trent Park to stand trial for the shooting of Allied soldiers in the war. For those shootings he received the death sentence which was later reprieved to life imprisonment. However, it was discovered from clandestine listening-in at Trent Park that he was responsible for burning down a village in Russia during a campaign on the Russian front and 'massacring the population as a reprisal for the accidental shooting of one of his pet dogs.' He also allegedly ordered the massacre of the population of another Russian village near Kharkov, and for these particular atrocities he never stood trial.

## OPERATION EPSILON

One post-war operation that had to be protected within British shores was the site at Farm Hall near Cambridge. It was here from May 1945 until October 1945 that MI19 held the captured German atomic bomb scientists in a joint operation with the Americans, codenamed *Operation Epsilon*. It was yet another unit of MI19 which came under the overall command of Kendrick, and he was stationed there for a time during Major Rittner's absence on leave due to sickness. Rittner was originally based at Latimer

House as a key member of Kendrick's team before his posting to Farm Hall.

Farm Hall represented one prime example why MI19 files could not be made public and released to the war crimes trials. Europe was entering the Cold War and nothing could be allowed to jeopardise *Operation Epsilon*, from which the British and Americans expected to obtain the most important scientific secrets in the new era.

Émigré listeners George Pulay, Herbert Lehmann, Heilbronn and a few others were transferred from Kendrick's other sites to a small M Room at Farm Hall to listen to the conversations of the top German scientists. At the end of the war, British and American teams of Field Security and Counter-intelligence had hunted in Germany for the scientists before the Russians got to them first. After their arrest the scientists were transferred to Farm Hall, and given no explanation for their detention. Once again MI19 had fitted the place with bugging devices. The small team of M Room operators eavesdropped, and ironically the scientists were overheard to comment: 'the British are too stupid to bug our conversations.' Amongst the files are copies of the scientists' reaction to the dropping of the atomic bomb on Hiroshima in August. Transcripts of the conversations have been reproduced in a book called *Hitler's Uranium Club*.

To underline the importance of ongoing operations, Major-General J.A. Sinclair of the Directorate of Military Intelligence Department told the Joint Intelligence Sub-Committee: 'nothing must be disclosed which would make more difficult the present or future exploitation of the means by which S.R [Special Report] material is obtained.' In a memo dated July 1945, however, the Directorate permitted S.R. material to be used for propaganda by the Political Intelligence Department as long as the original source was never revealed. The reason for this modification was that the Allies had now captured German Government archives; many of which were being translated, ironically, by German-speaking refugees serving in other units of the British and American forces. The capture too of German Government officials who were willing to divulge some of the country's closest secrets meant that information in some M Room transcripts could now be used for propaganda purposes. However, this did not extend to releasing the files of war crimes and atrocities. Nor did it mean that the files could be accessible to the general public.

## CHURCHILL AND THE M ROOM

What did Prime Minister Winston Churchill make of the MI19 bugging operations? His views became clear in a Personal Minute issued to the Secretary of State for War and General Ismay for the Chiefs of Staff which has been preserved in CAB121/236 at the National Archives. Dated 16 February 1944, Prime Minister Churchill wrote:

> 'The records of conversations between enemy prisoners of war at the Combined Services Detailed Interrogation Centre afford an excellent insight into the German character and the results of the Nazi regime. I am informed that special files have been kept of the more remarkable conversations under subject headings and that these contain accounts of atrocities that have been committed by the enemy, details of which have been preserved by Section 19 [MI19] of the Military Intelligence Directorate. If a summary of these conversations were prepared by a skilful writer, with a number of the conversations in original as annexes, this might prove a most educative book for the public after the close of hostilities. The Foreign Secretary and the Minister of Information advise me that Major Eric Linklater, who is at present working in

the War Office, would be likely to make a success of this work. Being a playwright as well as a novelist, he should handle dialogue with effect. I should be glad if this proposal could be made to Major Linklater, it being understood that the question of publication would be considered later.'

It is not known whether Major Linklater was ever approached with the Prime Minister's request. Nothing was subsequently published after the war. However Churchill did receive a favourable response from intelligence chiefs at the time which basically, after much discussion, endorsed his idea at a meeting of the Joint Intelligence Committee. Their unified reply to the Prime Minister was brief but affirmative: 'The Chiefs of Staff have considered the proposal in your minute. They are strongly in favour of the course of action you propose. They suggest that the objections to publishing this material before the close of hostilities would not apply after the defeat of Germany, though we might still be at war with Japan.'

It was to be though, a parallel scenario to the evidence which was gathered by the listeners on war crimes. In the end British Intelligence refused to release the files or knowledge of their contents into the public domain, or acknowledge the unit's existence and clandestine operations during the war. Consequently over 100,000 secret transcripts from the M Room remained closed until 1999.

# SIXTEEN

# THE LAST CALL

ON 7 MAY 1945 Germany signed unconditional surrender. War was finally over. On a personal level for Kendrick it had been a long road to victory against a country which he had fought against in the First World War, and one which he had closely monitored for the Secret Intelligence Service from Vienna during the 1920s and 1930s. The Second World War became the closing chapter in Europe's struggle with German nationalism and Nazism. It was a milestone, too, for the secret listeners. On the day that Germany capitulated, Fritz and Susan attended a friend's wedding in Letchworth, Hertfordshire. Celebrations were already evident everywhere. The town was decorated with flags and bunting. The following day, 8 May, was VE Day and a Public Holiday. Susan was recalled to Wilton Park by her immediate boss Major Le Bosquet who saw no reason to slack because the war in the Far East was far from over. That evening Fritz went alone into central London for the victory celebrations:

'Piccadilly Circus was crammed full of people, some sitting on roof of buses, others hanging out of windows or climbing lamp posts. It was a unique experience. We made our way through the crowds to Parliament Square, where we listened to a speech by the King, which was broadcast through loudspeakers in the street – nobody spoke a word, and with the evening sun shining on Big Ben, it was an impressive atmosphere. We then proceeded to Buckingham Palace, where after a short while the Royal Family appeared on the balcony, which was draped in red and gold. It was now getting dark, and we went back to Whitehall, where we heard and saw Churchill make a short speech from the balcony of the Home Office, which was lit up by searchlights.'

European hostilities may have ended, but MI19's work with German PoWs was far from over. The task of deciding the PoWs future took up much of the time. Some of that included re-education of, especially lower rank, prisoners in readiness for their repatriation to a post-war democratic Germany. During the later half of May 1945 there was concern that some high-ranking officers may commit suicide to avoid justice. One such person was Rear Admiral Scheer who had been transferred to a PoW camp at Grizedale. A memo from a Major, on behalf of Kendrick, wrote to MI19 headquarters about Scheer (WO208/5622):

> 'We have reason to suspect that the above [Scheer] has a phial of poison hidden on his person or in his belongings. Although a search has been carried out we have failed to locate it. As this PoW has now been dumped to Grizedale, you will no doubt wish to inform the Camp Commandant without revealing the source of our information. Care will also have to be taken, of course, to ensure that PoW does not know that we suspect him.'

The Joint Intelligence Committee decided that the centre at Latimer House would close due to the end of European hostilities. MI19's activities were to be concentrated in the Allied occupied zones of Germany under the name CSDIC (WEA). Latimer House closed on 1st September. Kendrick's headquarters was transferred to Wilton Park. The site also became No. 300 PoW Camp and it was here that a programme of denazification and re-education of German prisoners took place in readiness for their repatriation to Germany. Just prior to leaving for Wilton Park, Kendrick collated copies of the personal files of all the senior German officers, consisting of a summary of their military career, circumstances of capture and character notes. On 1 September Norman Crockatt sent them to the head of MI6 with a covering letter (WO208/5622):

> *'Dear C,*
>
> *The enclosed notes on Senior German Officer prisoners of war who passed through our hands at Cockfosters were compiled for DMI [Director of Military Intelligence]. The latter has now gone on leave pending handing over and has returned his folder to me. It occurs to me, however, that either you or he (in his future appointment) might find some use for these jottings, and I am, therefore, sending them to you.'*

Trent Park eventually closed after the German Generals and Senior German officers were repatriated. The site was then used by the Ministry of Education as an emergency teacher training centre, then a residential teacher training college and later by the University of Middlesex. Today, at the time of writing, its future is uncertain because the house and immediate grounds are for sale.

What happened to the German Generals who had 'entertained' British Intelligence for, in some cases, up to three years in captivity? Figures like von Arnim and Meixner had left already in the early summer of 1944. Others, like Bassenge, were eventually repatriated by 1947.

The fate of one particular General is of particular interest. On 22 February 1944, Cramer was repatriated to Germany because of his severe asthma. Was that the real reason? He was not the only General to suffer ill-health. Or did he go back with a mission on behalf of British Intelligence? He had already expressed to a British officer before his repatriation that he wished to tell Hitler that the German struggle was hopeless and it would lead to Germany's ruin. Given his anti-Nazi views, was it safe for him to be repatriated? His personal MI19 file records: 'it is believed he has been arrested by the Gestapo.' Cramer arrived back in Germany but was subsequently arrested for his involvement in the July assassination attempt on Hitler. He was held until 5 August by the Gestapo at Prinz-Albrecht-Strasse prison in Berlin. From there he was taken to Ravensbrück concentration camp. Due to some act of mercy he was released to a hospital in Berlin, then placed under house arrest. After Allied forces crossed into Germany he was taken up by the British Army as Commander-in-Chief of all German PoWs in Holstein.

## THE SECRET LISTENERS

What happened to the secret listeners? The work of the M Room operators continued for at least another year into 1946. Some transferred to the British zone of Allied-occupied Germany for similar intelligence duties. Others like Peter Ganz, George Pulay and Heilbronn transferred to Farm Hall near Cambridge where, as mentioned previously, they bugged the conversations of the German atomic bomb scientists. Prior to the transfers, a big 'farewell dance' was held for intelligence staff. As Mess President it fell to Fritz to act as host. He later wrote to his parents that he found the duty quite exhausting, having to ensure that the numerous guests were always supplied with drinks.

Although demobilization was a way off, for the German-Jewish émigrés working for MI19 it was the end of an evil regime which had destroyed their life in Germany, persecuted and murdered members of their family and friends. It was the end of a regime which had systematically annihilated 6 million of Europe's Jews. For the listeners there could be no going back to Germany to reclaim what was lost or rebuild their lives there permanently. Britain was now their home. They looked forward to being granted British nationality and being fully accepted by a country which they had served so loyally as 'enemy aliens'.

With the closure of Latimer House, Fritz's future seemed uncertain and it looked as if he might be posted to Germany on similar intelligence work. He and Susan therefore decided on a wedding date before he received news of his new posting. The date was set for 6 June 1945 – the first anniversary of D-Day. According to protocol Fritz asked permission of his Commanding Officer. Kendrick readily gave it. The day before the wedding, Susan was still on duty, so Fritz prepared the wedding food in readiness for the reception. Rationing was still in force but they managed to scramble together a decent buffet:

> 'I bought 15 loaves of bread, and various items to put on them, like spreadable cheese, liver sausage, gherkins, etc., and we were busy for several hours doing it. We had finished by 11.30, arranged everything for the next day, put damp towels on the sandwiches, and I returned to my pied-à-terre for the night. Susan was going to make a fruit-cup the next morning, consisting of cider, some gin, lemon-juice and cherries. We also provided sherry, whisky, Marsala, orange juice and lemonade. A wedding cake was decorated with the words "Fritz, Susan, 6.6.45".'

At 11am on Wednesday 6 June 1945 Fritz married his bride at Hampstead Registry Office in London. That day they received twenty-five telegrams, one of which came from Fritz's parents in Portugal who were 'with them in spirit.' The next day the new couple left for Cornwall for their honeymoon.

That September Fritz was separated from his new bride and transferred to Bad Nenndorf in the British zone of Allied-occupied Germany. There he would continue similar work with the Intelligence Corps; this time under the command of Colonel Stephens who had headed MI5's interrogation centre at Latchmere House during the war, and where German spies and prisoners were 'turned' to become double agents. How did Fritz feel to be stepping back on German soil for the first time since having fled for his life six years earlier? This time he was in British Army uniform. It was a moment filled with apprehension, and one which has remained with him:

> 'We crossed the border with Germany by train as it was getting dark, which was a pity, as now it was getting really interesting. When we got to the Rhine we crossed on a bridge built by British Army engineers, which was just wide enough for the rails, so that the carriage windows were "hanging over". We all felt a little uneasy while the train moved across at a snail's pace. Having left the Rhine behind us, the train picked up some speed, and we managed to get some sleep. The first town we reached in daylight was Osnabrück, and the destruction we saw can hardly be described in words. I had read many newspaper reports about damaged towns, but unless one has actually seen it, the sight is impossible to visualize. Between Osnabrück and Bad Oeynhausen, where we got off the train, we had a long break because the engine did not have enough steam, and there we took the opportunity of setting foot on German soil again. Our thoughts were not exactly "Home, sweet home". It seemed strange to see the German railway officials again, in their rather splendid uniforms with gold braid. If they still have the Nazi-emblem on their caps the lower part with the swastika had been filed off, so that only the wings of the eagle remained, and the

same applied where the emblem was still on a building: the swastika had been blotted out somehow. The rest of Bad Nenndorf seemed to be a hospital area for what was the German Army, and dozens of crippled ex-soldiers were walking about, which was rather depressing. The civilian population does not seem to like us particularly, judging by the looks they give us, which is not very surprising as we have thrown them out of their houses and are an army of occupation.'

On 1 October 1945, while Fritz was in Germany, Susan received her discharge from the ATS because married women were given preference for demobilization. She had attained the rank of Staff Quartermaster Sergeant, equivalent to Sergeant Major in the Army. She left with an excellent personal reference from Kendrick who wrote that she had: 'performed her duties, which were mostly of a clerical nature, in a very satisfactory and efficient manner during the two years she has been with this unit. She has a pleasant personality, is adaptable and conscientious.' Susan's first civilian job was with the Preparatory Commission of the United Nations in London, where she worked as supervisor in the Duplicating Section.

As a new year 1946 dawned, Fritz had his first opportunity to return to Berlin, the city of his birth. He used the opportunity to visit extended family and friends who he hoped had survived. One person he visited was the sister of a refugee-soldier in the 'alien' Pioneer Corps orchestra. She had survived in hiding during the war. Fritz later wrote of that moving occasion:

> '*The joy of these people to get news of their relations abroad and to see and speak to somebody "from the other side" is indescribable. They suck you dry, so much do they want to know - they don't want you to leave. Then they offer you something to*

*eat. And if you refuse, they are offended, and if you accept, they have less to eat. A difficult situation!'*

On 27 June 1946 Fritz was finally demobilized and returned to England. The following month, on 31 July, he typed a letter to his former Commanding Officer, Colonel Kendrick, asking whether he would act as a referee for various job applications to publishing firms:

*'Dear Sir,*

*Four weeks ago I returned to civilian life from CSDIC (WEA) – a very welcome change after almost 6 years in uniform! But to the 3 years I was part of CSDIC I shall always look back as the most pleasant, interesting and satisfying part of my army career. My present plans are to use the experience in editing, translating, etc which I gained in CSDIC (WEA), and to try and find some promising opening in the publishing trade. But without connections it is apparently not very easy to get in anywhere.'*

In a hand-written reply, Kendrick wrote 'I shall be pleased to do anything I can and am delighted that your wife has got fixed up in what must be an interesting job.' Fritz finally received British nationality nearly four years after the country which adopted him, entrusted him with some of their most important secrets. His post-war civilian jobs included being Officer Manager, Company Secretary/Accountant, and Accountant/Credit Controller (Qualification: FCIS). He and Susan have two sons, and have been married for over 67 years.

The German-speaking émigrés who were drafted into MI19 played a significant role in Britain's race to gain an upper hand over Nazi Germany. British Intelligence owes a great deal to the listeners who, due to the top-secret nature of their work, received no special medal or recognition for their achievements. In post-war civilian life they settled down and most of them married and had families. They went on to make a valuable contribution to business, education and academic life, politics, economics and the arts. One of those was Fritz's friend, secret listener Peter Ganz who had a distinguished career in academia as a Germanist and medievalist. This included appointments as lecturer at Royal Holloway College, London; lecturer in German Philology and Medieval Literature at Westfield College (London), Reader in German at Oxford University, then Emeritus Professor of German; Fellow of Hertford College, Oxford and Resident Fellow at Herzog August Bibliothek (Wolfenbüttel). During his time at Oxford, Ganz reached the pinnacle of his career and became pre-eminent in his field and acted as facilitator in establishing contacts between German studies in England and Germany. In recognition of this, in 1973 he received the Grosses Bundesverdienstkreuz by the Federal Republic. He died on 17 August 2006.

With George Pulay, Fritz lost contact after the war but, in a twist of fate, he recently met up with George's daughter Jessica Pulay, and his nephew, the actor Roger Lloyd-Pack. The only other known surviving listener is Eric Mark, who now lives in Belgium.

## COLONEL THOMAS JOSEPH KENDRICK, OBE

After Latimer House closed, Kendrick was based for a year at Wilton Park until its closure on 9 August 1946. Afterwards he transferred to the Interpreters Pool at Aldershot for a short time. Thereafter he continued to work for MI6 from his house Briarsholme in Oxshott, Surrey. For his services to American Intelligence he was honoured with the award of the Legion of Merit. His citation, signed personally by Harry Truman, read:

*Colonel Thomas Joseph Kendrick, British Army,*
*rendered exceptionally valuable services as commanding officer*
*of a special center for interrogation of enemy prisoners of war*
*for the British War Office from June 1942 to May 1945.*
*He willingly made available to the United States intelligence*
*units all facilities at his command, and contributed greatly*
*through his earnest cooperation to the effective training*
*of American intelligence personnel*

Kendrick continued to work for MI6 until his retirement in 1948. In *The Art of Betrayal* Gordon Corera aptly summed up the British Secret Service as: 'a self-perpetuating gentleman's club for members of the establishment with a naughty streak'. This was Kendrick's world, and traces of his life of secrets survived in the family home after his death. Kendrick's grandson, Ken, recalls a suitcase in the attic with gadgets in it - hairbrushes with secret compartments and fountain pens with compasses hidden in them, and silk maps of Europe carried by his spies.

Kendrick died in 1972 at the age of 91. A Roman Catholic funeral service took place in Cobham, Surrey, and was followed by burial in the municipal cemetery in Weybridge. 'I attended his funeral,' says grandson Ken Walsh. 'I stood next to my mother and noticed some chaps in long raincoats. I asked her who they were. She replied: "Oh, they're from the Foreign Office and MI6." As we left the church they shook hands with us. They were just like spies out of a film.'

Even in his twilight years Kendrick never spoke about his work. Until recently, MI6 did not officially exist. Kendrick went to his grave carrying many secrets. The cloak of secrecy surrounding his life adds to the sense of mystery, enhanced by the shadowy figures at his funeral.

# EPILOGUE

## DARK SECRETS

The release of MI19's vast cache of files at the National Archives has yielded some surprising results which have been under-used by historians of this period. Most importantly, they shed new light on how much British Intelligence knew about war crimes and the mass extermination programme of the Jews of Europe. The material from the M Room shows just how much was known about Germany's technological developments, military secrets, the operational workings of the Nazi war machine and conditions inside enemy territory. Transcripts add to our knowledge not only of the war and the British Secret Service, but to the known facts about the Holocaust. This is evident in one particular conversation, undiscovered by historians until the publication of this book, which records a previously unknown mutiny by SS guards in a concentration camp in 1936/7. It is of surprise to learn that these SS were shot for their action. Information has also come out of the transcripts that, in the early days, some German Military Commanders advocated the shooting of SS who committed atrocities against Jews, Russians and Poles. These commanders lost their posting, and Himmler set up special courts to try SS officers – effectively meaning that they were never brought to trial and the killings could carry on unhindered. Significantly too, the material highlights the part of the German Army in atrocities and the Holocaust, and dispels the myth that they played no part in it.

Transcripts and Summary Intelligence Reports show that the thousands of snippets leaked by German PoWs over the course of the war fitted into the overall jigsaw which had an impact on, for example, winning the Battle of the Atlantic, the discovery of Peenemünde and the rocket programme. Details like this provided vital technological information on Germany's military capability which could not have otherwise been ascertained from aerial reconnaissance. In the end, the work of the M Room operators at Trent Park, Latimer House and Wilton Park enabled Britain and America to win the intelligence game. Had the files from MI19 not been released in 1999, and with the passing of the generation of eye-witnesses, the story of the M Room and its secret listeners may never have come to light. A final quotation from the late Peter Hart who was immensely proud of his role as a listener:

> 'It is the duty of the older generation to leave an authentic record of their experiences during the Second World War for the benefit of posterity. Without it, history would simply be hearsay.'

# APPENDIX

# INTELLIGENCE STAFF AT MI19 [CSDIC]

A complete a list of names of Intelligence Staff as possible has been compiled here, however there may be some unexpected omissions. It does not include non-Intelligence personnel from other units who also worked at MI19. At the height of its operations, MI19 employed nearly 1,000 staff across its three sites.

Overall Commandant: Col. T.J. Kendrick, O.B.E.
Assistant Commandant (Intelligence): Lt. Col. CM Corner M.V.O
Assistant Commandant (Administration): Lt. Col. F. Huband, M.B.E., M.C., D.C.M.
Commandant at Wilton Park: Major L. St. Clare Grendona and the postal address is c/o G.P.O. Beaconsfield, Bucks.

## ARMY INTELLIGENCE OFFICERS

Source: a group photograph outside Latimer House.

Capt H. G. Abrahams, Capt F. G. Adams, Capt G. E. Austen, Capt S. F. Austin, Lt. A. J. Bauers, Lt. Blyth, Major C. H. le Bosquet, Capt R. Boothroyd, Capt M. O. Brigstock, Capt. Brodie, Lt. A. Buesst, Lt. J. G. Bullock, Capt J. E. Burgoyne, Capt C. E. Calderari, Major F. Cassels, Lt. K. O. Chetwood-Aiken, Lt. W. Cochraine, Capt G. P. Copping, Capt B. le Cren, Capt M. D. Davidson, Lt H. W. Davis, Capt. S. H. Davis, Capt C. L. Deveson, Lt. Col H. V. Dicks (camp psychologist), Lt. F. E. Edmunds, Lt. E. Egger, Lt. H. R. Evans, Lt. R. D. Fermo, Lt. E. M. Fitzgerald, Capt W.

E. Foss, Capt W. P. Gatliff, Lt. H. S. Gervers, Lt. Gross, Capt R. Hamilton, Capt. W. Hartje, Capt C. C. Hay, Lt. J. S. Heber, Capt M. Hilton, Lt. A. E. Hind, Lt. J. Hunter, Capt W. J. Ingham, Capt. H. R. Jahn, Capt J. E. Johnson, Capt. C. F. Joolman, Capt E. E. King, Capt G. A. Kitchen, Capt L. V. Lang, Lt. F. Lonergan, Lt. Macintosh, Capt E. W. Marin, Capt N. S. Marsh, Capt E. A. Morton, Lt. L. Muirhead, Capt I. T. Munro, Capt F. W. Murray, Capt A. B. Nash, Capt. A. H. New, Lt. A. Oakey, Major L. E. Parkin, Capt J. E. Parnell, Capt C. D. Perring, Capt H. Phare, Capt L. L. M. Pokorny, Lt. E. A. Poupard, Lt. F. W. Read-Jahn, Capt C. H. B. Readman, Lt. H. W. Reynolds, Major T. H. Rittner, Capt A. C. Robertshaw, Capt H. B. Romberg, Lt. M. Rowe, Lt. G. A. F. Sandor, Capt. W. H. Serin, Lt. D. Simon, Capt. A. G. Speirs, Lt. O. H. Strafford, Capt L. G. Struthers, Lt. G. A. Thompson, Capt B. S. Vickerman, Capt J. Walmsley, Lt M. Walshe, Lt. J. A. Weber, Lt. E. W. Zundel, Female officers: Subn L. F. Addey, J/Cmdr M. R. K. Bennett, Subn E. Bernert, J/Cmdr M. B. Boak, Subn E. W. Bobby, J/Cmdr M. Braun, Subn S. J. Caldwell, 2/Subn M. Crutchleigh-Fitzpatrick, 2/Subn A. G. M. Doyle, 2/Subn P. G. R. Doyle, J/Cmdr K. M. Falwasser, J/Cmdr M. J. Frise, Subn M. Grugeon, Subn S. P. Hall, Subn J. P. Horrigan, Subn E. Iles, J/Cmdr G. H. Leigh, J/Cmdr H. M. Lishman, Subn J. E. Little, Subn B. Maile, J/Cmdr T. Masterson, J/Cmdr R. Morris, Subn G. Ouseley, J/Cmdr V. M. Robins, Subn P. M. Rubin, J/C A. D. Skoyles, Subn M. Sworder, 2/Subn L. M. Thomas, J/Cmdr E. M. Thwaits, Subn F. F. Watt, J/Cmdr J. D. Woodhead, 2/Subn H. Zillwood

# SECRET LISTENERS

The names below are as complete a list as possible of the German-speaking refugees who served as secret listeners for MI19. In some cases their anglicized names are also given and the date of transfer from the Pioneer Corps into the Intelligence Corps. Some names have been added from a photograph of listeners taken outside Latimer House:

Robert Aufhäuser

Hubert Bailey

Peter Baines

Rudolph Bamberger (Bambi)

Otto Lothar Barber (b. 1924) = William Peter Barber, transferred 4 Oct '43

Fritz Becker (b. 1923) = Frederic Benson, transferred 25 June 1943

Fritz Bierer = Fred Bentley

Walter Beevers

Erwin von Bendemann (b. 1906) = H I Bertham, transferred 25 May 1943

Peter Bendix

Bentham

Berchstecher

Blake

Wilhelm Bonwitt (b. 1910) = Ernest Brent, transferred 8 July 1944

Bratu

Garry Casey

Hans Freiderich Eisler (b. 1920) = Sean Graham, transferred 5 July 1944

Emanuel Ekler (b. 1906) = Eric Ellis, transferred 26 November 1944

Bruce Eldon

Max Ernst Emanuel Erlanger (b. 1917) = Ernest Max Langley, transferred 17 May 1943

Kurt Ernst (b.1919) = Brian Keith Henson, transferred 4 October 1943

Erskine

Friedrich Falk (b. 1907) = Frank Falk, transferred 24 May 1944

Werner David Feist (b. 1909), transferred 18 January 1944

Fleiss

Hans Francken (b. 1908) = Hermen Geoffrey Francker, transferred 28 August 1943

Ludwig Heinrich Franken (b. 1908) = Lewis Henry Franklin, transferred 9 July 1944

Felix Konrad Fullenbaum (b. 1904) = Felix Kenneth Fraser, transferred 28 August 1943

Peter Ganz (b. 1920), transferred 16 August 1943

Hans Gochler (b. 1909) = John Gay, transferred 18 January 1944

Lev Golodetz (?), transferred 17 February 1945

Constantine Goloubitzky (b. 1918), transferred 27 September 1941

Eberhard Leo Hans Gottstein (b. 1914), transferred 8 December 1944

Innozenz Grafe

Graham

Ludwig Kurt Grunwald (b. 1924) = Kenneth Grandville, transferred 4 October 1943

Oskar Hamm (b. 1907), transferred 3 June 1944

Heilbronn

Kurt Otto Heinsheimer (b. 1911) = Frank West, transferred 25 July 1943

Walter Oscar Heller (b. 1921) = Walter Oscar Hellier, transferred 17 November 1944

Francis Hellman

Peter Klaus Herz (b. 1914) = Peter Anthony Hart, transferred 8 July 1944

Adolf Hirschfeld (b. 1908) = Alan Henley, transferred 8 July 1944

Hans Ernst Hoffmann (b. 1912) = John Ernest Housman, transferred 8 July 1944

Albert Hollander (b. 1908), transferred 31 March 1943

Willie Hornstein (b. 1893) = John William Horton, transferred 22 May '43

Franz Huelsen (b. 1902), transferred 23 March 1943

Erich Huppert (b. 1911), transferred 21 May 1943

Henry Jakobs

Jellinek = Jellicoe

Hans Kallmas (b. 1908) = Herbert Kellett, transferred 8 July 1944

Wolfgang Kals (b. 1912) = William Kennedy

Fritz Katz (b. 1918) = Frederick Geoffrey Katz, transferred 8 January 1944

Karl Heinz Peter Kaufmann (b. 1912), transferred 5 April 1943

Leo Kaufmann (b. 1915), transferred 8 January 1944

Leon Kendon

[Johnny King – British, non-German speaking draughtsman]

Siegfried Kissin (b. 1908) = Stephen Fred Kissin, transferred 20 June 1943

Erich Konrad (b. 1911) = Eric Arthur Conrad, transferred 15 May 1944

Konrad Paul Korn (b. 1917) = Paul Michael Douglas, transferred 17 May 1943

Ernest Korpner (b. 1909), transferred 26 June 1943

Kraft

Herbert Kyval (b. 1914), transferred 23 December 1944

Jimmy Leader

Walter Leatham

Herbert Lehmann

Lindsay

Carl Heinz Lipmann = Charles Lipton, transferred 8 July 1944

Alexander Lowy (b. 1913), transferred 10 February 1943

Fritz Lustig (b. 1919), transferred 19 May 1943

Siegfried Maennlein (b. 1902), transferred CSDIC (UK) 8 July 1944

Otto Mandel (b. 1901), transferred 8 December 1944

Mann

Robert William Mannheimer (b. 1918) = William Manners, transferred 8 January 1944

Männlein

Marefield

Erich (Meyer) Mark = Eric Mark

Tonie Marshall

Claus Mayer

Hans Adolf Mayer (b. 1911) = Herbert Marshall, transferred 31 May 1944

Wolfgang Mayer (b. 1908) = William Joseph Mayer, transferred 8 July 1944

Joseff Philipp Merfeld (b. 1903) = Peter John Morton, transferred 15 March 1944

Arthur Morgenthau (b. 1913) = Arthur William Morgenthau, transferred 8 May 1944

Robert Neave

Neuhaus

Neumann

Heinrich Nickelsberg (b. 1912) = Hilary Nichols, transferred 17 June 1944

Rees Nichols

Rudi Oppenheimer

Helmut Orgler (b. 1918), transferred 23 September 1944

Erich Peritz (b. 1907) = Eric Stephen Pearce, transferred 8 July 1944

Oskar Henryk Prentki (b. 1901), transferred 16 October 1942

George Pulay

Johnny Rapp

Sabersky

Heinz Jürgen Sahlmann (b. 1921) = Henry John Saunders, transferred 17 January 1944

[Bill Sales – British, non-German speaking draughtsman]

Edward Solomon Salti (b. 1920), transferred 10 January 1942

Teddy Schächter

Eric Schaffer

Godfrey Scheele

Robert Schneider (b. 1922) = Robert Lacey, transferred 4 October 1943

Ernst Schönmann (b. 1905) = Ernst Arthur Scott, transferred 18 January 1944

Scot(ty)

Segell

Francis Seton

Father Shipton

Hubert Simon

Sirot

Werner Stark

Spiller

Hans Stern (b. 1913) = David Stern, transferred 19 June 1943

Richard Paul Adolf Stern (b. 1917), transferred 20 August 1943

Sterne

Hans Strauss (b. 1908) = Hugh Spencer Strauss, transferred 17 November 1944

Frank Stevens

Wolfgang Tietz (b. 1913) = Leonard Deeds, transferred 18 January 1944

Albert Tugendhat (b. 1901), transferred 17 May 1943

Franz (Peter) Türkheim (b. 1917), transferred 17 November 1944

Michael Ullman (b. 1917), transferred 17 November 1944

Fritz Carl Ullstein (b. 1909), transferred 17 January 1944

Vigart

Wilhelm Vollbracht (b. 1906), transferred 8 December 1944

Max Mendel Wassermann (b. 1901) =Martin Steven Warner, transferred 18 January 1944

Fritz Wechselmann (b. 1906) = Arthur Fred Wellmann, transferred CSDIC (UK) 8 July 1944

Norbert Wegner (b. 1922) = Norman Willert, transferred 4 October 1943

Fritz Weis (b. 1913) = Fred Wells, transferred 8 July 1944

Peter Weisz (b. 1920), transferred 15 March 1944

Freddy Wellmann

Wulwick

## TRENT PARK

Secret Listeners known to have worked in the M Room at Trent Park, provided by the Intelligence Corps Museum:

Bentham, Berchstecher, Blake, Garry Casey, David Feist, Franken, Felix Fraser, Johny Gay, Graham (surname), Oscar Hamm, Allan Henley, Harry Jakobs, Leon Kendon, Kraft, Lindsay, Charles Lipton, Mann, Bobby Manners, Mannlein, Marefield, Eric Mark, Tony Marshall, Claus Mayer, Wolfgang Meyer, Nichols, Sabersky, Eric Schaffer, Scot (or Scott), Shipton, Sigell (or Segal/Segel ?), Francis Seton, Sirot, Werner Stark, Frank Stevens, Vigart, Warner, Well, Freddy Wellmann, West, Wulwick

# THE K ALBUM

The source is an original booklet called "The K Album" which consists of photographs and names of Air Intelligence Section at MI19 [CSDIC], under Felkin. Found amongst Kendrick's family papers.

S/L. W. L. Antrobus, F/L W.B. Atkinson, S/L L. P. Bamford, S/O C. R. Baring-Gould (Mrs Bottenheimer) (female), S/O E. J. Bembaron (female), F/L R. Benson, F/L C. R. Bingham, S/L B. E. Bishop, S/O H. M. Black (female), Capt E. H. Boehm, S/L A. K. Boning, Capt M. P. Borchert, S/L G. W. Bragg, S/O J. Y. Brooks (female), Capt L. A. Brunner, F/L E. Campbell, F/L V. I. Clark, F/L M. D. M. Cockraine, F/L R. J. Cole, F/L L. E. Collier, Flt/O K. R. Costello (female), S/L G. L. D. Cox, F/L D. Culver, Capt C. C. Davis, Flt/O J. E. M. Davis (female), S/L L. V. Davis, W/C R.M. C. Day, F/L J. F. R. Druce, Lt-Col E. Englander, S/O F. Fairburn (female), F/L W. Forbes-Watkins, S/O E. A. Ford-Hutchinson (female), W/C R. H. Francis, Capt W. A. Frank, S/L H. R. Gray, F/L B. B. Gregory, S/L H. O. Gregory, F/L R. H. Gould, Major K. M. Grubb, Flt/O V. L. A. Gundry-White (female), W/C P. de Haan, S/O M. E. Harcourt, S/L L. F. Hartje, F/L D. F. Haslewood, F/L M. A. Hicks, Lt-Col J. D. Holtzermann (US), F/L A. R. J. Humphrey, S/L John X. Hunt, F/L J. C. Hutchinson, F/L R. Hirsch, Commandant G. Ittel (French Air Force), S/L L. A. Jackets, S/L T. E. James, S/L W. Jamieson, W/C G. B. Jepson, S/O M. Jopp (female), S/L H. H. Keen, Capt W. M. Kloetzer, S/O C. M. Krause (female), S/L P. N. Labertouche, F/L S. A. Lane, S/L C. M. Lawler-Wilson, F/L N. E. Leigh, F/L P. K. Lickford, F/L J. R. Littlefair, F/L E. A. Littlefield, Capt S. R. Litton, F/L M. J. Longinotto-Landseer, F/L J. Lord, S/L Ludovici, F/L A. J. R. Lyon, F/L I. Macrae, Capt G. D. Mandelik, Flt/O S. M. Manduell (Mrs Jackets), W/C C. H. March, F/L H. G. R. March, S/L W. W. Marks,

Flt/O E. J. Masterman (female), F/L E. H. Mayer, Flt/O E. M. Mayes (female), Lieut J. H. Mehl, F/L E. E. Medland, S/L N. Miller, W/C W. L. Minter, F/L G. I. A. Moes, F/L J. E. Mullholland, W/C J. B. Newton, W/C Newton-John, F/L P. G. A. Norman-Wright, F/L E. C. Norris, F/L J. G. Nowell, F/L J. Odde, S/O O. Oppenheimer (female), Capt F. E. Overley, S/L J. E. H. Park, F/L A. Parkin, F/L Pelham-Toll, F/L E. C. Peters, F/L V. J. R. D. Prendergast, Capt Pyper (S. African Air Force), W/C R. M. Rickett, F/L G. M. Robbins, F/L J. S. Robinson, F/L B. P. Roche, W/C H. N. Roffey, Capt H. Rosenhaupt, F/L Ruse, Capt O. A. Saborsky, S/L E. Sankey, Capt C. D. Schneider, S/L J. F. A. Segner, S/L R. Scrivener, Flt/O L. M. Sieveking (female), S/L R. H. Siddons, F/L A. J. Sington, F/L W. M. Skeffington, W/C V. O. Slesser, S/L C. H. Smith, S/L D. A. G. Smith, Capt M. M. Sommer, W/C Peter Soren, S/L G. W. Spenceley, S/L C. K. Squires, S/L H. M. Stokes, Capt M Sulkes, S/L B. B. Sullivan, F/L A. Taylor, F/L J. L. S. Taylor, Flt/O I. D. Thornhill (female), Capt Willis Thornton, S/L J. P. C. Tooth, Major Max Van Rossum Daum, F/L S. Y. Vitalis, Capt R. E. Vollprecht, F/L C. H. R. Wade, Lt-Col E. M. Warburg, F/L H. J. Ware, F/L G. C. Waterston, S/L H. Webb, Capt H. E. Weingartner, Flt/O H. M. Weir, Capt J. M. Whitten, F/L R. R. Witter, F/L A. C. Wilberforce, S/L T.S. Wyatt

## NAVAL INTELLIGENCE STAFF

John Connell, Lt-Cdr Cope, John Everett (Canadian), Ralph Izzard, John Marriner, Harry Scholar (Czech), Dick Weatherby, John Weatherby, Charles Wheeler, Lt-Cdr Donald Burkewood Welbourn, Colin McFadyean. Women: Evelyn Barron, Jean Flowers, Ruth Hales, Esme McKenzie, Celia Thomas.

# BIBLIOGRAPHY

The National Archives at Kew (listed separately below) hold the transcripts of conversations of over 10,000 German PoWs held by MI19 during the war; private papers and photographs from the late Col. Kendrick's family; unpublished memoirs of Fritz Lustig, unpublished memoirs of Lt-Cdr Donald Burkewood Welbourn, RNVR (ref: 99/6/1) at the Imperial War Museum and The Intelligence Corps Museum at Chicksands. This book is also based on extensive interviews with secret listener Fritz Lustig; his wife Susan (née Cohn) and also surviving relatives of secret listeners.

## THE NATIONAL ARCHIVES

In the National Archives there are in excess of 100,000 intelligence reports from the interrogation and eavesdropping on the conversations of German PoWs held by the three camps of CSDIC. It is not possible to list all of those which have been consulted for this book and therefore only the most significant have been listed below:

W0208/4970 – the Story of MI19, also CSDIC Survey from 3rd December 1939 – 31 December 1940

W0208/3455 – Camp 10 and Camp 20; Survey Report for 1 January 1941-30 June 1941, also Survey Report for 1 July 1941-31 December 1941 and 1 January 1942-30 June 1942

WO208/3457 – details of the equipment used in the "M" Room

WO208/3433 – includes report on the German Senior Officers and their Nazi/anti-Nazi views

WO208/3504 – list of the 59 German Generals held at Trent Park with profile information and photographs for each where available

WO208/5550 – Summary report on the views of the German Generals, 1943

WO208/4137 – contains conversations about the secret weapon programme and Peenemünde

WO208/4167 - conversations of the German Generals at Trent Park, including details of war crimes and atrocities

WO208/4168 – Special Reports German Generals

WO208/4177 – lots of material on atrocities and war crimes discussed by the German Generals, as well as their reactions to being shown photographs of Belsen concentration camp

WO208/4363, WO208/4165, WO208/4166, WO208/4178 – summary reports of conversations of the German Generals at Trent Park, including details of war crimes and atrocities, also summary reports of life at Trent Park including excursions and Christmas celebrations

W208/5016, WO208/5017, WO208/5018 – military intelligence summary-reports, including information on the rocket programme (V-2 and V-3) and failed 20 July 1944 Putsch

WO311/632 – correspondence on evidence of war crimes not to be used in the war crimes trials

AIR 40/3070 – Secret Recordings of conversations of Luftwaffe pilots, bombing raids and being shot down, some of it as early as 1940

AIR40/3093 – conversations of lower ranks, includes details of Peenemünde and the V-2 rocket programme

AIR 40/3102 – conversations on Y-Gerät, Knickebein from U-boat crews and lower ranks

AIR 40/3106 – reports from lower ranks which include mention of atrocities and war crimes

AIR 40/3108 – report on first PoW, Lieutenant Wilhelm Meyer

CAB121/236 – Joint-intelligence Committee discussions on accommodation for CSDIC, originally marked to be kept under lock and key. Also Winston Churchill's personal memo on CSDIC and reactions to it by intelligence chiefs

Files from the Judge Advocate General's Office (JAG) have also been consulted. War crimes files are in WO 208, WO 309, WO 32 and WO 361.

## PUBLISHED WORKS

Bernstein, Jeremy. *Hitler's Uranium Club: The Secret Recordings at Farm Hall*, Copernicus Books: 2001

Fry, Helen. *K is for Kendrick: Britain's Secret Agent*, forthcoming: 2013

Fry, Helen. *Inside Nuremberg Prison*, Amazon: 2011

Fry, Helen. *The King's Most Loyal Enemy Aliens: Germans who Fought for Britain in WW2*, Sutton: 2007. Available in paperback and e-book as *Churchill's German Army*, History Press: 2010

Gilbert, Martin. *Auschwitz and the Allies*,

Hart, Peter. *Journey into Freedom*, Authors OnLine: 2003

Hoare, Oliver (ed.). *Camp 020: MI5 and Nazi Spies – The Official History of MI5's Wartime Interrogation Centre*,

Neitzel, Sönke & Harald Welzer. *Soldaten: On Fighting, Killing and Dying*, Simon & Schuster: 2012

Neitzel, Sönke (ed.). *Tapping Hitler's Generals: Transcripts of Secret Conversations, 1942-45*, Frontline: 2007

Oppenheimer, Paul. *From Belsen to Buckingham Palace*, Witness Collection, Beth Shalom: 1996

# ACKNOWLEDGEMENTS

I first stumbled across the story of the secret listeners whilst researching for two books, *Jews in North Devon during the Second World War* (2005) and *The King's Most Loyal Enemy Aliens: Germans who Fought for Britain in the Second World War* (2007). During this time I have interviewed a number of veterans and their families to build up a body of works which encompass the subject of the German and Austrian refugees who served in the British forces in the war. Writing this first book to come out about the secret listeners and their work in the M Room, would not have been possible without the help of a very special veteran. My heartfelt thanks go to veteran Fritz Lustig who has been waiting for it to be fully told. His wife Susan also worked for MI19 and has been incredibly supportive of this project. Fritz and Susan have provided extensive, invaluable firsthand accounts of life and work with the Intelligence Corps in MI19 at Latimer House and Wilton Park under their Commanding Officer Colonel Kendrick. Fritz has also given of his time to read and edit every chapter of the book. His meticulous care for detail, dedication and passion to see the story told, has made the writing of it most enjoyable.

This book could also not have been written without the huge, dedicated and practical help of the grandchildren of the late Colonel Kendrick: my sincere thanks to Barbara Lloyd and Ken Walsh for providing material and photographs for this book and for being willing to be interviewed extensively about their grandfather's life. Much appreciation too goes to great-granddaughter Anne-Marie for genealogical information and to relative John Vignoles for biographical research. Thomas Kendrick's biography *K is for Kendrick* is due out in 2013. Also my thanks to Jessica Pulay and Roger Lloyd-Pack for information about the family's escape from Vienna and the story of Jessica's father George

Pulay who was a secret listener. Also to the late Peter Hart, a secret listener, for help from his memoirs, and Adam Ganz for information on his father Peter Ganz's work as a secret listener at Trent Park.

I hugely indebted to historian and researcher Phil Tomaselli for his unparalleled expertise and help on intelligence material from MI5, SIS and Foreign Office sources in the National Archives. Phil is author of a number of books on the secret service and military intelligence, including *Tracing Your Secret Service Ancestors*. Thanks to Fred Judge for his help with archival material on the Intelligence Corps, Special Forces and MI6/SIS. Also my thanks go to Major Alan Edwards OBE, Corps historian at the Defence Intelligence and Security Centre, Chicksands and Joyce Hutton, archivist there, for their help with material from the archives relating to Army intelligence. Also to Colonel John Starling and Norman Brown of the Royal Pioneer Corps Association. To dedicated staff at the National Archives who have enabled me to find the most obscure references to piece together this story; and Bridget Clifford, Keeper of Tower History & Collections at the Royal Armouries Museum at HM Tower of London. Thanks too to Oliver Leiva at the University of Middlesex for information on the history of Trent Park. Many of the official reports and archival material for this biography have been typed up by Alexia Dobinson – with many thanks.

Thanks to my special friends Colin Hamilton, Trudy Gold, Claudia Rubenstein, Sheila Hamilton, Louisa Albani and also to staff at Kenwood House café for all their support. This journey has been encouraged by my writing partner in fiction James Hamilton, to whom I owe much. Together under the pseudonym JH Schryer we have fictionalised some of the WW2 stories in our novels *Goodnight Vienna* (2009) and *Moonlight over Denmark*. We are working together on a number of other novels of historical fiction.

Huge thanks to my family and sons Jonathan, David and Edward for their loyal support and encouragement over the years. A special commendation goes to my eldest son Jonathan who has accompanied me on several trips to the National Archives and worked methodically and carefully for hours through Secret Service files. He has also photographed key documents and found references which I missed. Finally, I owe Mary Curry a debt of gratitude for seeking me out ten years ago and sparking me to embark on this journey.

# THE AUTHOR

Historian and biographer Helen Fry has written over 24 books on the Second World War and aspects of Anglo-Jewish history. These include: *Churchill's German Army*; *Music and Men; Freuds' War, Inside Nuremberg Prison, Denazification, German Schoolboy, British Commando,* and *From Dachau to D-Day.* Helen graduated from the University of Exeter with a Ph.D in 1996. She teaches at the London Jewish Cultural Centre, and is an Honorary Research Fellow at the Dept of Hebrew & Jewish Studies at UCL. In fiction under the pseudonym JH Schryer she has co-written two novels: *Goodnight Vienna* and its sequel *Moonlight over Denmark.* Helen is currently writing film and TV scripts on some of her optioned works. She was interviewed for the Channel 4's documentary Spying on Hitler's Army, and been working on documentaries for ITV and BBC. A member of the prestigious Biographers' Club, she can be found on Facebook and Twitter. Her website: www.helen-fry.com

# INDEX

Made in the USA
Middletown, DE
18 August 2017